D1600469

CHARLES SMYTHE

PIONEER, PREMIER AND ADMINISTRATOR OF NATAL

DAPHNE CHILD

Charles Smythe

PIONEER, PREMIER AND ADMINISTRATOR
OF NATAL

CAPE TOWN

C. STRUIK (PTY) LIMITED

1973

C. STRUIK (PTY) LIMITED
Africana Specialist and Publisher

By the Same Author

Saga of the South African Horse   1967
Yesterday's Children   1969

ISBN   86977 030 6

Printed in South Africa by Printpak (Cape) Limited
Dacres Avenue, Epping, Cape

In fond memory of

EUPHEMIA JANET SMYTHE
('EFFIE')

ACKNOWLEDGEMENTS

I am grateful for help received from the following:

Mr Robert Gorneman of Durban, who so skilfully prepared old family photographs for use as illustrations.

The staff of the South African Library, Cape Town, especially Mr W. Tyrrell-Glynn, Assistant Director.

The Chief Librarian, Ministry of Defence Library, Whitehall, London.

The staff of the Richmond-upon-Thames District Library, Surrey.

Mr Rowan Smythe for his kindness and courtesy to me at all times, and for giving me every encouragement in my work.

Mr and Mrs A. Mervyn Wood for looking out documents and photographs, and in Mrs Wood's case for relating favourite family anecdotes for inclusion in this book.

DAPHNE CHILD

CONTENTS

Page

ACKNOWLEDGEMENTS vi
LIST OF ILLUSTRATIONS ix
AUTHOR'S NOTE xi
CHAPTER ONE 1
CHAPTER TWO 17
CHAPTER THREE 31
CHAPTER FOUR 47
CHAPTER FIVE 63
CHAPTER SIX 77
CHAPTER SEVEN 97
CHAPTER EIGHT 111
CHAPTER NINE 127
CHAPTER TEN 143
CHAPTER ELEVEN 161
CHAPTER TWELVE 185
CHAPTER THIRTEEN 199
CHAPTER FOURTEEN 209
CHAPTER FIFTEEN 225
CHAPTER SIXTEEN 241
APPENDIX I 255
APPENDIX II 257
BIBLIOGRAPHY 261
INDEX 263

LIST OF ILLUSTRATIONS

Facing Page

1. Charles Smythe as a boy 36
2. Methven Castle, north front, 1870 36
3. Charles Smythe in 1872 37
4. Guy Dawnay (left) and Frank Rhodes, 1872 . . 37
5. Mr John King, 1872 52
6. Mrs Janet King, 1872 52
7. 'Strathearn' in 1884 53
8. 'Strathearn' when the trees had grown . . . 53
9. Charles Smythe (*Local History Museum, Durban*) . 132
10. Margaret Smythe in 1890 132
11. Effie, age four 133
12. Mungo (left) and Edric, who became the father of the South African V.C., Lieut Quentin Smythe . . 133
13. Loyal Zulu, scouting for the British (*Illustrated London News*, 1879) 148
14. 'Lynedoch' waggon about to start for town . . 148
15. Charles Smythe as Speaker of Legislative Assembly of Natal 149
16. Return of Natal Volunteers, 1900 196
17. Winston Churchill and Lord Elgin (*'Punch cartoon, April*, 1906) 197
18. British Lion (to his cub Natal) "Go it, young 'un. I like to see you fighting your own battles. But, if you want me, I'm here." (*'Punch, May*, 1906) 197
19. The National Convention, Durban, 1908 (*Parliament Library, Cape Town*) 212
20. South Africa's first Provincial Administrators, 1912 . 213

Standing (left to right)   J. Rissik (Transvaal)
                       W. Ramsbottom (O.F.S.)

Sitting (left to right)   C. Smythe (Natal)
                       F. de Waal (Cape)

AUTHOR'S NOTE

'FAREWELL TO THE HIGHLANDS' is not a biography of the Hon. Charles John Smythe so much as a record of his achievements; I have not attempted to analyse his character, or assess the value of his political work. The book is intended to take the place of the autobiography he planned to write when he retired from his post as Administrator of Natal.

Mr Smythe died before he had completed more than a few pages of his life-story, but he left behind a set of diaries (hitherto unpublished) and many letters covering the period 1868 to 1918, which are valuable Africana. I have quoted from the diary and letters as extensively as possible in tracing the career of this successful pioneer-farmer and politician, and have sketched in the background history for the benefit of anyone unfamiliar with it.

Readers may disagree with some of Mr Smythe's views, but they should remember that these are views which were expressed fifty-five to a hundred years ago. Neither his descendants living today, nor I as his editor, necessarily share his opinions.

CHAPTER ONE

'FAREWELL TO THE HIGHLANDS, farewell to the north . . .'
Perhaps Charles John Smythe remembered this line from a poem
by Robert Burns as he gazed out of a railway-carriage window
one day in *February, 1872,* and watched the Scottish landscape
gliding by. He was leaving behind the Perthshire countryside
he had known from childhood and was going south to London,
far from home, family and friends. And London was only a
stopping-place on a long journey which would take him further
south still, for at Southampton he was to board a ship and sail
six thousand miles to the Cape of Good Hope at the foot of
Africa, and from there go on up the coast to Durban in the
British colony of Natal.

Charles planned to take up farming when he reached his
destination. He had a scheme in mind which he had set down in
his diary, (the keeping of a journal was to become a life-long
habit), and had written:

'I intend when I get to Durban to go to a sugar plantation.
People say that the coast is unhealthy, but as I shall get there in
winter it will not be so bad. If I do not like it I shall go up-country
and look at the sheep-farming . . . of course if I like the sugar I
shall stay on.'

Charles loved Scotland and was devoted to his parents and
brothers and sisters, but at the same time he longed for fresh
scenes, new faces, and the opportunity to strike out for himself
in an environment quite different from anything he had known
before. He had heard that a man could do very well in Natal if
he was prepared to work hard and put up with rough colonial
ways and lack of comfort. Charles was only nineteen, and was
energetic and full of confidence, keen to prove that he could make
a success of the career he had chosen. So it was farewell – for a
few years, at any rate – to the Highlands, and farewell to the
north. C.J.S. was going south.

1

The mailship *Norseman* (1,386 tons), in which he was to make his voyage to Cape Town belonged to the Union Line, which had not yet amalgamated with Donald Currie's Castle Line; she was 'not much bigger than the Harwich and Rotterdam ferry-boats', and was a strange-looking vessel propelled by sail as well as steam.

His cabin companions were two young men named Herbert and Frank Rhodes, eldest and second-eldest brothers of Cecil Rhodes, a promising youth whose business flair was already recognised on the Diamond Fields at Kimberley. Herbert had left Cecil in charge of his claims on the Fields when he went back to England for a brief visit; they had previously farmed together on a small cotton estate in Natal which Herbert still owned. Frank Rhodes had never been to South Africa before, and was coming out on holiday, not to settle; he had decided to make the Army his career, and was waiting to take up a commission in a crack cavalry regiment, the 1st (Royal) Dragoons.

It was not by mere chance that Charles found himself sharing a cabin with the Rhodes brothers. Herbert had been partly responsible for his emigrating to Natal, and treated him as a protégé. He had, in fact, gone to the trouble of booking Charles's passage for him. The two had been brought together by Charles's uncle and aunt, Mr. and Mrs. Archer-Houblon, who lived at Hallingbury Place in Hertfordshire and were friends of Herbert's father, the Rev. Francis Rhodes, rector of nearby Bishop's Stortford. When Mrs. Archer-Houblon heard in *December, 1871*, that Charles was thinking of going farming overseas it occurred to her that Herbert would be the very person to help him. It was a lucky thing that he happened to be at home just now and was on the point of returning to Natal. Charles should go out there with him, live on his estate and learn to grow cotton. It would be a splendid arrangement!

The Archer-Houblons were so captivated with this idea that they called on Herbert straightaway and requested – one might almost say commanded – him to take their nephew to South Africa and give him a job. Herbert took the line of least resistance and agreed to do as they asked. Charles knew nothing of all this until his mother received word of it from her sister. He wrote in his diary:

January 4th [1872]: 'While I was dressing Mama came up to my room and read me two letters from Aunt Georgie saying that they had seen a young Mr. Rhodes, son of the rector of Bishop's Stortford, who had just come home from Natal, and they had asked him if he would take me out with him and he said he would. It sounds very well indeed, and I think I shall go and see the man.'

He was thrilled that such a good opening had come his way.

Two days later Charles arrived at Hallingbury Place hotfoot from Scotland, only to be met with the news that the Natal plan had fallen through. Herbert had told the Archer-Houblons that he had decided to dispose of his cotton lands as soon as he could, and in future spend his time on the Diamond Fields. All hope of his taking young Smythe as a farm assistant had vanished. Charles could not even discuss the matter with him, as he had gone off to visit an aunt and would not be back at Bishop's Stortford for a fortnight.

Charles was angry and disappointed, but was not the sort to admit defeat and return meekly home. Herbert had let him down – very well then, he would go to Natal on his own. But first he needed to find out more about the Colony. He must put some questions to Herbert's father:

January 7th [a Sunday]: 'Walked in to Bishop's Stortford to church in the afternoon. Afterwards went to the rectory to see old Mr. Rhodes and had a long talk with him, but did not gather as much information as I wanted.'

January 8th: 'Saw Mr. Rhodes again and got a good deal more information from him'.

Still in search of facts and figures, Charles went to London next day to visit a relative, Frank Drummond, who was said to know a lot about South Africa. But Drummond had little to tell.

Charles now realised that there was nothing for it but to obtain the facts he needed direct from Herbert Rhodes. He knew that the rector's son was staying at Sleaford near Lincoln, so he consulted a railway time-table and then wrote and asked Herbert for an interview; he could fit in a visit to Sleaford before going back to Scotland. A favourable reply came by return post.

January 10th: 'Met young Mr. Rhodes at the station [at

3

Sleaford]. He took me to his aunt's, Miss Peacock's, house where we talked about Natal. Dinner at 6, and away at half-past.'

Charles's diary gives no details concerning his conversation with Herbert. All we know is that when he left for home that night it had been settled that he should sail for Natal with the Rhodes brothers the following week. One imagines Herbert saying, breezily, 'Sorry about the cotton-farming plan, but cotton's a dead loss anyway – that's why I'm giving it up – gets boll-worm in it, you know. But you come out to Durban with me all the same, and I'll get you introductions to one or two of the big sugar-planters there. Sugar – now *that's* the crop that earns money! Not cotton.'

Charles spent the next few days in a frantic rush to get ready for the voyage, but at the last minute the impulsive Herbert changed his plans again:

January 18th: 'Telegram from Rhodes to say that he was not going out to Natal till the *25th of February*, so I shall not go out till then either. I am sorry that I am not going away next week, now that I am all ready for it. It is a great bore to have it all over again. I hope Rhodes does not mind my coming out with him.'

January 31st: 'This month has been a very eventful one, at the beginning of it I knew nothing about this Natal business.'

February 3rd: 'Wrote to . . . Rhodes . . . asking him to take my passage for me.'

February 7th: 'I heard from Rhodes, saying he would take my berth for me.'

February 9th: 'Heard from Rhodes, enclosing a ticket for the *Norseman* steamer to sail on the *26th* of this month, from Southampton. The passage money from London to Natal is £38.–17/–.'

Charles wrote to Herbert, thanking him and sending the money for his ticket. The £38.–17/– covered first-class accommodation on the ship, which he thought quite reasonable. His new Martini-Henry rifle had not been expensive, either; he had got it 'with case and all the necessaries and 500 cartridges, all for £15'. A pair of revolvers in a case had cost £6, and he had also bought a medicine-chest, a charcoal-filter for straining water, and a supply of soap.

On *February 23rd* Charles arrived in London from Scotland, after 'a most touching farewell scene with Mama'; the parting from his parents and brothers and sisters had been a strain, for the Smythes were an affectionate family. He wondered if, after all, he was making a mistake in leaving them and going off to Africa. But his moment of doubt had been forgotten by the time he went aboard the *Norseman* at Southampton on the morning of the *26th*, and when the ship weighed anchor that afternoon and he knew the voyage had really begun his spirits soared. He stayed on deck until the cold wind drove him indoors, then went down to join Herbert and Frank in their cabin and get ready for five o'clock dinner.

Charles Smythe had little in common with the Rhodes brothers, although all three men were ex-public schoolboys, (Frank had been at Eton, Herbert at Winchester, and Charles at Trinity College, Glenalmond). The vicarage at Bishop's Stortford was a middle-class home which was typically English, whereas Charles came from an historic estate in the Scottish Highlands, and his kinsfolk belonged to the aristocracy and landed gentry of Scotland. Charles's father, William Smythe, had inherited the imposing Methven Castle near Perth, a building erected in the mid-seventeenth century by one Patrick Smythe of Braco. Among his forbears was James Graham, first Marquis of Montrose, the great soldier and statesman. An earlier and even more illustrious ancestor was the sixteenth-century Dutch ruler, William the Silent, Prince of Orange, under whose leadership the people of the Netherlands had fought to free themselves from Spanish tyranny.*

Methven Castle, where Charles grew up, was four storeys high and massive rather than beautiful; it had originally consisted of a square block with a round tower at each corner, the towers topped by pointed Gothic roofs, but there had been a later, more ornate, addition with crow-stepped gables, tall chimneys and stone balustrades. The interior walls were hung with family portraits and an assortment of old swords and dirks.

---

* See Appendix I.

5

The country surrounding Charles's home was thickly forested, and as a boy he spent many happy hours roaming Methven Wood where the Scots under Robert Bruce had fought a fierce battle with the English in *1306*. These ancient oaks were only a part of the extensive woods on the property, for there were large plantations as well; it was no wonder that he learnt to love and value trees and felt that no landscape was perfect without them.

An estate such as Methven required a huge staff to maintain it; William Smythe and his family were surrounded by about fifty retainers including gardeners, grooms, dairymaids and household servants, and lived in a style which few people can afford today. The members of the staff were well treated, (a ball was given for them from time to time in the servants' hall of the Castle, with a tea-party the day before for their children), but Charles and his brothers and sisters were made to understand very early in life that insurmountable barriers existed between themselves and their father's employees, and that class distinction was something which could not be ignored. Society was divided into rigid castes, and everyone knew his or her place.

Charles's mother, Emily, encouraged him to be proud of his ancestry, for like William Smythe she had distinguished family connections; she was the daughter of General Sir John Oswald and his wife, Lady Charlotte Murray, granddaughter of the 3rd Duke of Athol. One of Emily's cousins was Lady Augusta Bruce, whose father, the 7th Earl of Elgin, had salvaged the famous marble frieze of the Parthenon in Athens in *1801* – the frieze known as the 'Elgin Marbles' – which was later acquired by the British Museum. Augusta was for many years an intimate friend of the Royal Family, and before her marriage to Dean Stanley of Westminster in *1863* she had held the important post of Resident Woman of the Bedchamber to Queen Victoria.

Like most children of well-to-do homes in Britain at that time, Charles spent his earliest years under the eye of a nanny and saw little of his parents. The nurseries at Methven Castle were in the charge of a Mrs. Bell, a kindly despot known affectionately as 'Pin'. Charles, who had been born in *1852*, had an elder brother named David, two younger brothers – Frank (Francis) and Wilfred – and a sister, Beatrice (Bice). There was also a

6

half-sister, Margaret, who became the wife of Viscount Strathallan and whose son, the 16th Earl of Perth, was to be the first secretary-general of the League of Nations.

Emancipation from the nursery world was slow, as Charles recalled many years afterwards. The first step was the privilege of joining the grown-ups after dinner:

'Arrayed in a white frock with broad, coloured sash, you were taken down to the dining-room door by 'Pin'. You walked in, the butler placed your small high chair for you, and you were given a dessert plate of old china and regaled with a biscuit and some fruit.'

After dinner everyone went into the drawing-room, and at eight o'clock 'Pin' would knock on the door and say it was time for the children to go to bed.

'The youngest would then be carried off. The others would follow at ten minute intervals. It was a long way from the drawing-room to the nursery, up a flight of stairs and along passages not particularly well lighted. It required some courage in a small boy, and mine evanesced by the time I reached the top of the flight of stairs – and I fled for all I was worth along the passages until I attained the haven of the nursery.'

The next step on the road to adulthood was dining with the grown-ups at two o'clock luncheon. Finally came the great day when David and Charles were given a bedroom to themselves and escaped at last from the nanny's clutches.

Charles began his education under a tutor he shared with David, then in *1862* when he was ten he was sent to public school. He got on fairly well during his seven years at Glenalmond, but took far more interest in outdoor sport than in lessons. Shooting became his passion, and by the time he was fifteen he was a very good shot; in the holidays he carried a gun and ranged Methven woods, hunting partridges, pheasants and hares. He did not distinguish himself at school, except that as a senior boy he was considered responsible enough to be made prefect of a table in the refectory.

Charles left Glenalmond in *July, 1869*, with no definite career in mind. His brother David was going into the Army, but he didn't want to follow suit. His mother was ambitious for him; she dreamed of his becoming a barrister and rising to the top of his profession, and was disappointed when he said he didn't think he had brains enough to be a lawyer, 'it requires such an awful lot of work and knowledge'. He was not aware of his intellectual powers, since he had never really made use of them. Yet he was shrewd enough to realise he could make good if only he had sufficient incentive. He wrote in his diary, 'I think I require new scenes and something to make me work harder.'

His father suggested that he should become a stockbroker, someone else that he should go farming in Queensland, Australia, but Charles turned down both proposals. Exasperated, William Smythe sent his son to a 'crammer' in Cumberland for a few months, and then in *May, 1870,* Charles left for the Continent to study German under a tutor in Hanover. He spent about a year, off and on, in Germany, and was there while Prussia and France were at war. The experience of 'living in lodgings of my own, quite by myself under no control' gave him self-assurance and he learnt the value of money through having to manage on the allowance his father sent him.

He returned to Scotland fluent in German, and his parents decided to enter him for the Indian Forestry Service, for which a knowledge of either German or French was an essential qualification. He sat the examinations in London in *November, 1871,* but when the results in the various subjects were announced a month later he found he had failed badly. Mr. and Mrs. Smythe were upset, but Charles did not really care as his heart had never been in the Forestry project.

Idly, he reconsidered the suggestions that had been made earlier, and settled on farming overseas as being the only career for which he felt the slightest inclination. He was on the point of making enquiries about Australia when his mother mentioned his plans to Mrs. Archer-Houblon. By return had come 'Aunt Georgie's' letter with its news about Herbert Rhodes and his cotton-plantation, and Charles's imagination had immediately been fired: Natal seemed to him, all of a sudden, to be the place where his future lay! His parents sighed with relief that he had found an aim in life at last; they didn't know the first thing about Natal, but if the Archer-Houblons approved of it it must be all right.

The *Norseman* took thirty-five days to reach Cape Town from Southampton, and the voyage was far from comfortable for the ninety-five passengers on board, even those forty-eight who were travelling first class. The cabin shared by Charles and the other two young men was minute:

'The size of the cabin is about 7 ft. by 8 ft., including the berths. I am in the upper one – young Rhodes [Frank] in the lower one and old Rhodes [Herbert] in the single one on the other side. There are no shelves nor any place for putting things, and it is so small we have to dress by turns.'

At any rate, the meals were satisfactory:

'They feed us very well, we have breakfast at 8.30 with hot meat. Cold lunch at 1, and dinner at 5. We are going to try to get either tea or supper at 9.'

But a few days later Charles was writing:

'The water . . . is very bad, they make it by distilling the salt water and it makes everything boiled taste horrid, potatoes, vegetables, etc.'

Many of the *Norseman's* passengers were going out to the South African Diamond Fields, and included several women who were adventuresses if not actual prostitutes:

'There are some very funny sort of ladies on board, one in particular who seems a regular – –!'

But he made friends with a number of the men, especially 'two very jolly fellows, friends of Rhodes, one called Studdy from Devonshire and the other the Hon. Guy Dawnay'.

Studdy was going diamond-digging, and the twenty-four-year-old Guy, (a son of the 7th Viscount Downe), was travelling to Africa to shoot, and planned to join an elephant-hunter on safari:

'Dawnay is going up as far as the Victoria Falls on the Zambesi, where very few people have been before. He expects capital shooting – elephants, giraffes, buffalo, etc.'

Thrown into such close contact with Herbert and Frank Rhodes, Charles soon discovered that the brothers were very different in disposition. He had immediately taken to Frank, who was only a year older than himself and was a man of exceptional charm, very popular with everyone. Herbert, aged twenty-seven, was less attractive and was inclined to be quick-tempered and arrogant; he had a very unstable temperament, and had tried soldiering, cotton-growing and diamond-digging in turns, but his restless nature prevented his ever sticking to anything. All the same, he was good company on the voyage.

Charles went ashore at Madeira with Herbert when the *Norseman* called at the island a week after leaving England:

March 5th: 'The quarantine boat came off about ½ to 7. Went ashore with old Rhodes and a Mrs. Phillips.'

They breakfasted at Reid's Hotel, posted letters home, then hired horses and went riding:

'A most beautiful ride up to the top of the hills and then to the convent, and came down from there in a sledge over the paving stones . . . went down into the town and met young Rhodes and the others.'

The party returned to the ship, which sailed soon after lunch.

'Got a splendid breeze in our favour when we got outside. A most glorious day on the whole. I managed to get on the horse much better than I expected, and the scenery was simply splendid. I do not think I ever enjoyed a morning so much.'

There would be no further ports of call until they reached Cape Town, so the *Norseman's* passengers settled down to amuse themselves as best they could:

March 8th: 'Read, knitted [Charles was making himself a pair of socks], played chess . . . Rhodes and Dawnay made a roulette table in the afternoon and play began in the evening. Rhodes was banker, at first lost a little but afterwards won something like £50. One man lost all his money and had to give him an IOU for £20. I staked a little and won 3/6d then left off. Then played whist with Rhodes, Studdy and young Carr for 6d a point.'

The roulette table was a great attraction:

March 22nd: 'Played roulette in the evening in the smoking room. The captain and Mr. Joseph were the bank and were broken by everybody backing 00. The board is evidently unfair. Cotton then took the bank and lost a good deal. I won two guineas.'

Gambling was not allowed on Sundays, which were observed as solemnly at sea as on land. A religious service was held every Sunday morning, either in the saloon or on the poop deck.

10

Charles had been disappointed to find that 'the ship does not seem provided with books or games', but the passengers overcame the lack of a library or shop by holding auctions from time to time among themselves. At one of these Charles 'sold a novel for half a crown and bought three others, a pot of peach jam and a bottle of chutney.'

There was no practical joking when they crossed the Line, instead the crew was mustered for fire-fighting practice:

'The fire bell was rung and the men turned out to exercise . . . then they had the hose fixed on and all in their places in about a minute.'

Ten days later Charles watched the crew take part in a very curious ritual:

'In the evening the sailors burnt the effigy of a dead horse as they have been a month out from harbour today and from tomorrow begin to receive wages, as before they start they get a month in advance.' [This ceremony was an old seafaring custom, and in performing it the sailors used a wooden effigy suspended from the shrouds. They had a saying that to do work which had been paid for in advance was *to work with a dead horse* because you could not expect to get anything out of it; as they usually squandered their advance pay before sailing, they felt that the first month at sea was profitless].

The heat during much of the voyage was very trying, and had led to quarrels breaking out among the passengers. One of the 'very funny sort of ladies' Charles had noticed at the start was a persistent cause of commotion:

March 14th: 'There was great excitement in the evening, a Mademoiselle R, who was in a cabin with a sick old lady, insisted on having the porthole and door both shut although it was sweltering hot. She had been very quarrelsome before on the voyage, and another lady in the same cabin had to leave it. She began making a row and Studdy, who was next door, told her to be quiet. The old lady was obliged to go into the ladies' saloon to sleep, and at last there was such a row that the captain had to come in. It was a great joke – everybody turned out of their cabins in all sorts of costumes, nightshirts and anything.'

March 15th: 'There was another scene with Mlle R in the morning, down in the cabin.'

11

March 30th: 'There was another row about 12 o'clock at night between Mlle and the passengers. I was asleep all through it, but it seems to have been even worse than the last'.

People on board the *Norseman* had plenty to grumble about besides noise: the ship's engines failed on at least three occasions, the pump that supplied the bathroom and condenser broke down, and there was an epidemic of whooping-cough. Bad weather added to the general discomfort, especially when the little *Norseman* was nearing Cape Town:

March 27th: 'Met a heavy gale from the South . . . as we could not steam against it we had to sail away to the S.W., getting tremendously pitched about.'

March 29th: 'We shipped a good deal of water, the second-class cabin was knee-deep sometimes.'

Table Mountain was sighted on Easter Sunday, *March 31st*, and the ship berthed at Cape Town docks in the late afternoon. Charles was not much impressed with South Africa's mother city:

'This is a very straggling town with a few English troops, the 86th Regt. [2nd Royal Irish Rifles] just now. It seems so funny to see English soldiers walking about after having travelled so many hundreds of miles from home.' [Cape Colony had been a British possession since *1806*, and British regiments were permanently stationed there.]

Charles and the other passengers bound for Natal disembarked at Cape Town, as the mailships sailed only as far as Port Elizabeth before turning round. They had to wait several days for the coastal steamer to Durban, but the time passed pleasantly; Charles visited the museum, the botanical gardens and the swimming-baths, and on *April 3rd* he went out by train to Wynberg to watch a cricket match between a team from the *Norseman* and a local eleven. The *Norseman* team was captained by Herbert Rhodes, who had been an outstanding cricketer when he was at school at Winchester. Next day Charles went down to say goodbye to friends on the mailship, which left for Port Elizabeth that afternoon. He was feeling depressed, as Frank Rhodes was ill with a bowel complaint and although better 'will not be able to go by the *Natal* [coaster] which is a great bore for me as I shall not know what to do.'

Charles and Frank had become great friends.

April 5th: 'Bought eight Waverley novels, a puggeree and some tinder . . . went to the fruit market and ate a lot of grapes, pomegranates and figs. Rhodes, Monkton and Dawnay dined at the officers' barracks, at mess. Rhodes is going to come on in the *Natal* and leave his brother.'

On the *6th* Charles and the others sailed for Durban, while Frank Rhodes stayed behind in Cape Town.

April 8th: 'Got to Mossel Bay about five in the morning. Went on shore with Rhodes and Dawnay . . . went rambling up the hills, then Rhodes and I hired a trap and drove to some caves, which were very fine. We had a most pleasant drive.'

The *Natal* left that afternoon for Port Elizabeth.

April 9th: 'Got into Algoa Bay at 7 o'clock in the evening. Rhodes and Dawnay played Blind Hookey in the evening. Rhodes lost £53 to him.' [Blind Hookey is a gambling game in which players make their stakes on pure speculation without looking at their cards first].

April 10th: 'Went ashore at Port Elizabeth with Studdy and Nisbett. Strolled about the town, went to the library. Botanical gardens after lunch with Rhodes [and others]. Rhodes and Wood tried who could keep their head under water longest. Rhodes won, he kept his under for 2 minutes and 8 seconds. [Herbert was a fine athlete.] Then went with Carr to the Club, and saw some English papers with an account of the Procession and of a man the day after presenting a pistol at the Queen when driving.'

The procession to which Charles refers was Queen Victoria's drive through London with the Prince and Princess of Wales, (later, King Edward VII and Queen Alexandra), to attend a thanksgiving service at St. Paul's for the Prince's recovery from typhoid fever; he had been very close to death. The man who pointed a pistol at the Queen the following day was a half-crazed youth not responsible for his actions, but the attempt on her life rocked Britain and the Empire.

The *Natal* spent only one day at Port Elizabeth, and as she left harbour, passing the *Norseman* at the mailship's berth, 'the captain burnt a blue light . . . by way of saying farewell'.

April 11th: 'Got to East London about 2. Landed one boatful of cargo, and passengers in a surfboat.'

April 12th: 'A few mackerel were caught . . . by lines towing behind the ship with a bit of red cloth for bait. Passed St. Johns River [the Umzimvubu] at 12 o'clock. Came on to rain hard in the afternoon, and a tremendous sea on. I have never seen a ship roll so much before.'

April 13th: 'Arrived opposite Natal [i.e. Durban] at 9 o'clock . . . waited the whole day hoping in vain for a boat which never came off. The harbour is one of the finest natural ones in the world, but there is a shifting bar of sand which spoils it. Vessels can only get in at high water, which was at 8 o'clock this morning, and pilots will not go in after dark, so we hope to get in tomorrow.'

The entrance to Durban Bay was a narrow channel between the Point and the end of the high Bluff opposite, and the sand bar across it closed the harbour to ships of any real size. Vessels obliged to anchor in the unsheltered roadstead were often blown ashore on the 'Back Beach', now Durban's main bathing beach, and wrecked.

April 14th: 'Expected to move this morning, but were disappointed bitterly. The *Bismarck*, another coast steamer, came out across the bar in the morning and sent the pilot she had on board to us, but he would not take us across, so we are in for another day. No boats came out, though the sea seemed to us as calm as it could be. They do not seem very anxious for their letters, as we have the mails on board and they keep us for two days within sight of land without getting them. Amused ourselves with signalling . . . to the flag station. Did nothing in particular, but any amount of grumbling.'

April 15th: 'At 8 o'clock we up anchor and steamed on to the bar. Stuck there for about 20 minutes [they were eased off with the help of a tugboat] and then got into the harbour.'

The wide expanse of Durban Bay lay before them, serene and as yet unspoilt, protected on the southwestern side by the Bluff and fringed by trees growing right down to the water's edge. The *Natal* glided to her anchorage, and Charles went ashore in a boat with his friend Nisbett and another man. At the Point they caught a train to take them two miles through the bush to the town.

14

Charles and Nisbett took a double room at the Royal Hotel, which faced on to the square known as the Town Gardens, and then went off to find a magistrate to obtain permission to pass their guns through the Customs. Herbert Rhodes joined them at the 'Royal', (which Charles described as 'a very good hotel... and they feed us capitally'), and after lunch they walked about the town:

'Bought some pineapples for 3d a piece ... Dinner at ½ past 6. Had bananas, oranges, and grenadillas [passion fruit] at dessert. I am not sure whether I like the latter or not. Rhodes felt seedy in the evening, left dinner and went to bed.'

Next morning Charles went down to the Point, got his luggage cleared at the Customs and brought it back to the hotel; to his relief he found everything in 'wonderful condition'. He and his friends discussed their plans:

'Rhodes is going to wait on here till his brother joins him – which will be very jolly as he will not be here for at least a fortnight ... Dawnay will also be here for some time, and Buttermer [another friend from the *Norseman*] who has got a lot of letters of introduction to sugar planters.'

Charles's first impression of Durban was:

'Not much of a town ... all the country round for miles is bush, with here and there a plantation. The bush is about twelve foot high and so thick it looks as if you could not go through it ... the mosquitoes bother a little at night, but they are not bad at this time of year.'

His real interest was of course in the sugar-cane farms, and he could hardly wait to get out into the country and see them. Life seemed full of promise, and in a few days' time he would be twenty years old!

Durban, second largest settlement in the Colony of Natal, was not such an insignificant place in *1872* as Charles Smythe's letters to his relations in Scotland may have led them to believe. Its wide streets were being hardened, and were bordered by houses, shops and offices some of which were double-storeyed. Brick and corrugated-iron had replaced wattle-and-daub and

15

thatch as building materials. Durban's Town Gardens were flanked by what Mr. (later, Sir) John Robinson called in his 'Notes on Natal, 1872' 'a handsome pile of public offices' (now known as the Old Court House), and other amenities included 'a bathing-stage [at the Bayside], public wells and pumps, a spacious gaol ... street lamps, masonic halls, and a bowling alley'. Behind the town rose the wooded heights of the Berea, dotted with houses and gardens approached by sandy lanes which, only twenty years before, had been tracks made by elephants roaming the indigenous forest.

The Colony was a much smaller country than South Africa's Province of Natal today. It was bounded to the north by the Tugela and Buffalo rivers, beyond which lay the territory of the warlike Zulus whose name fifty years earlier, in the reign of the terrible Shaka, had been known and feared as far north as Lake Malawi. In *1872* Zululand was in a state of turmoil, torn by strife between rival chiefs struggling for supremacy, and refugees spilled into Natal to join the 300,000 Zulus already living peaceably there. The Natal Zulus were called 'kaffirs' to distinguish them from their kinsmen across the Tugela; the word 'kaffir' means 'unbeliever' in Arabic, and was not used by the whites in a derogatory sense in those days, as it is now.

The European population of Natal was barely 18,000. Most of the settlers were British, over three thousand of whom lived in Durban and another four thousand or so in the capital, Pietermaritzburg, fifty-four miles inland from the port; nearly all the others were farming folk. Pietermaritzburg, which was the seat of the Lieutenant-Governor, His Excellency, Robert Keate, was connected with Durban by electric telegraph, but there was no rail link between the two towns.

CHAPTER TWO

CHARLES WROTE HIS DIARY in a series of strong, well-bound notebooks, and had reached the last page of one of these during the voyage to South Africa. His final entry had been:

'With this volume I end probably the happiest time of my life, with no cares about money or anything else. Henceforth I shall have to work hard, keep up a character, and make a name in a new world without one person that I know beyond the two months' acquaintance. I hope I shall be able to do it.'

It was a challenge, and he was determined to succeed. He would begin by putting his money affairs in order:

April 17th: 'Went to the London and South African Bank and heard from them that £200 had been paid to my credit [by his father, through the Union Bank of Scotland]. I found that to get any interest upon it I have to have it first for three months and then to give three months' warning before I drew it, so I cannot draw any before this day six months. I therefore deposited £160 at four per cent on those conditions, leaving the other £40 for my expenses in that time. Received from them a cheque-book.'

(In a letter to his mother he mentioned this transaction and added, 'Say to Father that I find gold is far the best thing to bring out, as they charge five per cent for changing English notes').

After his visit to the bank Charles called at a magistrate's to apply for a permit to buy gunpowder, then spent the afternoon cleaning his guns while Herbert Rhodes and Dawnay went to a croquet party.

April 18th: 'Studdy, Nisbett, Rhodes and Dawnay started at 6 by coach [the daily four-horse omnibus] for Pietermaritz-burg. [Dawnay and Rhodes were going to the latter's cotton farm near Richmond.] Before he left Rhodes introduced me to a man called Grice, with whom I am going to see a sugar

17

plantation . . . Saw Buttermer off by train to Umgeni . . . feel very lonely being quite by myself without knowing a soul here. Got out my concertina and played on it.'

On the *19th* Mr. Grice called to make arrangements for the visit to the plantation, and next day he and Charles set out on horseback for Mr. Andrew Kennedy's farm – one of the largest sugar estates in Natal – at Sea Cow Lake, a few miles north of Durban. Grice's sister and a Miss Beningfield had gone on ahead.

'Overtook them and got on all right till we came to a drift [ford] over a small river [the Umgeni] that was swollen by rain. We had to dismount, take off our saddles and go across in a boat while kaffirs swam our horses across.' [Recent floods had swept away the bridge.]

When the party reached Sea Cow Lake they found that the farmer was not at home, but his wife entertained them hospitably. Kennedy turned up late that night, 'having had to walk from the drift, his horse not being able to cross as it had risen so since we left.'

April 21st: 'My birthday, though I never remembered it was till the evening . . . Grice and I and Mr. Kennedy went for a walk over the plantation. They have nearly 1,300 acres under sugar and coffee, he has two sugar mills and a coffee mill. The largest concern in the Colony . . . I had a long talk with Mr. Kennedy, hoping he would let me come on to his plantation, but he did not propose it so I did not like to.'

Charles was disappointed that no offer had been made him, but did not give up hope that the planter (a fifty-five-year-old pioneer from Lancashire) might change his mind and take him on as an assistant or overseer. He decided to keep in close touch with the Kennedys, and started back for town feeling that the visit to Sea Cow Lake had not been altogether a waste of time.

When he and Grice and the ladies reached the Umgeni they found it still running high, and there was no-one to swim their ponies across:

'We took the saddles off and tied the horses' bridles up tight and drove them into the river; they all got safely over, after being carried down a good way by the current.'

As soon as Buttermer returned to Durban he and Charles hired horses from the Royal Hotel's stables and went to see

18

another of the local sugar estates:

April 25th: 'Started with Buttermer at about 11 for the Reunion plantation . . . sent our bags on there by a kaffir. It is about ten miles from here.'

They spent two days looking over the farm and mill, but Charles thought the place compared unfavourably with Kennedy's. On their return to the 'Royal' they found that Rhodes and Dawnay were back.

The following morning was a Sunday, and Charles attended Matins at St. Paul's Anglican church. The service was conducted by the famous Bishop John William Colenso,* the cleric at the centre of a furious religious controversy which was still raging:

'Went to St. Paul's . . . at 11, and heard Bishop Colenso preach. Did not think much of him. He did not do or say anything particularly striking.'

After lunch Charles walked to the botanical gardens with Buttermer, Rhodes and Dawnay.

Next day Buttermer said goodbye to his friends from the *Norseman*, and left for Pietermaritzburg; he had been offered the run of a 6,000 acre farm for three years, rent-free, and was to join in partnership with the owner's son to stock it. Wishing he were as well placed, Charles went off to mull over his own plans while he watched Herbert Rhodes playing in a cricket match. Later, he and Herbert discussed his affairs:

May 1st: 'I talked with Rhodes, who said he did not think I could get a better plantation to go on that this [Sea Cow Lake] where there is both sugar and coffee grown.'

With Herbert's encouragement Charles approached Mr. Kennedy again:

May 2nd: 'Rode to a coffee estate with Kennedy where there was a coffee pulper at work which he wished to see as he is putting up a coffee mill.'

There was still no offer of employment, but the farmer went so far as to suggest that Charles come to stay at Sea Cow Lake for a time; the young man could board with his sister, Mrs. Phillips, who lived with her son and daughter in a house near

---

* See Appendix II.

his own. Charles was delighted. He had just bought a hack called 'Lucknow' from Mr. Duncombe, the landlord of the Royal Hotel, so would be able to get about the estate easily and ride in to Durban whenever he pleased.

May 4th: 'I settled with Mrs. Phillips I should give her £5 a month exclusive of horse feed and kaffir's wages to look after the horse, but she could not take me in for a month. Mrs. Kennedy kindly invited me to come . . . and stop till Mrs. Phillips is ready.'

May 6th: 'Asked Duncombe where I could hire a kaffir and he got me one. I am to give him 7/– for the first month and his food, and if I like him 8/– the second month.'

Charles hurried off to buy a currycomb and brushes for his pony, and showed off his paces to Dawnay when they went riding together:

'Dawnay possesses two steeds for hunting purposes, far inferior to mine . . . "Lucknow" is a very good animal, warranted the fastest $\frac{1}{4}$ of a mile horse in the Colony.'

He left the hotel and moved his belongings to the Kennedys', but found next morning that his newly-hired groom had 'bolted'. To add to his chagrin, 'Lucknow' put a foot in an antbear hole and tossed him off into the mud while he was riding through the sugar-cane with his host. His stay at Sea Cow Lake had begun badly, but at any rate he managed to pick up a great deal of information about farming from Kennedy, and was shown the machinery in the new mill 'where they were working the centrifuge which separates the sugar from the treacle.'

May 9th: 'Rode into Durban to look for my kaffir but could not hear of him so shall get another. It was the Thanksgiving Day in Durban for the recovery of the Prince of Wales. They had services, and in the evening a bonfire at which three oxen were roasted for the kaffirs of whom there were about a thousand, and then they danced their war dance.'

On the *11th* Charles was in town again, this time to meet Frank Rhodes, who had at last arrived from Cape Town; there was a lively reunion at the 'Royal', in which Herbert and Dawnay joined. The party was a farewell occasion too, for the Rhodes brothers would be leaving in a few days' time for the

Diamond Fields. Guy Dawnay was going away too; he had arranged to go big-game shooting in Zululand before he trekked up-country. Charles expected to meet these young men again, so said goodbye quite cheerfully.

When he got back to the Kennedys' house he found the family opening letters and newspapers from overseas, for the *Natal* in which Frank had come up from Cape Town had brought the fortnightly English mail. There were two news items of outstanding interest:

'The S.S. *Penguin* made the quickest voyage on record to the Cape from England in $24\frac{1}{2}$ days. . . . Mr. Musgrave is appointed Lieut. Governor of Natal' [in succession to Keate].

Charles had found mail from Scotland awaiting him in town, and sat down at once to answer it. In a letter to his mother he wrote:

'Maggie [Margaret] will be interested to hear that the river literally swarms with alligators, as she warned me so against bathing in the rivers. The lake which is about half a mile from the house used in addition to have hippopotami [sea cows] but there are only two left and these are very shy and cunning. I have not seen any bad snakes yet, though there are a good many about. The greatest plague is undoubtedly the ticks, which if you go into any grass or bush cover you and are very difficult to get rid of except by rubbing yourself with oil. The climate is most splendid, and they say that for the next four months we may count on the same fine weather without a drop of rain.'

Even in the dry season the coast was unhealthy, as he soon discovered. He began to feel off-colour, and took medical advice the next time he was in Durban:

May 15th: 'Went to Dr. Lyall's and told him I did not feel well, and he said I had a touch of fever. Gave me some pills and recommended a warm bath in the evening and a cold one in the morning.'

This rather odd treatment was successful.

Charles got on very well with Mr. Kennedy whilst staying in his house, and went with him every day to inspect the mills or the lands. He could learn very quickly if sufficiently interested, and soon grasped the financial aspect of sugar and coffee farming

21

despite the fact that he had had no business training or experience of any sort. In a letter to his father he wrote:

'Sea Cow Lake. Mr. Kennedy's.
May 17th, 1872.

'Dear Father,

'I dare say you would like to hear what sort of an estate this is. At the nearest point it is about 5 miles from Durban. The area is 4,000 acres, of which there are 1,200 under sugar and 150 coffee; the rest is uncultivated bushland. It is very well supplied with water, as the Umgeni bounds it on two sides and the little Umhlanga on another.

'Mr. Kennedy has been out here 16 years, and was one of the first who began planting sugar here. He had little capital to start with, and consequently had to raise money by mortgage when he got his machinery. He made it pay very well for ten years, but then he wanted more machinery and land so he went Home [to Britain] and made a company [the Umgeni Sugar Company] he getting half the shares and being made manager at £800 a year. This was about five years ago, and now they have got a splendid sugar mill and gone in a little for coffee. They expect a dividend of 10½ per cent for this last year. The total outlay on the estate has been about £65,000 on the 16 years.

'I was talking with Mr. Kennedy about what was the least capital that one could begin on – he said certainly not less than £10,000 or you are sure to get into difficulties. The machinery cannot be got to be of any use under £3,000. Their new mill here cost nearer £10,000. The cost of good sugar land anywhere near here is about £3 an acre, and then you have to clear it at about £8 more.

'The great difficulty is transport. They are very lucky here in being only 5 miles from the Umgeni railway-station, which is the only railway [in Natal] except the one from the harbour to Durban, each of them being about 2 miles long. The only means of transport is by bullock waggons, 14 or 18 oxen to one waggon, with 1 or 1½ tons of weight. They have 500 oxen here, of which they lose about 15 per cent every year by sickness. They are trying tramways on some estates now, but it is too hilly here I think.

'Coffee has hardly been tried enough; it is paying enormously now as they are able to sell it at £70 or £80 a ton, but the question is whether it will pay when they get only the export price which is £50 or £60.

'Mr. Kennedy says before he invested all his capital in this concern he made a very good thing of lending his money on mortgage at 12 per cent, of course only doing so on the first mortgage . . . all mortgages are obliged to be registered at Pietermaritzburg to be legal . . .

'There is a dreadful disease here among the horses . . . that kills about 30 per cent. A horse may be quite well to all appearance, and in two hours is dead. They have no remedy of any kind for it. I hope my horse will not get it. [This was the terrible horse-sickness which killed thousands of beasts every year in South Africa; the cause was then unknown.]

'I am glad to hear you have got the drain finished all right at Methven . . . they do not go in for anything of that kind here, not even in Durban.

'Goodbye, dear Father,
'I remain your affectionate son,
'C. J. Smythe.'

William Smythe must have been very pleased with this letter. Charles's month at the Kennedys' was very full; when he was not at the mill he was trying his hand at taxidermy, stuffing birds he had shot, and he learnt to make bullets in a bullet-mould in the kitchen. He rode into Durban on a shopping expedition, arranging for an iron bedstead to be sent out in preparation for his move to the Phillips's, and he bought bedding at Messrs. Harvey and Greenacre's store. 'Lucknow' was put up at the Royal Hotel stables while he was in town. Charles had engaged a groom named John for his horse, at 12/– a month plus rations.

Every Sunday an Anglican clergyman, the Rev. Mr. Shears, came out to Sea Cow Lake to hold a religious service on the verandah of the Kennedy home, and neighbours rode over to attend. A Mrs. Turton accompanied the hymns on a harmonium which was 'a present to the congregation from the clergyman'. On one occasion Bishop Macrorie, Colenso's rival, came to preach the sermon. Charles found that the local Anglicans

23

were bitterly divided and feelings were running very high. 'People fight more about Colenso and Macrorie here than I should have thought possible'. He had not yet taken sides himself.

On *June 1st* he made his move from the Kennedys' to Mrs. Phillips's home; it was a house typical of the humbler settler dwellings of the period:

'You open the front door and find yourself in a living-room in which everything is done, eating, sitting, washing, ironing.'

Four doors led out of this apartment, three to bedrooms and one to 'a small kitchen and pantry where my kaffir and theirs sleep. All the rooms are about the same size, about ten feet by twelve. There is no ceiling, only a bit of canvas is stretched over the top of the wall with a galvanised roof above. The furniture is composed of old packing-cases, except five wooden chairs and one wooden table which we have in this room' [the one he shared with Mrs. Phillips's son, Tempie].

It took Charles a week or two to settle in. He put up shelves and a gun-rack in his bedroom, and tried (unsuccessfully) to get a kaross of silver jackal fur as a blanket for his bed. With his servant John's help he built a thatched shelter paved with bricks for his horse, and constructed a manger. He was so confident that his stay at Sea Cow Lake would be a long one that on his next visit to Durban he took out a quarter's subscription to the local newspaper, 'The Natal Mercury', which was published thrice weekly.

He sent his mother an account of how the Phillipses lived:

'There is no butcher nearer than Durban, and we send two or three times a week for meat and groceries. We bake our own bread; breakfast at eight consists of mealie [maize] porridge, meat, bread and jam [he liked the home-made jams – guava, Cape gooseberry and Indian sorrell]. Dinner at 1.30 of meat and perhaps pudding; tea at six or half-past, of bread and jam.'

He added:

'Clothing and boots are the most difficult things to get here, they are all ready-made and very dear.'

Charles often went hunting while he was at Sea Cow Lake: *July 3rd:* 'Killed my first buck, a reedbuck . . . my kaffir carried it home and skinned it.'

24

A few days after that he shot a 'boa constrictor', (it must have been a python), about seven feet long, and later on two blesbok. The buck were very good eating:

'My kaffir is always in a great state of joy when I shoot one, as he gets some of the meat which, as they never get anything but mealie porridge, is a great treat. He is a very sharp fellow, and we get on very well.'

On one occasion Charles shot and wounded an eight-foot crocodile in the Umhlanga River when he was out with his gun, and found it lying dead next day. His servant skinned it on the spot, and Charles proudly carried the skin home.

He often came across poisonous snakes on his hunting expeditions, and once a friend who was with him killed an eight-foot mamba, deadliest snake in Natal:

'We buried it carefully, as the kaffirs said that if they tread on one of its bones months afterwards they will get poisoned by it.'

Charles was enjoying the leisurely colonial life, and although he still visited Mr. Kennedy's sugar and coffee mills regularly he was spending more and more time riding and shooting or working in Mrs. Phillips's garden. He often went in to Durban for the day, had "tiffin" (lunch) at the Royal Hotel, and met friends there. His evenings at the Phillips's were spent in making music on his concertina to entertain the family, playing bezique or chess with Tempie, or taking his turn in reading aloud from a novel. He had begun to carry on a flirtation with Miss Phillips.

On *June the 13th and 14th* the winter race-meetings were held in Durban, on the flat ground at the foot of the Berea, and there was general excitement over them. Charles thought the racecourse very disappointing:

'There is no grandstand, everybody comes in their own waggon or carriage or on horseback.'

He was much better pleased with the dances he attended in Durban and in the North Coast village of Verulam in *July* and *August*:

August 14th: 'We have been very gay here since I last wrote, actually had two balls. The first one was at Verulam, about twenty miles from here, a county ball. The Kennedys went up in their trap and I rode beside them.'

25

He had sent John on ahead with his evening clothes, and changed at the hotel but was unable to get a bed there for the night. Dancing began at 8.30 p.m., and continued until half-past four in the morning:

'I was much surprised to see everybody so smart, much better got up than I expected, and not my idea of a Colonial ball. I went back to the hotel . . . lay down on a bench for an hour, then rode back here, and pretty tired I was – but I had a bath and was all right . . . It is rather a bore after coming in tired like that to have to rub down your horse, as my kaffir was bringing back my bag.'

The Durban ball was grander than the one at Verulam, with more guests, a sit-down supper, and music provided by the band of the 75th Regiment (1st Gordon Highlanders) from Pietermaritzburg. Dancing went on until 5 o'clock, and then Charles escorted Mrs. Kennedy and Miss Phillips to their lodgings before returning to the 'Royal', where he had left his hacking clothes, to smoke a pipe with a friend. Afterwards he lay on the floor in his friend's room, in a dressing-gown, for 'a snooze from 5.30 till 8'. His summing-up was, 'Awfully jolly ball.'

Charles had been delighted to find one of his old schoolfellows from the Highlands among the dancers:

'Saw Mitchell Innes, who was with me at Glenalmond, at the ball, he has been out here three years and is going to stock a farm up country.'

It was perhaps Mitchell Innes who gave him news of Herbert Rhodes:

'I hear that Rhodes has gone off to the Gold Fields, but I have never heard from him since he left here. There is not much talk about the Gold Fields – people seem to say that it requires machinery, therefore will only pay companies.' [These were the alluvial gold-workings of the Eastern Transvaal, not the Witwatersrand reefs which were as yet undiscovered]. Charles had written in his diary on *July 20th*, 'I have not heard anything of the Rhodeses since they left, and do not expect to.' Yet he was rather hurt that they had not kept in touch with him.

Guy Dawnay, on the other hand, had not forgotten Charles. He returned from Zululand in *November*, decided to visit

Kimberley en route to the Victoria Falls, and offered young Smythe a seat in his waggon for part of the journey. Writing to tell his parents this thrilling news, Charles said he planned to go as far as Kimberley with Dawnay, then turn back and stay for a time at the farm near Ladysmith in northern Natal where Buttermer was living:

'Buttermer says he will put me up for a bit and show me stock-farming.'

Mr. and Mrs. Smythe were not as pleased to hear of this trip as Charles expected, for they felt that by now he should have settled down to steady work on a sugar estate. His letter was doubly vexing because he had informed them, as an after-thought, that the Lieut. Governor of Natal, Mr. Musgrave, had taken a house in Durban for three months so as to meet the coast people; the Smythes knew the Governor well, (the Musgraves were a distinguished Scottish family), and they believed it would be in their son's interest to call on him. Now that he was going off on trek the opportunity would be lost.

But Charles was not interested in the Lieut. Governor, and he no longer cared about getting in with influential sugar-planters and others on the coast. He was not sure that he wanted to take up sugar or coffee farming after all, for he had discovered some of the snags; as far back as *September* he had noted, 'Bark disease has appeared on the coffee . . . a great pity as coffee seemed to be about the best thing going.' Also, the cost of labourers' rations had risen sharply and mealies were expensive, 30/– per muid instead of the usual 10/–.

The greatest drawback of all, however, was the shortage of labour:

'There is a great scarcity of black labour just now . . . the evil is that the kaffirs will not work as long as they can grow their mealies and pay 7/– [a year] for their hut tax, which they can earn by half a month's work . . . we now employ nothing but coolies [Indian labourers] about the mill as they are not so likely to go away as the kaffirs.'

Charles had been surprised to find Indians in Natal, but the reason for their being there was, as he said, that the Natal Zulus would not do agricultural work if they could help it. The sugar planters had been particularly hard hit, as cane-cutting

27

was a job no white immigrant would take on. In desperation the planters had persuaded the British Government to import indentured labourers from British India, and the first party had arrived in *1860*. Other Asiatics – mostly of the shopkeeping class – had emigrated to Natal at their own expense, and by *1872* the Colony's Indian population was well over 5,000.

The majority of the Natal Zulus lived in large, clearly-defined 'reserves'; these had been the creation of the British Government of *1844*, which had persuaded or compelled the black population to move into them when it took over the country. (The Africans had been in a disorganised state at the time, many of their clans shattered as a result of the upheavals of Shaka's day.) The number of Zulus in the reserves had increased enormously during nearly thirty years of peace under British rule, and many had found new homes for themselves on Crown land or had become tenants on the white settlers' farms.

Every married Zulu had his kraal or group of beautifully-constructed beehive huts, where he dwelt with his wives and children; he was by tradition a warrior and stock-owner, whose wealth was gauged by the size (not the quality) of his herds of cattle and flocks of sheep and goats. He left the tending of his mealie plot to his wives, as he was a proud man and considered work such as planting, hoeing and reaping to be beneath his dignity; he was quite different in every way from the toiling peasants of Europe and Asia. In *1872* there was still enough grazing land available to the Natal Zulus to enable them to cling to their out-dated pastoral way of life, but it would not be long before a lot of them would have to look for some other way of making a living.

The white colonists wanted to see the reserves broken up and the tribesmen employed in regular work on the farms or in the towns. Their motive was selfish, but their instinct was sound because the current system was doing the Zulus no good; under the British Government's laissez-faire policy they were stagnating instead of learning to adapt to Western civilisation. Under Natal's Representative form of government it was Britain, not the settlers, which was ultimately responsible for the Africans' welfare, but their education had been shamefully neglected – there were no schools for them except at the mission-stations, and they had few opportunities of learning European professions or skills. Mr. (later, Sir) Theophilus Shepstone, the Secretary for Native Affairs, had had plans for their advancement, but was hampered by lack of funds.

Shepstone, known throughout South Africa as *Somtseu*, had been guide, friend and virtual ruler of the tribes in the Colony since *1856* and had an insight into the mind of the African which few Europeans have had; he spoke the Zulus' language like one of themselves, understood their customs and laws, and found much to admire in their culture and character. He passed on a great deal of information about them to the novelist, Henry Rider Haggard, who worked under him for a time when he first came to Natal in *1875* as a young man. Haggard collected further information from *Somtseu's* head attendant, the old warrior *M'hlopekazi*, and from Mr. Fynney, the chief interpreter. Later, he wrote the epic story of the Zulus in four of his books – 'Nada the Lily', 'Marie', 'Child of Storm' and 'Finished'.

CHAPTER THREE

CHARLES'S JOURNEY TO the Diamond Fields with Guy Dawnay was due to begin in *mid-December, 1872*, and he had a good deal to do before they left:

December 10th: 'I have been busy getting everything ready for my trip, loading cartridges, etc. I shall take 300 for my rifle and 250 for my shotgun. People say the roads are in a dreadful state with all the rain.'

He had bought a sturdy pony called 'Pompey' for the rough travel, and would leave 'Lucknow' at Sea Cow Lake in the care of his servant; John had gone away for a time, but had sent a brother as a replacement:

'They have an agreement that when one is tired of working and wants to go home the other comes from home to take his place. Not at all a bad plan for the master.' [Zulus who took jobs in town always tried to keep one foot firmly planted in the country. This is how the migrant-labour system came about.]

Just before Charles set off he received an unfriendly note from Mr. Kennedy, which annoyed him very much. A messenger brought it to him when he and the flirtatious Miss Phillips were resting under a peach tree after midday dinner, Charles lying with his head in the girl's lap. The wording of the letter made him so angry – his diary does not reveal what it was – that he rushed off straight away to see Kennedy and the two men had a row. Charles must have realised that there was not much chance after this of his being taken on at the sugar estate when he returned from the Diamond Fields.

A few days later he and his friend Guy were well on their way:

December 22nd: 'Managed to get our two waggons started from Durban on the *14th*, but as the roads were very bad Dawnay and I did not start to ride up till the *18th*. Left after tiffin at the 'Royal', reached Padley's (25 miles) where we slept, and came on to Pietermaritzburg next day (35 miles). We

31

overtook the waggons just outside the town. [The ox-waggon journey from Durban normally took three days, not five] ... Pietermaritzburg is an awfully dirty town built in the Dutch style.' [It had been founded by the *Voortrekkers*, Dutch emigrants from Cape Colony, in the late *1830's*; Rider Haggard described it as 'a charming town of the ordinary Dutch character, with wide streets bordered by sluits of running water and planted with gum trees.']

The two young men took rooms for the night at the Plough Hotel, then went along to the Club where to his great surprise Charles found not only Herbert Rhodes and Studdy, but Fairleigh and Campbell, friends of his whom he had not seen since he was at school. It was extraordinary how often he met old-boys of Glenalmond in South Africa! He discovered that Herbert Rhodes had not been to the Gold Fields, as he had thought; he had found Cecil seriously ill at the Diamond Fields and had carried him off to spend six months trekking leisurely up the old missionary road through Botswana. Frank had stayed behind in Kimberley to keep an eye on the claims.

Next morning Charles and Dawnay rode after their waggons and soon caught up with them:

'Found they had not been able to get up the Town Hill, so rode on to the Umgeni [at Howick] to wait for them.'

Charles was much impressed with the Howick Falls where the Umgeni River, which he had often crossed near its mouth at Durban, plunged over a high cliff.

December 24th: 'We did another twelve miles, and then I had my first night under canvas.'

They camped at Curry's Post, the two white men in their tent while the half-breed drivers and the Zulus slept under the waggons.

Christmas dinner next day was a meal of fried mutton and bacon, rice and plum pudding, and on the *26th* they began trekking at four in the morning, outspanned at Mooi River for breakfast, inspanned again in the afternoon and did another twelve miles to reach Griffin's Hill. They arrived at Bushman's River (Estcourt) hoping to be able to get a damaged waggon wheel repaired, but the blacksmith was 'on the spree' and they had to wait there. To add to their troubles, some of the oxen had fallen ill; one had to be shot, another died, and they hurriedly dosed the rest. The last day of *1872* found Charles 'trying to kill time at a little roadside canteen with little money and a prospect of not getting on.' At any rate, the inn was 'wonderfully good, considering the town only consists of six houses.'

By *January 2nd, 1873*, Dawnay had lost eight out of his thirty-two oxen, and by the *8th* fourteen were dead. He and Charles now decided to leave the waggons at Estcourt in the charge of a friend, and go on on horseback carrying clothes, waterproofs and revolvers in their saddlebags. Buttermer had ridden down to Estcourt to join them, and the three set off for his farm near Ladysmith. Charles left 'Pompey' at the farm as the horse had a sore back; he bought another pony there, named 'Blesbok'.

From Ladysmith Charles, Dawnay and Buttermer turned westwards towards the Drakensberg Mountains and made their way up Van Reenen's Pass. On the plateau beyond lay the Orange Free State which, like the Transvaal, was a Boer republic independent of British rule. To reach Harrismith they were obliged to cross two streams running so high that the water was up to their saddles, and further on was the deep Wilge River which they had to cross in a boat with their horses swimming behind.

There was trouble on the far bank of the Wilge, because a Boer whose farm bordered the river insisted that the young men pay a toll of a shilling each to pass through his land, and when they refused to pay he threatened to sue them. Sure enough, on arrival at Harrismith they were served with a summons. They consulted a lawyer about the matter, hung about for two days in what Charles described as 'a stupid little town with nothing to see', but won their case when it was brought before a magistrate. They were very glad to be free to ride on to Bethlehem next morning.

January 13th found them twenty-two miles nearer the Diamond Fields, and on the *14th* they covered the very long stretch to Winburg, offsaddling at intervals. After that came a thirty-mile ride to a farmhouse where they stayed the night and which turned out to be infested with bugs! In disgust they left their beds and went out to doss down in a waggon. This experience,

33

coupled with the Harrismith incident, made Charles jump to the conclusion that the Boers were an unsavoury lot. He would have been amazed if he had known that, thirty years later, he would be accused of being a "pro-Boer".

On the *16th* they reached Bloemfontein, 'a much nicer place that I expected', Charles said, and from there Buttermer took him to visit a farm owned by one of his friends, while Dawnay rode on. The two men made the final stage of the journey to the Diamond Fields in a Cape cart drawn by four horses, but were held up at the flooded Modder River and had to spend the night sleeping under the cart. At last, on *January 25th*, they drove into Kimberley.

Charles sought out Dawnay and went with him to the Kimberley Club, and here he found Frank Rhodes, Nisbett and other men he knew. Frank introduced him to his nineteen-year-old brother Cecil, who had completely recovered from his illness and had just bought Herbert's claims. (Herbert planned to go to the Eastern Transvaal Gold Fields after his visit to Natal.) Charles heard that Cecil would be leaving the Diamond Fields in a fortnight's time and going overseas to study for the entrance examination to Oxford University; he had set his heart on winning an Oxford degree, and had already made more than enough money to cover his fees and expenses. He was booked to sail from Cape Town on *February 10th* with Frank, when the latter returned to Britain to take up his Army commission, and had arranged for C. D. Rudd – who became his partner in the largest of his enterprises – to watch over his business interests in Kimberley in his absence.

Charles went with his friends to see the famous 'Big Hole' which once had been Colesberg Kopje:

'It is a most wonderful sight, thousands of men digging, buckets flying along a network of wire ropes . . . Imagine a large hollow with bits of ground thirty foot square of different depths down to a hundred feet below the surface, covered with a perfect network of wire ropes with buckets on them for bringing out the earth – some 1,000 niggers and white men standing on long platforms with windlasses connected with wire ropes. The rattle of the buckets and pulleys, a scorching sun, and, about a hundred feet from the edge of the hollow where the buckets are emptied, niggers washing various sieves and white men sorting.'

With his quick grasp of detail Charles had immediately observed exactly what was going on:

'The process of working is this: a man has a thirty-foot claim, or a quarter, an eighth or even an eighteenth of one; the digger committee made the platform and windlasses, and a man has to pay for his windlass. He then fastens a wire rope, a guide from the platform to his claim, and then puts on a couple of buckets with soil, and they are hauled up by the windlass and carried by ropes to where the man is sorting; then it is taken and passed though a coarse sieve by his niggers and then through a very fine one to get the sand out. The coarse stuff is pounded up with wooden mallets by niggers and then poured through the fine sieve, and what remains is thrown on the sorting table. There sits the sorter white man and scrapes the gravel over with a piece of iron, picking out the diamonds when he sees them . . .

'I went and sorted at one of Rhodes's claims with Dawnay and Buttermer. I found one little diamond and Buttermer another, also same garnets . . .'

January 26th [a Sunday] 'At two o'clock started in a trap with the two Rhodeses and Dawnay for Klipdrift, the river diggings [about twenty-five miles away]. Got there about six. Very pretty place, and the Vaal, a much bigger river than I expected, running through it with trees along the edge . . . went to church in the evening, a nicer one than at New Rush' [Kimberley].

The young men stayed the night at the local Club, and next morning after a bathe in the river Charles and Dawnay went to see the diggings. They found them 'almost deserted, scarcely anybody working', and picked up some 'pretty stones'. On the way back to Kimberley they met a vast crowd of Africans leaving the Diamond Fields en route for home, all carrying guns. The sight was something of a shock to Charles, who had not known of the enormous traffic in firearms at the diggings; nearly every African who worked there bought a gun to take back to his kraal.

January 29th: 'In the evening went to call on the Grices with Cecil Rhodes, and then went to one of the gambling halls where

35

I played for a bit.' [He was destined to meet Cecil only once again, but was to hear a great deal about him in the years to come.]

Charles thought Kimberley a very unpleasant place and had no desire to stay and join the throng of fortune-hunters there:

'The heat is something awful, and the houses being all built of galvanised sheet-iron of course are no protection from the heat . . . Diamond digging does not pay up here at all. The only people who make money are the claim-holders who let out their claims to a man who pays all working expenses and gives them half the profits. Also, the buyers and brokers do a very good trade.'

Charles and Buttermer returned to Bloemfontein from Kimberley by post-cart. 'A beastly journey . . . I would far rather ride than go in the post-cart,' Charles said. They reached the Free State capital to find 'everybody excited about a prospect of war with the British', for the Boers were involved in a heated dispute with Britain over the question of the ownership of Griqualand West and the exact position of the Free State's western boundary. Picking up their horses at Buttermer's friend's farm the two young men, joined by Dawnay, rode back to Estcourt. They found only fifteen of Dawnay's oxen left out of the original thirty-two. Charles commented:

'The number that are dying all along the road are dreadful, so we are not exceptional. Nearly all the transport-riders who go up lose some.' [Red-water and other cattle diseases were very prevalent.]

He had kept his eyes and ears open during the journey from Durban to the Diamond Fields, and had collected a lot of information about farming prospects. In one of his letters home he told his parents:

'All up from Pietermaritzburg to the Drakensberg is chiefly stock and sheep farming . . . the great disadvantage being that you almost always require two farms, one for summer the other for winter. Angora goats seem to be . . . likely to do well. Land about here is from 2/6d to 5/– an acre.

'With the Free State I was not at all favourably impressed.

36

1. Charles Smythe as a
   boy

2. Methven Castle, north front, 1870

3. Charles Smythe
   in 1872

4. Guy Dawnay (left) and
   Frank Rhodes, 1872

It is badly watered, almost all the farmers depending on large artificial dams for catching a supply of water. It is subject to long and severe droughts. No wood except along watercourses. Sheep-farming does very fairly in some parts . . . the farm where we stopped at Bloemfontein had 8,000 sheep on it, but there the transport of the wool is heavy and there are a great many diseases to contend against . . .

'The Transvaal, where we are going, is the best country, everybody who has been there talks of it as much better than Natal, well-watered . . . in parts of it sugar and coffee grow well. They are talking of making a railway from there to Delagoa Bay which, if they do, will make it cut out Natal altogether. Land is rising in price there fast. A few years ago you could get a farm there for a bag of coffee, now they are up from 1/- to 2/6d an acre. I believe it would be a good thing to buy a farm there . . . the drawbacks are the length of transport for everything and being under Dutch government [Charles always referred to the Boers as Dutch] and surrounded by Dutch. The president [the Rev. Thomas François Burgers] seems to be a very pushing man, and no doubt if once they get a means of transport they will go ahead.' [The Pretoria to Delagoa Bay railway was Burgers's favourite project, as it would give his country access to a port free of British influence; he raised a loan in Holland to finance the building of it, but the line was not open until *1895*, when Paul Kruger was President.]

Dawnay managed to hire more oxen at Estcourt to replace those he had lost, and on *February 17th, 1873*, he and Charles left for Pretoria with two waggons on the next stage of their journey. Charles knew he ought to turn back and look for a settled job, but could not resist the chance of going at least as far as Pretoria. The route to the Transvaal capital was via Ladysmith, Newcastle ('not much of a place, only twelve houses'), and Heidelberg. Charles thoroughly enjoyed the leisurely life of trekking by ox-waggon:

'When one is on trek the days are pretty much the same . . . at daybreak the niggers let the oxen loose from the waggons where they are tied all night, and make a kettle of coffee. We get up at sunrise . . . and have a cup of coffee, then the oxen are inspanned and we trek for three hours – or more if we do not come to water.

37

Then we outspan and have breakfast – porridge if we can get milk at a farm; meat, rice, coffee and biscuits. We stop till about three in the afternoon, then inspan and trek for about two hours to water, when we stop for the night – pitch the tent where Dawnay and I sleep, and have dinner of meat and rice and jam in the tent, have a pipe, talk and turn in about ten. It is very jolly except when it rains and then it is a great trouble getting anything cooked, but we have not had much.'

Food was no difficulty: they shot for the pot and bought fowls and mealie cobs at farmhouses – and once they bought a sheep's carcase, cut it up, and salted some of the meat.

There was dull country between the Drakensberg and the Vaal River, but from the Vaal to Heidelberg came what was for Charles the highlight of the trip:

'We had about four days' trekking through the game veld, and there we had fine fun. Think of large plains covered as far as you can see with herds of game consisting of wildebeest, blesbok and springbok!'

He and Dawnay had their ponies with them, and tried hunting on horseback, Boer fashion:

'The way they shoot is for several people to go out and try to drive one of the herds from one to the other. The buck always runs in a straight line, so the thing is to try and cut them off . . . the great thing is having a horse that will stand firm, because you have to gallop after the herd as hard as you can, then jump off, fire your rifle at them, on again and after them as they go away all right for some distance with two or three bullets in them. My horse will not stand a bit, and if loose always ran back to camp after a shot, leaving me very much out of it . . . With a rifle the least pull either way makes a tremendous difference at 400 or 500 yards which is the usual distance, and when one's pony's rein is over one's arm and he is jigging at it it is not at all easy to keep steady.'

With so much game about, Charles and Dawnay expected to catch sight of lions on the prowl, ('where Dawnay was shooting in the Zulu country there are a good lot'), but few were seen although transport-riders told them that 'a little higher up they have to tie the oxen between the waggons and light fires to keep the lions off.'

Passing through Heidelberg, the waggon party reached the Transvaal capital on *March 15th* and outspanned by a stream about three miles beyond. Charles's impressions of Pretoria, (founded in *1853*) were:

'Not much of a town, about half a dozen stores, and grass growing all about just as if it had been carried from somewhere and dropped in the veld.'

They tried to post letters to Britain, but found these would require Cape Colony as well as Transvaal stamps, and there were none to be had:

'At last we met a doctor who said he would send our letters with his to an agent in Cape Town, who would re-post them.'

From Pretoria onwards they were accompanied by a white hunter named Moore, whom Dawnay had engaged for his shooting expedition to the Victoria Falls. Charles could not afford to trek further, as he had run short of money and had already had to borrow from Guy, 'the kindest fellow I ever met', but he decided, all the same, to continue as far as Rustenburg; he had heard good reports of sugar and coffee farming there, and it might be worth while going to see for himself. The waggon track led them through a fertile valley lying in the shadow of the Magaliesberg, and further on they crossed the Crocodile River, 'the beginning of the Limpopo', near its source. They were camping in a hollow when they were caught by a sudden storm:

'We had to pile all our bed-things and selves on the table to keep dry.'

On *March 24th* the young men arrived at the farm 'Thorndale', home of the celebrated hunter, Henry Hartley, and were invited to spend a day or two there:

'He was the greatest elephant-hunter in Africa, but being clubfooted has always shot on horseback, and Dawnay got a lot of information from him. He is a fine old man with a long white beard, and told us lots of hunting yarns . . . he has not been hunting for the last two years, as the last time he was out he was very much smashed by a rhinoceros.'

Charles, Dawnay and Moore had Sunday dinner and supper with him, played whist in the evening and sat talking till midnight.

Hartley had bought his Magaliesberg farm in *1841*, and

used to set out from this base every winter with his sons to hunt and trade in what is now Rhodesia; his personal tally of bull-elephants was 1,200. He had been a great favourite of Mzilikazi, founder of the Matabele nation. Whilst in Rhodesia he had come across many ancient gold-workings, and with the German geologist, Karl Mauch, had discovered the Tati Gold Fields on the Rhodesia/Transvaal border in the *1860's*. He never completely recovered from the terrible experience of being tossed and trampled upon by a wounded white rhino in *1869*, and died in *1876*.

When his guests set off again on *March 26th*, Hartley rode part of the way with them; Charles had a very interesting chat with the old hunter, and heard some news which he thought might be useful:

'He says the Doppers are going to trek away further west, as near Pretoria is getting too civilised for them, and there will soon be farms for sale very cheap.' [The Doppers were a religious sect bitterly hostile to President Burgers; some three hundred families, the so-called 'Angola *Voortrekkers*', left the Transvaal in the *1870's* to escape his 'heretical rule', and many of them died of fever or starvation on their trek to Portuguese territory.]

Charles was delighted with Rustenburg, which he and his companions reached on the *28th:*

'A very pretty little town with lots of gardens. Bananas grow well, and pineapples.'

Dawnay stocked his waggons with provisions, because there would be no chance to do so further on.

From Rustenburg they trekked to an African chief's kraal, a huge settlement of about a thousand huts, where Dawnay hoped to engage another waggon-driver to replace one who had 'bolted' in Pretoria. (The man had taken fright on hearing accounts of the dangers awaiting them on the way to the Falls.) The chief welcomed the white men, invited them in, and ordered wooden stools to be placed for them in the shade of his 'audience trees' covered with drying mealie cobs. He squatted on the ground while his tribesmen sat round him chewing wild sugar cane, and Dawnay talked to him with the help of an interpreter and explained what he wanted. His reply was disappointing:

'He said he could not let any of his people go, as three had been killed by Lobengula [the Matabele king] last year. We heard a great deal about the different chiefs' quarrels . . . which was useful to Dawnay . . . He then gave us some kaffir beer and sugar cane . . . in return we gave him some sugar with which he was much pleased. The kaffirs came and talked to our boys and frightened two of them who were Basutos so much by telling them that the Matabele were sure to kill them that they bolted on Sunday night, so Dawnay is very short-handed now, only four Amatongas and one halfcaste driver.'

On *March 31st* came the parting between Charles and the other two, and he watched wistfully as his friend's waggons disappeared in a cloud of dust, heading west:

'I hope I shall see Dawnay again, certainly a better fellow never lived . . . I hope he gets on all right, there is a very bad bit of country between this and Bamangwato [in eastern Botswana, near present-day Serowe] where he has to do 43 miles without water . . . no joke in this hot weather, as oxen cannot do more than three miles an hour.' [To reach the Victoria Falls Dawnay would have to travel more than six hundred miles, which would take him at least six weeks.]

Charles rode back to Rustenburg and from there to Pretoria, calling at farms on the way and enquiring about coffee-growing prospects in the Transvaal; he found that farming conditions in that country were not as good as he had thought:

'The farms are very cheap here, from £700 to £1,500 for farms from 4,000 to 6,000 acres, but everything has to be grown by irrigation as there is no rain sometimes for six months.'

At Pretoria he sold 'Blesbok' and thought himself lucky to get £5 for him, 'as horses here are dying by the thousands of horse-sickness. Salted horses, those who have had the sickness, cost from £60 to £100.'

He made the return journey to Natal by post-cart and horse-bus, after arranging for his luggage to go down to Durban on one of Messrs. Zeederberg's transport waggons. He observed with alarm that the post-cart driver was 'pretty tight' when they left.

'Changed horses after three hours and a half. Then on again to Heidelberg four hours, where we arrived about six o'clock. [They spent the night there.] Up at daybreak and started.

41

Nobody but me in the post-cart. Changed horses twice and crossed the Vaal River. Got to an iron house that Welch [the transport company] has put up for passengers, by five o'clock. Had nothing to eat but the food we brought with us, and some eggs. The up post-cart came in about an hour after, with two passengers and the driver. We all slept there.'

April 6th: 'Started very early before sunrise and drove for seven hours to MacPherson's store where we stopped an hour and had a capital dinner. Then on again and got into Harrismith by dark.'

April 7th: 'Started after breakfast . . . in a bigger bus with three passengers . . . had lunch at Smith's on the Berg, and got to Colenso by night. Awfully rough travelling over the roads.'

April 8th: 'Started from Colenso at sunrise, got about halfway to Bloukrantz when we found one of the wheels was on fire, the axle of the cart having bent so that the oil had all run out.' [Wheels often caught fire in this way.]

Luckily they were within five miles of a blacksmith's, where the repair was done.

At Estcourt Charles bought a horse, and from there rode down to Durban and then on to Sea Cow Lake. He found that an old school-fellow of his from Glenalmond had been engaged as Kennedy's new estate manager.

April 21st was Charles's birthday and coming-of-age, but he did not feel in the mood for rejoicing. His hopes of getting 'the surveyorship of a small estate' had come to nothing, and he realised that without some practical knowledge and experience his chances were poor. Writing to his mother, who was worried at his being without a job, he said:

'I could easily get employment as a field overseer . . . the pay is from £5 to £10 a month without rations, but the work is decidedly not intellectual, and pretty hard.'

He was very depressed, and the death of 'Lucknow' contributed to his unhappiness.

To please his mother he called on the Lieut. Governor and Mrs. Musgrave, and was invited to lunch. A few weeks later he set off on a round of visits to sugar and coffee estates on the Natal north coast, and at the Reynolds's home met Mitchell Innes, whose marriage to Miss Reynolds was to take place in three days' time. Mitchell Innes had bought eight thousand acres of land up-country, and was going in for stock-farming. The only other guest in the house was Bishop Colenso, and Charles played a game of whist with him which he described as 'very jolly'.

By *mid-June* Charles had decided to leave Natal and go back to Scotland for a time. He felt that the Phillips family had had enough of him, and he was finding life very dull. 'It is killing work this, having nothing to do.' He rode to Duff's store and bought gifts to take home: two monkey skins and a civet cat skin, and some assegais, wooden snuff spoons and other 'kaffir curiosities'.

Before he left he took part in Durban's winter races:

'I got a fine cropper at the races. I jumped a hurdle and my horse put his foot in a hole, sent me spinning! I did not hurt myself, no more did he, but lost the mouthpiece of my pipe.'

At the meeting he came across his Scottish friend Fairleigh, who introduced his brother:

'They are going up to see Cetewayo the new Zulu king's coronation, which is to be a splendid turnout of five thousand warriors to dance, and any amount of men to be killed. People are afraid he will attack the Dutch in the Transvaal, as it is the correct thing for a king to begin his reign by making war on somebody.'

His predictions of bloodshed at the coronation show that he had heard of atrocities committed by the Zulu kings Shaka and Dingaan, but in fact there was no question of a massacre taking place, nor of an attack on the Transvaal, when Cetewayo was installed as paramount chief in *1873*. Theophilus Shepstone performed the investiture himself, with impressive ceremonial, in the presence of British troops; he hoped that the unrest caused by the rifts between the late King Mpande's sons would cease when Cetewayo was recognised as sole heir to his father. Cetewayo was powerful, but Shepstone's influence with the Zulus was great enough to keep him in check.

Charles left Sea Cow Lake on *July 14th*, after spending a last evening with Miss Phillips, she seated in a big chair with Charles 'leaning over her, reading a story with her, her head almost touching mine and our hands often meeting'. He confided to

43

his diary, 'Poor darling, I am sorry to leave her so lonely and ill', but his feeling for her was really only superficial.

He sailed from Durban in the coaster *Zulu*, transferred to the mailship *Asiatic* at Cape Town, and reached Southampton on *August 21st*. A day or two later he was back at Methven Castle in Scotland, and there he stayed for the next few months, spending much of his time shooting, fishing and playing games. He kept in close touch with Natal news while he was away; the 'Natal Mercury' was sent to him regularly, and he received frequent letters from Mrs. Phillips.

Early in the New Year Charles met Frank Rhodes again, in Edinburgh. On *January 15th, 1874*, he had driven to the barracks where the 1st (Royal) Dragoons were stationed:

'I met Frank walking, as I was halfway there, and he got into the cab and drove to the barracks with me. He gave me lunch and showed me his room and the stables, and then we walked back to Edinburgh, where we parted.'

Frank was to leave for Sandhurst in a week or two's time. He told Charles that he had had news of Dawnay up to October, and that he (Dawnay) expected to be back in England in *March*. Charles was very glad to know that Guy had survived his hunting expedition.

The two young men had had a long discussion about Natal, and the Colony was very much in Charles's thoughts when he went that same month to stay with his uncle and aunt near Bishop's Stortford. On *January 23rd* he called on old Mr. Rhodes and to his surprise found Cecil at the vicarage, and this led to further talk about South Africa. Cecil was on the point of returning to the Cape; he had begun shuttling back and forth between Oxford and Kimberley, leading a dual life as student and businessman, and would continue to do so until he had taken his degree in *1881*. The Rev. Mr. Rhodes gave Charles news of Herbert:

'Old Rhodes showed me a letter from Herbert, in which he said he was finding about an ounce of gold a day up at Lydenburg.' [The alluvial Gold Fields at Lydenburg in the Eastern Transvaal had been opened the year before, and Charles had seriously thought of going there himself when he was in Pretoria in *April, 1873*. He had had the offer of a lift in a Government

44

surveyor's waggon, and wished now that he had accepted.]

He spent the next few weeks travelling on the Continent, and returned to England on *March 12th* just in time to watch a very splendid Royal procession: Prince Alfred, second son of Queen Victoria, had recently been married in St. Petersburg to the Grand-Duchess Marie, daughter of Tsar Alexander II of Russia, and the bride was making her first public appearance in Britain as Duchess of Edinburgh, driving through London with her husband and the Queen. The city was illuminated in the evening of the processional day, and Charles found 'a great crush' in the streets.

The marriage of the Duke and Duchess of Edinburgh had been of especial interest to the Smythe family, as Cousin Augusta Bruce and her husband, Dean Stanley, had attended the glittering Royal wedding; at Queen Victoria's express wish the Dean had married the couple according to Anglican rites after the official Russian Orthodox Church ceremony. The Tsar had personally presented Lady Augusta with a valuable gold trinket-box as a memento of the occasion.

During his holiday on the Continent Charles had been thinking constantly of Herbert Rhodes and the Transvaal Gold Fields, and on *March 17th* he wrote to old Mr. Rhodes, asking him for the latest news from Lydenburg. On *March 19th* he posted a letter to the agent of the Union Company, enquiring about a steamer passage to South Africa.

March 20th: 'Heard from old Mr. Rhodes, saying he had not heard from Herbert since I saw him, and dissuading me from going out.'

March 24th: 'Wrote to engage berth in steamer.'

Charles wasn't going to listen to the sort of advice he didn't want to hear. He had made up his mind to try his luck digging for gold. If Herbert could find an ounce of the stuff every day, so could he. He had managed to persuade his parents to fall in with his schemes, and next day noted in his diary that William Smythe had said that £500 and a bequest of £100 would be sent to him in South Africa, £50 for his expenses on arrival and £150 a year in the future, payable half-yearly.

On *April 2nd* Charles's brother David, who held a commission in the 79th Highland Regiment (The Queen's Own Cameron

45

Highlanders) wrote to say he had seen Frank Rhodes and heard from him that Guy Dawnay was back in England. Charles sent off a letter to his friend, who replied by return saying he was very sorry not to have the chance of seeing him before he sailed. He had had very good sport on his shooting trip, he reported, and his 'bag' had been 140 animals, including thirteen elephants, ten giraffe, five sable antelope and five rhino! (Many nineteenth-century hunters killed as many animals in a season, and it was no wonder that Africa's big game faced extinction.)

On *April 7th, 1874,* Charles sailed from Southampton, bound for Durban.

CHAPTER FOUR

CHARLES'S SECOND VOYAGE to South Africa was even more uncomfortable than the first had been:

April 25th: 'Have been awfully troubled with bugs ever since I came on board in my berth, and am trying sleeping in many different places. I have fixed on the saloon table till daybreak, and then to my bunk as they do not bite then.'

The only fortunate thing about the trip, from his point of view, was that he made friends with two other young men who were going out to the Transvaal Gold Fields and arranged to join forces with them. Their names were MacCallum and Wood. When the ship reached Cape Town the trio spent an uproarious evening celebrating their arrival; MacCallum took his bagpipes and played in front of several of the hotels in the town, 'while another fellow took round the hat'.

They disembarked at Durban on *May 15th*, and immediately began making plans for their journey to the Gold Fields. Charles was anxious to leave as soon as possible, as the Royal Hotel, where he was staying, was expensive. 'It is much dearer than it was, 10/– a day!', he complained. The young men thought of buying a buck-waggon and taking up a load of flour to sell, but finally settled on going by post-cart with the minimum of luggage and '£100 each, with which we hope to make our fortunes'. They would carry their money (gold sovereigns) in money-belts made for the purpose. Most of their clothing had been packed into a large trunk which would follow them by transport-waggon. Charles left his guns with King, the Durban gunsmith. He wrote home:

'If after six months we find the Gold Fields are not paying, we shall come down and look out for something else, but at present we are bitten with gold fever . . . if we lose all our £100 we think of joining the new Mounted Police at 6/6d a day, which is pretty good pay for a private.' [Mounted police had

47

been raised in Natal following the recent rebellion of Chief Langalibalele. One wonders how Mrs. Smythe received the suggestion of her son becoming an ordinary trooper.]

Charles, MacCallum and Wood left Durban on *May 23rd, 1874:*

'We had to get a span of oxen to pull the post-cart up the hill at one point.'

But worse was to come:

'Between Newcastle and Wakkerstroom [a village just inside the present-day Transvaal border] it was the most fearful road I ever had the pleasure of travelling on, even in this Colony.'

The two-hundred-mile stretch from Wakkerstroom to Lyden-burg was equally appalling:

'Our work consisted in getting out and walking at every hill though we had four horses . . . and changed horses about every three hours. We stuck fast in mud holes about five times, and had to get out in them and pull the cart out . . . At one place we came to a stream where the cart stuck in the middle and away went the leaders with all their harness, and we saw them no more. The wheelers broke their traces, and were only kept from running away by the pole [of the Cape cart]. The driver and kaffir were pitched out . . . We patched up the cart and inspanned the two horses that were left, and had to walk for four hours to the nearest farm.'

They reached their destination utterly exhausted.

June 12th: 'The first person I met in the Lydenburg Hotel was Herbert Rhodes. He is looking very ill. He went down to Delagoa Bay and got the fever and was very near dead of it, but he is getting much better now.' [Illness was not the only cause of Herbert Rhodes's haggard appearance; he was leading a dissolute life on the Gold Fields, and drinking heavily.]

Charles and his friends did not remain at Lydenburg but pushed on to the diggings at Pilgrim's Rest, which were said to be richer:

'All the men who work steadily we hear are doing very well, and the gold is scattered over a great area of ground. A twelve-pound nugget worth about £600 is the biggest that has been found yet . . . it is a beautiful country about here, high mountains and lots of bush and water . . . The camp [known as Middle

Camp] is much smaller than I expected, as it is scattered all up the creek for about two miles and a half. It is all tents.'

He and his friends bought a large tent and pitched it about a mile up the creek. Then they set about finding a claim to work:

'We of course had lots of offers of claims but did not buy one, and now we are going to work a claim of a Dr. Hyde, a brother-in-law of Mrs. Kennedy . . . we are first to pay all our expenses out of what we find and then give him a quarter of the profits, which is a very liberal offer.'

Charles had sought out a man named Cameron and presented a letter of introduction which Herbert Rhodes had given him, and Cameron may have helped him find African labourers:

'We have managed to get two kaffirs, which is luck as they are very scarce now, being frightened by the cold weather.'

June 12th: 'We had our first day's work in the claim today, and very hard work it is, and my hands are all blistered in consequence . . . the gold is found in the old bed of the creek which is covered by almost six feet of surface soil, then a sort of gravel, then big boulders among which is the gold . . . We first have to strip the surface soil . . . of about twelve square feet and get down to the gravel, which we intend to wash tomorrow by putting it into a long narrow box with cross bars in it, through which a strong stream of water flows; all the dirt and small stones are washed away, and the gold however small is so heavy that it sinks to the bottom.' [The residue was put in a flat tin basin, which was dipped in water and shaken till at last the sand had all disappeared and the gold was left glittering at the bottom.]

There was little hope of making much out of a single claim, so Charles and the others seized the chance of getting another:

'There has been a new rush reported about twenty miles from here, and Dr. Hyde's partner went over yesterday and is going to mark us out a claim; so directly it is publicly reported one of us will have to go over there to keep it open, or else in three days' time anybody may jump it.'

June 28th: 'We have got, up to now, 24 cwts of gold, worth here £4.–12. It is not exactly making a fortune, but helps to pay expenses which are 25/– a week for each of us and 30/– a week for kaffirs. To pay expenses we require to find 6 cwts a day.'

Charles was enjoying himself at Pilgrim's Rest:

'It is great fun, the work . . . we begin by getting up about 7 . . . have coffee and bread and butter, cold meat if we have any. Go down to the claim about 8.30 and work till 12. One of us goes up before that to cook the dinner . . . We rest till 2, then back to the claim . . . work till 5.30, wash, have tea, read, write in the evening, turn in about ten . . . the great excitement of the day is when we pan off after we have stopped work . . .

'We have made our tent much more comfortable . . . we have each got a bed by nailing a piece of canvas on two sticks and nailing them to posts in the ground . . . we have also got a table . . . we have a stream close by for water and washing, which is a great luxury' [as the creek water was too muddy to use].

A typical Sunday dinner, cooked by Charles, consisted of 'oxtail soup with compressed vegetables in it, beefsteaks done on a gridiron, and rice and dried peaches stewed.'

Camping was less amusing in wet weather:

'The great bore is to get any food cooked when it is raining, as we have no fireplace and if we start a fire in the tent we are choked by the smoke.'

Charles, MacCallum and Wood kept very much to themselves at Middle Camp:

'We live quite alone, our tent is about 200 yards from any other . . . we know very few fellows here.'

The diggers were divided into two very different groups, one quiet, respectable and law-abiding, and the other just the opposite. The first group, to which Charles belonged, attended the church services held every Sunday, supported a small library and newspaper, and tried to live in as civilised a way as possible; the second, which Herbert Rhodes had joined and in which he was well to the fore, was a wild, gambling, drinking set. Among the diggers were men and women from all parts of South Africa, as well as people from Britain and the United States and many experienced gold-miners from Australia.

There were a number of Scotsmen at Pilgrim's Rest, and one of them sought out MacCallum because their surname was the same. 'Rather a character' was Charles's opinion of him, but he was good company. When he came to dinner one evening in

September he brought a bottle of champagne and a bottle of French claret, 'the first liquor that has been drunk at dinner in the tent'. This 'other' MacCallum told Charles he was claimant to the Scottish earldom and estates of Breadalbane, and was going home at Christmas time to renew his case. (A claim to this title had been made in 1863 by a Major Charles Campbell, but without success.)

After about ten weeks' hard labour Charles and his companions found that their claim had not paid, so they decided to move. A whole month's effort had brought them only three ounces of gold, which they sold for £11. Bad weather had hampered their work, and the cold had made conditions wretched. There had been several nights of such severe frost that 'all the water was frozen hard in the basins, and we had a job to get to sleep . . . for the cold'.

Things went better at their new claim. 'Last week we got 2 ozs 5 cwts,' Charles noted, early in *August*, but there were disputes with the Africans about their pay and they had to give them more money, (35/– for the coming month, and £2 the month after). The Africans knew they were indispensable to the diggers, and could afford to demand what were then high wages.

Labour troubles seemed endless. When one African worker died the rest became scared, saying they would die too, and half of them made off without their pay. The difficulty of getting and keeping assistants was Charles's only real complaint, and he did not share the general dissatisfaction at Pilgrim's Rest with the way the Gold Fields were run by the Transvaal government:

August 9th: 'There was a public meeting of diggers in the camp yesterday, to try and get up a self-government for the Fields . . . I did not go down, as I had no grievances against the Government.'

A so-called 'Diggers' *Volksraad*' or Parliament was elected a little later on, and Herbert Rhodes became a member of it. Charles came across Herbert occasionally, 'looking very seedy from the effects of the [malaria] fever he got at Delagoa Bay,' but they had nothing in common and the friendship lapsed.

On *August 23rd* Charles wrote to tell his parents that he and

51

his friends had bought a claim of their own:

'MacCallum works it with four niggers while Wood and I work the one we were in, with four other niggers . . . the one we bought is close beside our other one . . . an advantage for moving big boulders as we can put all the niggers on to pull at the block-and-tackle which we use for taking them out.'

Early in *September* they bought another claim and let it to white diggers, 'they paying their own expenses and giving us a fourth of the finds'.

'We keep a most exact account book', Charles wrote, sending his parents a statement of expenses for the three and a half months in which he had been at Pilgrim's Rest with MacCallum and Wood:

'House food, etc. .. £86. 0. 11.
Working a/c .. .. £39. 8. 7.
Kaffirs' wages, etc... £44. 19. 0.
Claim .. .. .. £45. 10. 0.

'Total £215.–18.–6., which minus the gold sold (£55.–18.–0) leaves £160.–0.–6., which we have spent . . . so you see the company's affairs are not very flourishing.'

Unexpected setbacks brought much disappointment:

October 11th: 'We got 30 cwt in one day and thought we were on to something good, and the next morning when we went down to work we found that one of the sides of the claim had slipped in, and we have got some tons of earth to move before we get to the gold again.'

All this time the young men had been awaiting the arrival from Durban of their trunk full of clothes and other belongings. When it finally reached them there was great rejoicing in the tent:

'If you fancy that we have passed four months here with nothing except what we brought up in a handbag apiece, you may imagine what it is to have a comparatively large supply of clothes and books arrive.' [Charles hated to be without books.]

In *November* the rains set in, and the diggers were miserably uncomfortable:

'All this week we have hardly had a dry thing to put on. Our tent is only single canvas, so leaks like anything . . . my waterproof sheet is too narrow for my bed . . . the floor is two

5. Mr John King, 1872

6. Mrs Janet King, 1872

7. 'Strathearn' in 1884

8. 'Strathearn' when the trees had grown

inches deep in mud ... One very unpleasant night I had, holding my waterproof sheet and mackintosh together over me while I was in bed, from two o'clock in the morning until seven with the thunder pealing almost continuously the whole time.'

To cap all, Charles fell ill with dysentery on his return from a short hunting trip.

The dream of making a fortune at Pilgrim's Rest had faded, and the three friends decided to give up gold-digging:

November 29th: 'We have sold up all our possessions here, but the sale did not realise much; we only got £13 for our claim and about another £13 for our tools, tent, etc. It has not been a very paying business ... there are a great many people leaving here now the weather is so bad.'

Charles may have seen Herbert Rhodes again before he left, but if so he made no mention of it in his diary. Herbert eventually trekked north from the Gold Fields and became an elephant-hunter and ivory-trader in the region of the eastern Zambesi. He died in *October, 1879,* in a shack on the lower Shire River in Malawi, burnt to death when, (so it was said), a cask of gin which he was opening accidentally caught fire. It was a terrible end to a wasted life. He was only thirty-four.

Charles was glad to see the last of Pilgrim's Rest, but when he and his companions took their places in a waggon bound for Pretoria on *November 30th* he felt depressed at the thought of having no definite plans for the future. He must go down to Durban to pick up the possessions he had put in store there – but what then? It seemed a pity to leave the Transvaal, especially as news had just come of fresh mineral discoveries:

'It is a wonderful country for minerals. There is a cobalt and silver reef just discovered about a month ago near Nazareth [Middelburg] and they say the ore is splendid.' [Cobaltite and safflorite were mined at Middelburg for years, but today South Africa's silver is obtained from the Witwatersrand mines, as it is alloyed with the gold.]

At Pretoria the trio broke up; MacCallum took his leave, as he was going to the Diamond Fields, and Charles and Wood set off for Natal by ox-waggon. Between Heidelberg and the Vaal River they passed through the game veld which had thrilled Charles when he was on trek with Dawnay, but the buck had been hunted so much since then that they were now very shy of man. They found the Vaal in flood and running so high that the oxen were soon out of their depth and had to swim, and the Sandspruit, further on, proved utterly impassable for the waggon. Charles and the other two passengers swam over, dragging Wood, (who could not swim), by a rope, and they took shelter in a store on the far bank. The date was *December 24th,* and they faced a bleak Christmas, but things turned out happily after all:

'On Christmas morning, the river having gone down about six feet, we managed to get the waggon through and inspanned near the store. We made a most beautiful plum pudding using a whole ostrich egg in it, [they had come across an ostrich nest in the game veld] and they asked us to dine at the store and gave us roast fowls and hare . . . we were all pretty tired of buck meat . . . so were very grateful.'

The hospitable shopkeeper was a Scot named Gibson.

Charles reached Durban in *January, 1875,* to find the town in a ferment. Chief Langalibalele's uprising the previous year had caused great alarm in the Colony, and there had been general satisfaction when his tribal lands were confiscated and he was banished for life to Robben Island, off Cape Town. But Bishop Colenso had gone overseas to protest against the severity of the punishment, and been supported in Britain; the British Secretary of State for the Colonies, Lord Carnarvon, had ordered a full enquiry into the affair, and had recalled the Lieut. Governor of Natal, Sir Benjamin Pine, Anthony Musgrave's successor.

January 17th, 1875: 'There is great indignation here against Bishop Colenso, and the country altogether is unsettled. If they insist on sending Langalibalele back I expect there will be a very pretty row. Also, Pine's recall is thought very unjust, as there is very little doubt that if any other governor had been here who did not understand the kaffirs there would have been a general insurrection here and an invasion from the Zulus who were quite ready to help him if he had had the least chance of success.

'It is all very well for the Peace Society and these sort of people to talk, but let them come and stop out here for a bit and see if they would not require to be pretty strict to their dear black brethren, who if they were to unite would be ten to one [it was nearer twenty to one] against the whites. I do not think they would supply them with guns and ammunition.

'There will be a very strong demonstration against Colenso when he lands, and if it were not for his age and cloth he would be mobbed. Altogether, the English Govt. is behaving shamefully . . .'

Charles was echoing the opinion of most settlers in Natal, who felt that the British Government had let them down; they were vastly outnumbered by the Zulus, yet there was only a handful of British troops in the Colony to protect them in time of trouble; they feared they might easily be overwhelmed. Langalibalele's defiance of Shepstone had been a great shock as it showed that the latter's influence had waned, and with Cetewayo's 60,000 warriors across the Tugela spoiling for a fight the whites were naturally uneasy. Rightly or wrongly, they believed that Africans must be very firmly handled and that a lighter touch would be construed as weakness. They were extremely resentful of people who criticised them from the safety of a country six thousand miles away.

January 31st: 'Bishop Colenso has returned [from England] but only four of his staunchest friends went down to meet him. He stopped two days in Durban but did not show his face . . . There are any amount of memorials getting up to Sir Benjamin Pine from the Colonists, saying how sorry they are he is going away, and that he saved the Colony from destruction.'

Charles was too young and active to remain depressed for long over his failure at the Gold Fields. He had no thought of returning home, but began looking about again for an opening in Natal. He told his parents that he might try stock-farming, since there seemed to be nothing for him in sugar:

'The great thing of farming is that you can hire a farm for £40 or so a year with option of buying, and if it does not succeed why you do not lose very much.'

He had bought another horse in Durban, and spent most of *February* visiting friends up the coast who might be able to give him news of stock farms for hire inland. (He spent a week with the Phillips family, but he and Miss Phillips had long lost interest in each other.)

On *February 23rd* he rode to Tongaat to stay with a settler named Munro, and it was here that a chain of events began which was to have a vitally important outcome for him. At Munro's he heard that there was a Perthshire man named Forbes living nearby, and as he could not resist the chance of talking to someone who came from the same part of the Highlands as himself he went to see Forbes next day; he was invited to spend a night or two, and his friendly host told him of yet another ex-Perthshire immigrant, a Mr. John King, who was one of the most respected and successful dairy-farmers in Natal. King lived on the farm 'Lynedoch' at Caversham in the Fort Nottingham district of the Natal Midlands, and it seemed likely he might be able to help Charles. Forbes may have suggested, 'Why don't you ride up to Caversham – it's about thirty miles beyond Pietermaritzburg. John King may have some land you can rent – anyway, it's worth a try.'

Charles seized on the idea of going to see Mr. King, and started on his long ride next morning. Looking back on that journey forty-three years later, he was to say that he had ridden to 'Lynedoch' with no particular object in view, 'in fact quite at a loose end', but by that time he had forgotten how urgently he needed a place to settle in in *1875*, and how full of hope he had been that something would come of his visit to Caversham. He reached 'Lynedoch' one afternoon at the end of *February*.

Margaret (Elizabeth Margaret) King, the farmer's younger daughter, was busy churning butter in the dairy when she caught sight of the handsome young stranger, on a tired horse, coming in at the yard gate. She said to herself, 'Oh, bother, I'll have to leave this job and go and make up a bed for the man,!' for it was taken for granted that a traveller arriving towards sunset would be put up for the night. She was not interested in handsome strangers, because at nearly twenty-two she was already engaged. She took off her apron and went out to greet him.

Charles never forgot his first impression of her as she took his hand: a good-looking girl in a long frock of white muslin

56

pin-spotted with green, her fair, curly hair piled on top of her head. Her eyes were strikingly blue, and her face had the slight tan of someone who spends much of the day in the sunshine. He thought her immensely attractive.

Margaret's parents received Charles in their usual hospitable way, but as soon as they heard who he was there was great excitement, for they had known his family in Scotland very well. Charles discovered, to his surprise and delight, that John King had been factor, or manager, of Methven for twelve years when 'Uncle Robert', (William Smythe's half-brother), owned the property. King had emigrated to South Africa in *1849*, before Charles was born.

Writing to his mother on *March 3rd*, Charles told of the meeting and said, 'You cannot imagine what a lot of home talk we have had!' He went on to say, ' "Lynedoch" is a splendid farm, and Mr. King is a very practical man . . . he is doing very well out here. There are two sons [Robert and James] . . . and two daughters [Grace and Margaret; Grace was Mrs. Charles Speirs] . . . also two aunts [the Misses Ellis] who live with them.'

John King was a pioneer who had arrived in Natal from Scotland in the ship *Henry Tanner* only a few years after the Colony became a British possession. Large parts of the country were then very wild and practically empty, as the *Voortrekkers* who had set up a short-lived Boer republic had nearly all departed, and the British authorities had shepherded the Natal Zulus into the newly-created 'reserves'. Britain had had no desire to annex Natal, but the Boer republic's unhappy relations with the Zulus had led to trouble on the adjoining Cape Colony border, and she had felt obliged to intervene. As the British Government did not want to spend any more money on Natal that it could help, white immigrants had been encouraged to settle in the Colony to act as a buffer between the Zulus and the Cape tribes, and to keep the Boers out. (It was cheaper to fill the country with settlers than to station a large military force there; settlers could be expected to provide for themselves!) Some five thousand British men, women and children landed at Durban during the years *1849* and *1850*. Few of them had any idea of the events which had prompted the annexation, or knew that the immigration agents' account of their new homeland was far too rosy.

John King and others like him had suffered great hardship in their early years in the Midlands, as there were no amenities of any sort nor any medical aid at hand. Lions, leopards and hyaenas preyed on their flocks, and the primitive Bushmen, armed with bows and poisoned arrows, frequently swept down from the Drakensberg to raid the stock. A company of infantry-men of the 45th or Nottinghamshire Regiment, (later, the 1st Sherwood Foresters), stationed at the small post they had named Fort Nottingham, tried in vain to keep the raiders in check.

In spite of almost insuperable difficulties King and his courageous wife, Janet, had managed to establish a thriving dairy farm, and from 'Lynedoch' they sent cheese, salted butter and raspberry jam regularly by ox-waggon to the market in Pietermaritzburg. Because of the scarcity of labour their children had to work in the fields and help with the animals; they had a governess, Miss Wilson, for a short time, but apart from this had no education.

In the years that followed, other settlers (most of them Scottish) joined the pioneers in the Fort Nottingham district, and a few Zulus came to live on Crown land, but the countryside was still very empty. So lonely was it, in fact, that when Miss Elizabeth Ellis lost her way in the mist one evening, while returning to 'Lynedoch' from the Kings' other farm, 'Gowrie', she knew it was useless to shout for help. She snuggled down for warmth beside a herd of domestic pigs gone wild, and waited patiently for daybreak!

Charles was much impressed with 'Lynedoch'. The old homestead stood in a green valley between the present-day railway-stations of Balgowan and Nottingham Road, protected to the north by a ridge of hills whose southern slopes were covered with indigenous bush full of yellow-woods and other fine trees. From the top of the range, and looking westwards, the peak 'Giant's Castle' – nearest point in the great curving wall of the Drakensberg – was clearly visible although it was over fifty miles away. There was much in the landscape to appeal to Charles as a Highlander: here was scenery on the grand scale, with steep, grass-covered hills, panoramic views, dark patches of forest, and streams rushing over boulder-strewn beds or leaping in cascades from high cliffs. The air was cool and bracing, for the altitude was nearly five thousand feet, and he heard that there was bitter cold in winter, with falls of snow.

He had intended to spend only a night or two with the Kings, but they pressed him to stay on. After a week John King made him a proposition, partly perhaps out of regard for the Smythe family, but mainly because he was a good judge of character and saw that Charles was intelligent, keen to learn and not afraid of hard work:

March 24th: 'After I had been here about a week Mr. King proposed that I should rent from him the farm "Gowrie" [4,500 acres] adjoining this ... he would help me in that sort of practical knowledge of farming in which I am deficient.' [Charles was to run the farm in partnership with Mr. King's elder son, James, profits and expenses to be equally divided. The lease was to be for five years with option of seven, and all improvements would be taken at a valuation at the end of the lease.]

Writing to tell his parents of the offer, Charles said:

'I propose beginning with 500 sheep, which at £1 apiece would be £500, and 25 mares at £10, which would make £750, then there would be a few cows and oxen, another £100.' He already had £1,000, and asked his father to allow him a further £500. He went on to say:

'There is a great demand for horses, and likely to continue, there is no horse-sickness up here ... but sheep are the best paying of all ... Mr. King proposes to put the same number of stock on as I do, and let me have the farm rent free.' [Initially, a rent of £15 a year for three years had been suggested.]

It was a wonderful opportunity, and Charles was delighted. He asked his mother to send him out a box of hard-wearing clothes, and then rode off to Durban early in *April* to apply (unsuccessfully, as it happened), for some Indian indentured labourers for 'Gowrie' as the labour problem was just as acute in the Natal Midlands as it was on the coast.

He found the port unusually gay, with society enjoying a round of balls and lavish banquets given by the temporary

Lieut. Governor of Natal, the very distinguished soldier and administrator, Sir Garnet Wolseley. The colonists were flattered – as Lord Carnarvon had hoped they would be – that such an eminent military man had been sent to set their affairs in order. They were rather startled, too; they hoped it meant that Britain had at last realised how defenceless they were:

'Everyone is very much surprised here at Sir Garnet Wolseley's appointment, and hope he will do good, as things are bad at present.'

Wolseley had a difficult role to play. Lord Carnarvon desired him to amend the Colony's constitution so as to curb the settlers' legislative powers, as he believed that even under the Representative form of government then in force they had too much say in the making of laws affecting the Natal Zulus. Britain could, of course, have altered the Natal constitution over the colonists' heads, but this might have caused a revolt. Much better, thought Carnarvon, to let the dazzling Sir Garnet try a little gentle persuasion.

The British Colonial Secretary was a man of foresight, who realised that mounting tension between blacks and whites in many parts of South Africa was hampering the country's progress; he wanted a uniform and more sympathetic native policy in the four states, as a preliminary to their federation. The first step towards achieving his aim was to gain control over Natal's legislature.

Under Representative Government, Natal had a Legislative Council of twenty members, fifteen of them elected and five nominated by the Crown. (The five were the Treasurer, Postmaster-General, Protector of Immigrants, Secretary of Native Affairs, and Attorney-General.) The Crown nominees, with the Chief Justice and the Commandant of Troops, formed an Executive Council presided over by the Lieut. Governor. The fifteen elected members of the Legislative Council represented the Colony's four thousand white male voters; there were no voters among the 350,000 Natal Zulus, although it was possible for a Zulu to qualify for the franchise.

Wolseley prepared a Constitution Amendment Bill increasing the number of Government nominees from five to fifteen to strengthen the Executive; this would prevent the elected members from having things too much their own way, as he thought they did at present. Charles's comment was:

'I think it is a good thing, as everyone quarrels so with his neighbour here that it used to be all wrangling and nothing done – still, it is a power which may be very much abused.'

He felt that it would be better, in these perilous days when the settlers' existence seemed so insecure, that Government officials and nominees should have firm hold of the reins; this was not at all the same thing as direct rule from Britain, for these men were on the spot and thoroughly understood Natal's problems. Charles was beginning to take a real interest in the machinery of government, though he had no plans ever to take up politics himself.

Sir Garnet's Bill was strongly opposed when it came up for debate, but he made only a slight concession, namely that the number of nominated members should be increased to thirteen instead of fifteen.

Before he made way for Natal's new Lieut. Governor, Sir Henry Bulwer, he brought about some important reforms in the administration of Zulu affairs and abolished the £5 Marriage Tax which the young men had so much resented. He urged Lord Carnarvon to annex Zululand at once – by peaceful means – before Cetewayo's power grew any greater, but his advice was not heeded. If it had been, the Zulu War might have been avoided.

CHAPTER FIVE

CHARLES PLANNED TO BUILD a house for himself on 'Gowrie', but he dreaded the thought of living there all alone; he asked his parents to try to find a suitable Scottish couple who wanted to emigrate to Natal and who would come and help him on the farm:

'The man must be very steady, a handy fellow willing to do anything, as the temptations to drink here are almost worse than at Home, and the woman would have to work a little and know a little about dairy work. You cannot think how lonely it would be on a stock farm up here without a soul but kaffirs for miles . . . There are passages granted by the Natal Immigration Aid Office for £10 passage money by the Union Company steamers, and also free passages which I must find out about.' [Luckily, as it turned out, nothing came of this plan.]

It would be months before his house was ready, and in the meantime Charles boarded at 'Lynedoch'. When he was not up at 'Gowrie' he spent his time helping Mr. King and learning all he could about agricultural methods and stock-breeding; there was little the old pioneer could not tell him about the problems peculiar to farming in the Natal Midlands, and how to deal with them. Charles greatly admired him for his knowledge and achievements, and told his parents:

'Mr. King is now very well off indeed, and known and respected by everybody; is in fact a landed gentleman.'

In the evenings, when the paraffin-lamps were lit, the family gathered in the sitting-room and Charles entertained them with his concertina or played bezique with Margaret. He very soon realised he had fallen deeply in love with John King's daughter, but because she was engaged he was 'pretty shy' of her and tried to hide his feelings. He was very unhappy on the occasions when her fiancé rode over to the farm and he saw the two laughing and talking together.

In *mid-April* the situation changed dramatically, quite without warning:

'About a fortnight after I returned from Durban, Lindsay came one morning and there was a row, and the engagement with him was broken off. I cannot say how delighted I was at this, as I had something like fallen in love with Madge [Margaret] myself.'

Charles was free to court Margaret openly now, and only held back because he knew he could not afford to marry yet. He believed she cared for him, but could not be sure of it, and she was content to keep him guessing for a time. It seemed that this situation might last indefinitely, and Margaret's brothers, who could not help seeing what was going on, must have thought it a strange sort of romance.

Early in *May* the Kings began making plans to attend the 'great [Pieter] Maritzburg week of dissipation' held annually in celebration of Queen Victoria's birthday (*May 24th*). As usual there was to be a series of events including 'a grand review of all the forces in the Colony, numbering about 300 men', an agricultural show, race-meetings, fireworks, a bazaar and 'amateur theatricals'. It was settled that Charles should ride into town with Jim, Bob and Margaret, as the parents were not going, and rooms were booked in advance. The party was to be joined en route by Grace and her brother-in-law, Bob Speirs, and a Mrs. Shaw. Charles thought the celebrations would probably prove very 'feeble' – though of course he did not say so – and had no idea that the visit to Pietermaritzburg would bring about a crisis in his love affair.

The riders were to leave 'Lynedoch' early in the morning of *May 24th*, but at the last minute Bob King was obliged to go on ahead and Jim decided to wait until later, so Charles found himself Margaret's sole escort for the first part of the trip. Nothing could have suited him better:

'Madge and I started about five o'clock to ride in. I was pretty sure by this time that she cared for me.'

They had never been together unchaperoned before, and the experience was thrilling; as they cantered along in the pale winter sunshine, delighted to be in each other's company, they wished they could prolong the hour for ever. But all too soon

64

they reached Day's farm, where Grace and the others were waiting for them, and there they had to separate.

The party of young people arrived in town as fresh as when they had set out, (a thirty-mile journey on horseback over rough tracks was commonplace in those days), found their lodgings and changed into the clothes they had brought in their saddle-bags. Then they went out to enjoy themselves. Charles's diary tells the rest:

'Madge, Bob and I went to the review in the afternoon, and down to see Mrs. Speirs in the evening . . . The next day Madge, Bob and I went to the races, and in the evening to the fireworks in the Market Square and after that to the bazaar. I only stopped there a few minutes but managed to get very cross with Madge, I do not know why.'

On *May 26th* Charles and Bob wanted Margaret to go with them again to the races:

'But she would not go, which did not improve my temper as I thought she had been humbugging me and was going to get rid of me now. I met Cooper [an acquaintance] and went to dine with him at the Club. Madge, Bob and I were going to some theatricals in the evening, and I very nearly did not go. However, I did, and got there late. After the first act I asked Madge if she would like to go out, and she came and we had an explanation and I knew she cared for me.'

They had declared their love for each other at last; he had asked her to marry him, and she had accepted.

Charles thought it better to keep quiet about the engagement for the time being; he asked Margaret not to say anything about it until he was established on 'Gowrie', and she agreed. All the same, his conscience was troubling him: 'I am not sure if I am doing right towards her.' He knew that he ought to have asked Mr. King's permission to propose to his daughter.

Needless to say, they could not keep the affair to themselves. A month after the visit to town Margaret told him she had been asked outright if she were engaged to him, 'saying everybody said so'. The pair played into the gossips' hands by forgetting to be discreet; when they went to a dance at the farm 'Fordoun' Charles wrote in his journal afterwards, 'Danced almost entirely with Madge'. It was no wonder that tongues were wagging.

The secret was blown sky-high early in *October* by a stranger, a minister from Pietermaritzburg who was spending a night or two at 'Lynedoch'. The man happened to overhear Charles and Margaret saying something uncomplimentary about him, and was quick to retaliate:

October 7th: 'Here's a nice go, the murder is out . . . when I came home in the evening Madge told me that the parson had taken Mrs. King aside and asked her if we were engaged . . . he said our conduct was not becoming, and that we were talked of through the country.'

Mrs. King questioned Margaret, who did not know what to say and referred her to Charles. The young couple spent a very uncomfortable evening, closely watched and not allowed to sit together, while the minister glowered at them from his chair. In desperation Charles 'went out to try and speak to Mr. King before he went to bed, but could not get hold of him'.

October 8th: 'I asked Mr. King if he would have any objections to my marrying Madge, and he said none but what would my people say, and that is the question . . . Gave Madge my ring [an emerald set in gold] and she wore it all the evening, so it is all out now . . . I think Mr. King is quite pleased, but am afraid Mrs. King is not.'

October 9th: 'Mrs. King has not said anything to Madge either one way or the other, and I have not had an opportunity of speaking to her alone.'

Charles had assumed that the Kings would be pleased for Margaret to marry him, but he knew his parents would disapprove. It was not the fact of his getting married that William Smythe and his wife would object to, but the fact that he had chosen as his bride the daughter of a former employee of Methven. The snobbish Mrs. Smythe would be particularly upset, for she had hoped he would marry into the Scottish aristocracy or landed gentry. Margaret, who had spent all her life in Natal, did not understand Charles's problem, but her parents did, very well.

Next day Charles wrote to his mother to break the news of his engagement, his fiancée sitting beside him and adding her message at the end of the letter. 'I hope they will not be angry at home', he thought, as he sealed the envelope. He would have to wait two or three months for an answer, living on tenterhooks all that time.

Luckily he had a lot to think of besides his parents' reaction. He had begun stocking 'Gowrie', and had bought 160 sheep, all of which had to be treated with McDougal's Mixture (sheep-dip) to free then from ticks. The foundations of his farmhouse had been put down and a Mr. Moreland had tendered to make and lay the bricks, but Charles quarried the building-stone himself, and cut timber in the bush on Bob Speirs' farm at the Dargle, beyond Fort Nottingham. He took a waggon to town and bought 5 cwts of galvanised-iron for the roof, four panel doors, a glass door and some sash windows. He would rather have had a thatched roof – 'thatch is much cheaper, but is much more dangerous in the winter [the dry season in Natal] on account of the grass fires'. The cottage was to consist of two small bedrooms, a dining-room and a sitting-room, with a six-foot verandah in front, and a dairy, kitchen, pantry and extra bedroom behind.

Charles and his partner were still critically short of help on the farm:

'There are no kaffirs on it, and there are none to be got here, at least they are too lazy to work . . . Bob and I went down to the thorns [i.e. thorn country] and were out for five days among the kaffirs there, trying to get some to work, but could not get one.'

The few men they had at 'Gowrie' were slack:

September 15th: 'Half the sheep were not brought home at night. The kaffir, Jim, who was herding them must have been lying in his kraal all day.'

Charles gave the idle shepherd a whipping.

Always on the lookout for labourers, he studied advertisements in the newspapers:

'There was a notice in the [Government] Gazette for application for liberated slaves, to be bound for three years, so we applied for twelve, but I am rather afraid they will be given to the coast people before we get a chance.' [These freed slaves were Zanzibaris and Mozambique Africans from Arab slave-dhows. captured in East African waters by the Royal Navy. A small number of them were landed at Durban between the years *1873* and *1879*; they were indentured as labourers for three years, then each man was given a plot of land on the Bluff. This was the origin of Durban's ex-slave colony.]

Towards the end of *December* Charles began watching his overseas mail anxiously, as his parents' response to his engagement news might arrive any day:

December 30th: 'They have got my letter before the important one, so I may expect an answer to it now.'

In the meantime he heard from the faithful Guy Dawnay, who sent warm good wishes. Dawnay, an intrepid traveller, had been to Lapland and was on the point of setting off for Abyssinia to shoot and to learn Arabic.

January 13th, 1876: 'I got my long-expected letter from home . . . about my intended marriage. A letter from dear old Father, neither approving nor defending it but simply laying the position before me from an unprejudiced point of view, stating all the disadvantages I should be putting myself under, but all most kindly put. Mother's, as was natural, was much stronger against it, very anxious for me to come home, etc.'

Replying to his mother's plea that he should return to Scotland at once, Charles wrote:

January 23rd, 1876: 'As to coming home just now, it is simply impossible and, dearest Mother, I am afraid you must make up your mind to my having my home out here and not with you.'

He admitted that his prospects in South Africa were nothing out of the ordinary:

'With luck one might make a fortune in this country, but all that a man has to expect is that with steadiness and sticking to his work he may make enough to keep himself and family if not in great splendour at all events very comfortably . . . Anyway, dearest Father and Mother, whatever happens, neither of you can have cause to think that it is for want of good advice and love on your part.'

More letters from home reached him on *January 27th:*

'My mother still full of regrets about my engagement. My Father sound and sensible as usual.'

When he answered these letters on *January 30th*, Charles told his parents that he intended getting married as soon as the house on 'Gowrie' was finished, but that building was held up because

68

of lack of timber. The wood would take a month to cut, at least three months to dry out, 'then a month to get it worked and put down, so I expect it will be six months before we get married'. That would set the wedding day at some time in *July* or *August*.

'I enclose a list of things I shall want for furnishing my house, if you will get somebody to buy them, and stop the money out of my allowance. The electroplate articles . . . from somebody like Mappin & Webb; dinner and bedroom sets in stoneware, some plain pattern; the tea-set in something better. The fenders must have no steel or brass about them.'

Charles spent the next six months building up his stock, and by *mid-May* he and Jim King had 360 merino sheep, 28 horses including a stallion they planned to enter for the Pietermaritzburg Show, and 80 head of cattle. The horses had given a good deal of trouble because they were always running away; there was nothing to stop them, as the countryside was unfenced. The last lot of mares bought from a farm twenty-five miles from 'Gowrie' tried time after time to get home – 'though herded in the day and brought up to the house in the evening, they make off through the night.'

The labour position had improved at last, and Charles and his partner had a white man, (a deserter from a ship), working for them for £3 a month and his food. They also had four Zulu labourers, who were paid £1 a month each. Charles thought the white artisans he had to employ as builders were grossly overpaid:

'My two carpenters, a man and a lad . . . are at day's wages, and very high, the man at 12/– and the lad at 7/–. It is a fine thing being a tradesman out here.'

Busy as he was, he never lost touch with current affairs, and was following newspaper reports of Lord Carnarvon's moves towards federation in South Africa with the greatest interest. The Colonial Secretary campaigned vigorously from *1874* until *1881* for the union of the Cape and Natal with the Transvaal and Orange Free State, but in Charles's view the scheme seemed impractical:

April 1st, 1876: 'I see South Africa has been mentioned in the Queen's Speech . . . as to Confederation it is a great mistake.

69

If it was done under British supremacy it would be all right, but the Dutch republic [the Transvaal] would not have that.'

By *July* all thought of politics was far from his mind, for the homestead on 'Gowrie' was finished and the household goods he had asked his parents to buy for him overseas had come. He hired a waggon to bring them up from town:

'There is no doubt the danger of transit in the thirty miles between this and Pietermaritzburg is much greater than in the other 6,000!'

But when he unpacked the things he found that only a sink and a cup had been broken on the long journey from Britain. He and Margaret thoroughly enjoyed furnishing their new home.

Preparations for the wedding-day were well in hand now, and early in *August* presents from friends and relations began to arrive: a toilet set, a pair of earrings for Margaret, two vases, a tea-tray and other gifts. But what meant more to Charles than the presents were the kind letters from both his parents which he received on the eve of his wedding. Replying, he told them he was very grateful, 'as I know how much your feelings must be against it'.

The young couple were married on *August 17th, 1876,* at half-past ten in the morning, in the sitting-room at 'Lynedoch' which Mrs. King had decorated with masses of pink peach blossom. The Rev. A. van Velden, the Dutch Reformed Church *predikant* from Pietermaritzburg, took the service; the Kings were Presbyterians, but their minister was away in the Cape and Mr. van Velden was acting for him. Mr. Shears, the Anglican vicar of Howick, (whom Charles had met earlier, at the coast), had been to visit him and Margaret and bless the match. In a letter to his mother, describing the ceremony, Charles wrote, 'It was a very quiet affair, there were only people from the four nearest neighbours.' The family was still mourning the death of Margaret's aunt, Miss Helen Ellis, so gaiety would have been out of place.

Margaret's wedding gown had been sent her by a relative in Edinburgh. It was made of ribbed silk, and because she was in half-mourning a delicate blue-grey shade had been chosen; the close-fitting jacket was trimmed with real lace and had swansdown at neck and cuffs, and the skirt was very full. She wore a veil of Limerick lace which had been sent with the gown, and a wreath of artificial orange-blossom. (The dress became a family heirloom, and the veil was worn by three of her daughters at their weddings, and by some of her granddaughters.) Looking at his bride as she came into the room in her finery, Charles's heart was very full.

He had expressed his feelings about Margaret King in a letter to his mother and father, though what he said naturally did not touch on the emotional side of their relationship:

'I think Madge will make me an excellent wife, she is so good and cheerful, makes the best of everything, and I know she will be the greatest assistance to me in farming, she knows so much about stock and is a much better judge than most of the farmers about here and certainly far better than I am, as you may imagine.'

In his diary he filled in some of the details concerning the wedding:

'The bridesmaids were two Miss Jaffrays and Maggie Amos. I gave them lockets, they cost £3.–10 each. We had a very good breakfast in the kitchen. I gave Van Velden £5. Madge changed her dress and we started to walk to "Gowrie" about half-past twelve. Mrs. King and Bob came up to receive us. Mrs. King broke a cake of shortbread over Madge's head.'

Mrs. King's odd-sounding behaviour was not really as strange as it sounds, for she was merely following an old Scottish marriage custom: a plate of rich shortbread, (which like wedding-cake symbolised fertility and good fortune), was flung over the bride's head when she and her husband reached their new home, and the omens were read by the way the plate broke. The more pieces there were, the happier the marriage would be; alternatively, the number of pieces indicated the number of children the couple would have. If the plate remained intact, the outlook was very poor!

Charles ended his account of that day – the most momentous of his life – with the words:

'Had tea by ourselves, and to bed about nine. And thus ends my bachelor's life and I think I could not have made a better choice of a wife anywhere. I only hope we shall get on well

71

together, and though my marriage is not regarded with favour at home I think if they were out here they would think I was right.'

___

Charles and Margaret settled into their little house very happily, and were particularly proud of their sitting-room with its carpet sent out from Scotland, its sofa, comfortable chairs and ornaments. In the centre of the room was an oval table 'very prettily made by the carpenter', piled with copies of 'The Illustrated London News' and 'The Field', and there was a bookcase filled with well-bound classics; few farmhouses were so well supplied with reading matter. In cold weather a log fire burned in the chimney-place.

In the evenings Margaret sat with her wool-work while her husband played his concertina to amuse her, but she wanted a piano and made up her mind to save the money for one out of her dairy earnings. (Farm butter was salted down in wooden barrels and sent to town to be sold for winter use; it fetched two shillings a pound, and was a very useful source of income.) Charles mentioned her longing for a piano in one of his letters to Methven, and William Smythe sent a gift of £25 towards the cost of buying one and having it shipped to Natal. Thanking him, Margaret wrote:

'It would have taken me a great many churnings before I could have made as much from my butter, and though Charlie's concertina affords a certain amount of music it hardly comes up to a piano.' [The instrument arrived at 'Gowrie' a year later; it had come all the way from Edinburgh and was nearly new, yet its cost landed at Durban was only £38.–10].

Margaret's letter told Charles's parents more about the new house, and she had to admit that she found it hard to keep the rooms clean:

'There is a loft above in which the mealies for the kaffirs are kept, and the walking about brings the dust down, which distresses me.'

Mrs. William Smythe thought the place too primitive by far, and said so the next time she wrote. Charles, very much on the defensive, replied:

'Dressing rooms are a luxury unknown in this part of the

world . . . even on the coast where things are done on a much better scale than here . . . The open drain you allude to from the kitchen is a most harmless thing, nothing goes into it but the washing of the milk pails and dirty water from the kitchen . . . We are not more than four hundred yards from the fountainhead, and a good deal of water is led past the house.'

Mrs. Smythe had also asked about food supplies, and was told in one of Charles's letters:

'They killed a beast at 'Lynedoch' last week and we got a quarter, so we shall live on salt beef for some time to come.'

Porcupine was another frequent item on the meat course, and was described as 'capital eating . . . very like good buck, and a most agreeable change from bacon and eggs which is the staple food when the gun season is over.'

Charles was working very hard to improve 'Gowrie'; he was building a byre for twenty cows and a stable for eight horses, and was enclosing the garden and field with a wire fence. Early in *1877* he bought a second-hand ox-waggon for £42, which was very cheap, and planned to put up a forty-foot waggon shed as soon as he could. He and Jim King had plenty of help, as a shortage of mealies had obliged some of the local Zulus to come forward; but they would not stay once they had earned enough to pay for a few bags of maize.

The astonishing physical strength of the Zulus never ceased to amaze Charles:

'I was driving poles in the waggon, and was just crossing a burn . . . when the kitchen boy who had come to help us unload them fell off and the waggon went right over his back. He was lying on his face, I of course thought he was killed as there was about a ton upon the waggon, but he only limped about for a couple of days and was all right again. I am certain it would have killed any white man.'

As usual, Charles took note of what was going on in Natal as a whole, not merely in his own district. He was especially interested in the railway-line which was being built from Durban to Pietermaritzburg, (Sir Henry Bulwer had turned the first sod at Durban on *January 1st, 1876*), as he knew it would eventually be extended right through the Colony:

December 3rd, 1876: 'Our railway is progressing but slowly, and we are paying an enormous price for it. I am afraid it is to be a job like most of the other works that are done by the Government here. The contractors are getting £8,000 a mile for it, and were to import by the contract two-thirds of the labour but have not done so yet and are trying to creep out of this clause, and as they pay very high wages to the kaffirs the sugar planters are grumbling awfully.'

He had another complaint:

'The Government tried to get a Property Tax through the Council this year, but it is postponed till next, and in the meanwhile a valuation Bill has passed to value all the land and improvements on it. It will come rather hard upon people like me who have just been putting up a good house and enclosures, while it will hardly affect . . . the landowners who are just holding land on a speculation and not doing a bit of good – letting kaffirs squat and burn down the timber and make their mealie gardens and run as much stock as they like for £1 a year, while they will not let it to white people except on exorbitant terms.' [Land occupied by Zulus was often ruined through soil-erosion caused by over-grazing and the removal of trees and bushes for firewood.]

Disturbing news of fighting in the Transvaal had reached the Midland farmers by the beginning of *December*, (this was the war between the Boers and the Bapedi chief, Sekukuni, which so far had gone very badly for the Boers), and Charles wrote to reassure his family in Scotland that he and Margaret were in no danger:

'The Transvaal war is not likely to affect us here much, though it does the storekeepers. I think England will take it [the Transvaal] over . . . I think the Zulu country will also be taken over at the death of the present king, as he has no children and there is sure to be a row among the kaffirs which will afford a good pretext to England to take it over.'

Charles's interest in outside events had vanished by the time *Christmas, 1876*, came round, for he knew that Margaret was going to have a child and he could think of little else; the news that he was to become a father had thrilled him. Because of her pregnancy his wife was unable to ride to church at Howick with him on Christmas Day, (which was just as well, as he got caught in a storm and did not reach home until late at night), but they both went to 'Lynedoch' to celebrate the New Year. The only thing that detracted from their happiness was Mr. King's ill-health; he had a bad leg and could not get about without a crutch or stick, and there was little hope of his getting better.

Early in *1877* farming families in the Midlands saw convoys of British troops, conspicuous in their scarlet tunics, making their way northwards towards the Transvaal border and everyone speculated as to what it meant:

March 18th, 1877: 'There is great excitement about the military movements here. The whole of the 13th Regiment [Prince Albert's Somersetshire Light Infantry] is marching up-country with seven guns. The 3rd Buffs [East Kent Regiment] have arrived at Pietermaritzburg and the 80th [2nd Battalion, South Staffordshire Regiment] has just landed at Durban. There have never been so many soldiers here before. It is supposed they are going to annex the Transvaal. It has put up the price of cattle and horses already, which is a good thing.'

Charles had obviously not heard that the Transvaal had been annexed by Britain already, on *January 1st*. The Boers had not succeeded in subduing Sekukuni, their country lay wide open to attack from Zululand, and Lord Carnarvon had decided to take over the republic 'to avert a general native war' and to further his scheme for federation in South Africa. The newly-knighted Sir Theophilus Shepstone had been given orders to ride up to Pretoria and hoist the British flag there, and although he took only a small party with him he met with little resistance; in fact, many townsfolk welcomed him as the country was nearly bankrupt. A large number of the backveld farmers, on the other hand, were fiercely resentful.

On *May 1st*, as Margaret's time was close, Charles took her into Pietermaritzburg and left her at Mrs. Baxter's, the midwife's, house to await the birth of her baby. He spent the next few weeks burning fire-breaks on 'Gowrie', as the most dangerous time of the year was approaching: ironstone boulders falling in the foothills of the Berg and striking each other often caused sparks which set the parched grass alight.

Margaret's child, a daughter, was born on *May 29th*, and Charles, very excited, wrote to his mother next day:

75

'It is a fine lassie with such a lot of darkish hair and dark blue eyes, but I think it will turn fair as it has very light eyebrows . . . I am glad it is a girl . . . its name is to be Euphemia Janet, to be called Effie. Janet is after Mrs. King.'

Charles did not need to explain the choice of the baby's first name. He had called the little girl after his paternal grand-mother, the lovely Miss Euphemia Murray, daughter of Mr. Mungo Murray of Lintrose and known as 'the Flower of Strathmore'. This was the young woman whose charms the poet Robert Burns had sung in his poem beginning 'Blythe, blythe, and merry was she . . .'

He paid Mrs. Baxter £13 for attending Margaret, (the charge was 25/– a week before the confinement and £2.–10 after), and had Effie baptised at the midwife's house by an Anglican clergy-man; his mother had sent her a beautiful christening robe, one he had worn himself. When the infant was about three weeks old he brought her and her mother home. To celebrate their safe arrival, and his new status as a father, he 'had the kaffirs in and gave them a tot and a piece of tobacco'. There was great rejoicing at 'Gowrie' and 'Lynedoch'.

CHAPTER SIX

MARGARET HAD NO-ONE to help her care for Effie, so Charles looked after the baby himself on his wife's butter-churning days. At other times Margaret tied the child on her back, Zulu-fashion, as she went about her work. There were no 'black nannies' in the *1870*'s, as respectable Zulu women seldom left their kraals. Effie was strong and healthy, and as blithe as her great-grandmother, the lovely 'Flower of Strathmore'; her doting father described her as 'such a jolly personage'. On Sunday afternoons he would put her and her mother in a rough sledge and take them to visit the neighbours at 'Fordoun', and she seemed to enjoy the ride over the bumpy track.

Ox-drawn waggons, carts and sledges were still the main means of transport in the country districts of Natal, but the railway-line was slowly nearing Pietermaritzburg and Charles knew that extensions were already planned:

June 11th, 1877: 'The railroad works are getting on, and I think there is little doubt now the Transvaal has been taken on that they will push on the railway to Newcastle directly this is finished. I had two of the railway surveyors here for a night, as they were coming down the future line.'

In *October* came news of the latest clash between whites and Africans in South Africa, this time in Cape Colony. It was the so-called Ninth Kaffir War, last of the many wars on the Cape's eastern frontier.

October 30th: 'I believe the irregularity of the mails is that the country steamers [coasters] are employed in the Cape transporting troops and provisions to the eastern frontier where they are at war with a kaffir tribe. It will not affect us at all, as though other tribes would have joined if these had been successful at first the whites have luckily not lost an engagement yet.'

On *November 23rd* came trouble of a different sort, a catastrophe directly affecting 'Gowrie': it was a severe hailstorm which struck about four o'clock in the afternoon, lasted only a quarter of an hour, but as Charles said, 'made a clean sweep of every growing thing we had'. Describing it in a letter to his mother, he told how huge, jagged lumps of ice had fallen, killing six sheep and injuring many more; the shepherd was cut about the head before he could take shelter. Charles' crop of oats was ruined. The corrugated-iron roof of the farmhouse was pierced in twenty places, and the noise of the hail drumming on it was deafening:

'Poor little Effie shook like anything and was as white as a sheet, and we could see she was crying though it was impossible to hear her.'

Charles realised that his home would need re-roofing entirely, but he would patch it temporarily with white lead. The damage was a bit of very bad luck, and he was naturally much upset. Yet he ended his letter with words which must have touched his mother's heart for a different reason:

'I forgot that my greatest and most important news ... is that Effie cut a tooth yesterday and another is making its appearance ... I wish you could see her, she is so bonny.'

Natal's summer storms could be lethal even when they did no damage to crops, as Charles saw for himself about this time: two Zulus in his employ had a very narrow escape from death one day, when they were caught in a thunderstorm half-way home from Pietermaritzburg, after taking in the wool clip. The men had outspanned the waggon to rest and feed the oxen, and were just about to yoke them up again when lightning struck:

'It hit the after yoke which was standing against the pole, rending it into splinters and knocking the kaffirs head over heels.'

The lightning ran along the chain, and if the oxen had been inspanned all sixteen would have been killed instantly. The Zulus were only stunned, and soon recovered:

'They are both away home now to get purified by the witch-doctors, as none of the other kaffirs will go near them until the witch-doctors have gone through a lot of ceremonies with them and given them roots [i.e. medicine concocted from roots and other ingredients] to prevent the lightning striking again.'

Charles argued with them about their superstition – he could make himself understood in Zulu fairly well by now – but his reasoning had no effect on them:

'They only answer that the white people are quite different from them, and that they are only dogs.'

The year *1877* ended in general gloom, with rumours of war rumbling like thunder-clouds on Natal's horizons. In the eastern Cape a Pondo rising was threatening, and there was trouble beyond the Tugela:

'The Zulus are disputing with Sir Theophilus Shepstone as to the boundary of the Transvaal, and are very impudent . . . the Pietermaritzburg Volunteers have got orders to be in readiness at six hours' notice, but whether it will turn out to be a piece of bragging of the Zulus or not has yet to be seen . . . the Zulus have an army of 60,000 men with guns.' [Shepstone would not support King Cetewayo in his claim to the so-called 'Blood River territory', a strip of land which the Transvaal Boers also coveted as it would give them access to the sea at St. Lucia estuary.]

The young couple at 'Gowrie' managed to shake off their feeling of foreboding at Christmas time, and gave a gay little dinner-party for four guests on Christmas Day. The menu was soup, roast beef (they had to send twelve miles to the nearest butcher), Yorkshire pudding, roast buck, potatoes, turnips and plum pudding. 'This is the grandest dinner we have ever had', said Charles, proudly.

He had good reason to feel pleased, for he was not only a father now, at the age of twenty-five, but a landed proprietor too. Half a three-thousand acre farm named 'Howard' had been put up for sale, part of which adjoined 'Gowrie', and his offer of 2/3d an acre had been accepted. He wanted to buy the other half of 'Howard' as well, but the owners, the Land Colonisation Company, were asking 8/– an acre, which he thought far too much. It gave him a sense of satisfaction to know that he had 1,500 acres entirely his own; he and Jim got on well in partnership, but he longed to be independent. He felt it was a move in the right direction when, in the New Year, a fresh arrangement was made whereby he took over the whole of the agricultural improvements and working expenses of 'Gowrie' except for expenses purely connected with the stock.

The first two months of *1878* brought the Natal settlers no relief from the menace of war. The Zulus were in resentful mood, Natal papers were full of reports of massacres in Zululand, and the missionaries were finding it impossible to carry on their work there.

January 13th, 1878: 'I wish the British Government would take over Zululand now, it has to be done sooner or later, as the kaffirs will never be thoroughly quiet till the Zulu chief is deposed, as he claims to be paramount chief from here to the Cape. Bishop Colenso has as usual been interfering in the matter. I do not think that anyone could be more hated than he is by the people here. His church has dwindled down to almost nothing, and if the other party did not rush to the extreme of High Church I think he would have no followers.'

The settlers were living under a great strain, and the unrest was fraying their nerves. Charles wrote to his parents on *February 23rd,* 'You have no idea what a drawback to the Colony these constant Zulu scares are.'

He launched into a bitter attack on Cetewayo:

'What I cannot understand is why they should treat a savage as a civilised king, a savage by whose orders hundreds of innocent men are killed every year. Who in conjunction with the British Government of Natal is the upholder of slavery in its worst form, the selling of women and girls to the highest bidder. The kaffir woman is the most degraded being there is, she is bought for her husband for ten head of cattle in Natal, [Charles was referring to the custom of *lobola*], she is then his absolute property. She hoes the fields and reaps the crops, cooks his food and makes his beer, while he does nothing, and the more wives the husband gets the better she likes it as there is less work for her to do [and less child-bearing]. How the British Government can allow such things here while it flaunts its philanthropy at home I cannot understand.'

Charles misunderstood Zulu marriage; a Zulu girl was not bought and sold, as he imagined, nor were matches arranged without the couple meeting first, as happens in some Eastern countries. A girl would be courted by a man, probably have limited intercourse with him, (though the begetting of an

80

illegitimate child was strictly forbidden), and he would approach her father or guardian and ask respectfully for her hand. The cattle given as *lobola* were a prerequisite of a legal Zulu marriage, a sign that a contract had been made. The *lobola* protected the wife because it prevented her husband from lightly abandoning her or getting rid of her. Each wife in a polygamous marriage had her recognised status, (the first wife was a person of importance), and her own hut where she lived with her children.

Most Victorian settlers in Natal, particularly those who were staunch churchgoers, thought polygamy and *lobola* shocking, and believed Zulu women to be very much misused. It did not occur to them that their own women had no legal rights, and were expected to be entirely submissive to their fathers or husbands!

In *mid-March, 1878,* the atmosphere in Natal was still very tense:

March 17th: 'Of course we are all very anxious to hear what is to be the end of all this talk about war. I only wish they would have it out here with the Zulus and have done with it, instead of the perpetual scare hanging over our heads. There could not be a better man than Sir Theophilus Shepstone to deal with them, as he understands them thoroughly, but unfortunately his ancient ally and now bitter opponent Colenso misrepresents everything that he does so much that I am afraid his hands are practically tied.'

The thought that Zulu warriors might come sweeping south into Natal was a nightmare to Charles, especially as Margaret expected to give birth again in a few weeks' time. This second baby would be only eleven months younger than the first. 'Effie cannot walk yet . . . poor little thing, she is very young to have a rival coming so soon,' he told Emily Smythe, when he wrote to break the news that she was to have another grandchild. He added that the cow which had been Effie's 'foster nurse' had just died of redwater. He had booked a midwife named Mrs. Biggs to attend Margaret's confinement, (it had taken him a whole day's hunt in Pietermaritzburg to find a nurse willing to come out to the farm), and was to fetch her early in *April*. Her charge would be £5.–10 per week, and £1 for delivering the baby. However difficult the birth, she would have to manage without the help of a doctor.

Charles' burden was lightened a little at the end of *March*, as his eldest brother David, who had resigned his Army commission, had come to Natal to meet Margaret and spend a few months at 'Gowrie'; he joined enthusiastically in all that was going on, and was a great help to Charles.

In one of his letters to Methven, David wrote:

'We have had great fun breaking in young oxen, they are not very wild though, and we get a riem [thong] over their horns and tie them to an old ox and then get them yoked. Some won't move at all but lie down and are dragged along by the other oxen till they think fit to get up.'

He listed the animals on the farm as:

'Cattle 117 (forty of them Madge's), 490 sheep, 1 goat (Effie's), 41 breeding horses, 3 riding horses, nearly 50 fowls, 7 ducks, 2 geese, 3 dogs, 3 cats ... plus any amount of fleas in the summertime and any amount of ticks on the cattle!'

David was happy to take on any job, from cutting timber in the bush to fighting grass-fires or catching young horses for branding. The colt-branding was rough work, for the animals had to be driven into a stone kraal where a noose was thrown over the head of one of them and pulled so tight that the beast nearly choked; when it fell the rope was loosened so that one of its front legs could be tied up to its neck, and trussed in this way it was carried out. The same performance was repeated with each in turn. The breaking-in of a colt for driving was done by tying it at the side of a trained horse; it would struggle at first, but when forced along by the other it soon gave in.

When Charles could spare the time he and his brother went shooting, and there were few days when David, who was a keen botanist, did not spend an hour or two in the veld on his own, searching for rare plants. He was making a collection of bulbs, seeds and dried ferns to take home to Scotland. The local Zulus, observing how energetic he was, soon had a nickname for him, he found:

'The kaffirs give most people names when they have been any time here, and mine is *Madumela* . . . *He Who Rushes At A Thing*, or does a thing furiously. Charlie was called *The Reed* when he was on the coast, but now he is called *Among the Reeds* [*Mhlangen*]. The kaffirs do not understand when you ask for anyone by their real name but only their kaffir name.'

David was fascinated by the Natal Zulus. He told his parents:

'We have had great fun . . . with a witch-doctor who smells out where lost things are. We had hidden half a crown the night before, and made him try and find it. He went through a long performance, but failed utterly to find it, so of course he said it was not fair . . . They do wonderful things in the way of finding missing cattle by cross-questioning, which is the principal part of the performance. In the Zulu country they smell out the *umtagati* or witches and then they are killed, [one is reminded of the dramatic smelling-out scene in Rider Haggard's 'King Solomon's Mines'] but of course they can't do that here.'

He was taken one day to see a Zulu wedding ceremony:

'We went to a dance at a kraal . . . there were two brides, it was a marriage dance – about two hundred kaffirs. It was a most curious performance. First all the bride's party and then the bridegroom's party came down from the other side, following each other and going zigzag all over the place. We did not stay till the end, as it lasts several hours, but I believe it finishes by the whole lot joining and clapping hands, and then they adjourn to eat and drink *tchwala* or kaffir-beer, slightly acid I think.'

David had been at 'Gowrie' only a few weeks when Margaret's second baby, another daughter, was born on *May 1st*. The birth was a difficult and painful one as the child weighed ten pounds, yet less than a fortnight later the midwife was sent home and by *May 21st* the young mother was well enought to resume her churning and make 12½ pounds of butter. The Rev. Mr. Shears came and christened the infant 'May Emily', and David Smythe was her godfather.

Charles could not relax, even though Margaret's confinement was safely over, for there seemed no end to his farming troubles this winter; there had been a plague of caterpillars, he had lost six head of cattle from redwater, and his stock was suffering badly because of the current drought. He was so short of labour that in desperation he took on a young tramp, a Frenchman, but he did not stay long and Charles let him go without regret:

'He is a very good example of how useless it is for a man to come here unless he has some trade or is willing to stay some time at nominal wages till he learns farm work. I put him to stone-quarrying, and he was no better than a kaffir and physically not as strong.'

In the background, dwarfing all other anxieties, was the constant fear of war: reports of fighting in neighbouring territories filled Natal newspapers. A day or two before May's birth Charles had written:

'The kaffirs [the Bapedi tribe] have broken out in the Transvaal, but I think will soon be subdued if the Zulus do not help them [this was Sekukuni again, egged on, it was said, by Cetewayo] . . . There has also been a rising among the Griquas and Pondos, just on the south border of Natal, but they will be easily put down. The worst of it is that the powder magazine in the European camp where all the white men and women had taken refuge blew up, whether accidentally or not is not known, and killed seven or eight people, injuring many more. A hundred of the Natal Mounted Police have gone down, and two hundred of the Buffs, though the place is really in Cape territory . . .'

The Sekukuni war did not end as soon as Charles expected, and reinforcements were called for:

July 29th, 1878: 'There are great military movements going on, all the available troops being marched up to the Transvaal . . . the military movements must be at enormous expense, ox-waggons being the only transport and there being no grass now along the roads for the oxen; they simply live on their fat and the half of them die, so that they [the British Government] have to pay four times the rate of transport now . . . than in summer.'

All this activity increased the normal hazards of the dry season:

'There is an enormous fire raging just now, some soldiers on the march up-country dropped a match into the grass and it is burning for miles.'

David, writing home, told a tragic story of another of these seasonal fires, one which had got out of control and burnt down three homesteads:

'Two of the houses were thought quite safe as they were across the Lions River, which is fifty feet broad there, but the fire jumped across and caught one house, and a piece of burning thatch was blown from it and lighted on the roof of the other, about 150 yards away across a broad road and a garden, and burnt it down too. The people were only able to save the things they had on!'

It says much for Charles's foresight, and his firm belief in Natal's future, that he decided at this time of gloom and uncertainty to buy more land. On *August 12th* he rode to Estcourt to attend the sale of the farm 'Vaalkop', (the name was changed later to 'Inchbrakie'), which he acquired very cheaply for 4/3d an acre. The farm, nearly three thousand acres in extent, was a beautiful stretch of country with the Mooi (Pretty) River running through it, and it marched with part of 'Howard'. He had to borrow from the bank in order to put down the 25% cash payment required. Soon after this his father sent him £600 so that he could buy the remaining half of 'Howard', but announced that in future Charles's allowance would be cut to £120 a year.

William Smythe sent David a sum of money, too. The young man had heard of a farm for sale in the Transvaal, north of Pretoria – six thousand acres for only £87 – and wanted to purchase it. Charles thought this quite a good speculation, as land in the Transvaal was increasing in value.

David had been at 'Gowrie' over four months now, and had recently been on a very enjoyable shooting expedition in the Drakensberg with Bob Speirs and four other men, two of them British officers. He wrote a full account of his trip to the family at Methven:

'I got two horses from the kaffirs . . . we had a cart with the tent and provisions, and had capital fun. The cart could not come up to the mountains, so we left it and the tent and took our provisions on our led horses to some caves which the Bushmen used to use, and stayed there for some days. The caves were full of Bushman paintings, most curious they are, and wonderfully well drawn. I tried to trace them, but could not as the stone was so rough, they are mostly scenes of hunting elands and of fighting. [Bushman art closely resembled prehistoric cave-paintings in France and Spain.]

'We had lovely weather on the whole, but the first night we were in the tent was bitterly cold with snow. The scenery was lovely, and I went right up to the top of the Berg, between 10 and 12,000 feet. I took my horse about halfway and climbed the rest. The view from the top was magnificent, the whole of Natal right away to the Zulu country while to the left one could see some of the Free State and to the right down to Kaffraria, and behind, Basutoland [Lesotho]. The shooting was not much though we got a lot of partridges . . . some ducks, quail, one oribi, and an eland which is a great rarity here . . . about three years old and the size of an ox . . . I brought some fern seed from the Bushman cave and some cones of a pine which is the only one indigenous to South Africa and which only grows up in the Berg and is very rare there. *Widdringtonia* is I think the name of it. There are two kinds of it, I have got both.'

David had only just returned from his trip when Britain made a significant move towards putting an end to the Zulu peril:

August 27th: 'Things are looking warlike on the Zulu border, as Lieut. General Thesiger [Lord Chelmsford] has come and a lot more troops and I think they are going to have a settling with Cetewayo . . .'

A fortnight later David wrote:

'They say Sir Bartle Frere [the British High Commissioner] is coming up himself [from the Cape] either this week or the following. General Thesiger went down the week before last to take possession of the mouth of the St. John's River in Pondoland, they met with no opposition and left a detachment of soldiers there. [The Pondo chief was paid £1,000 in return for the cession of Port St. John's to the Crown, but Pondoland was not annexed to Cape Colony until much later.] They have sent off the 13th Regiment and the Frontier Horse against Sekukuni in addition to the Volunteers, and will I think soon quiet him.'

The belief that war with the Zulus was imminent prompted

the white farmers in Natal to form rifle associations for their own defence. Charles Smythe rode over to the Dargle to an inaugural meeting of a rifle association there, and noted in his diary:

'We are all getting Government carbines for which they charge us £6.–12. so that in case of a row we may be all armed with a weapon that will take the same ammunition.'

September 24th, 1878: 'The state of affairs here is an extraordinary muddle. There are three states, the Transvaal, Griqualand East and [Griqualand] West, being governed quite contrary to their constitution without any legislative assembly. [There had been serious rebellions in both parts of Griqualand, and things were still very unsettled.] I fancy the Home Government wants to drive us into Confederation, which would be a very good thing, but we do not like joining other states like the Cape and Transvaal which are heavily in debt, while our [Natal's] revenue is always over our expenditure . . . Sir Bartle Frere was to arrive here on Monday from the Cape on his way to the Transvaal, where I hope he will see the necessity of ending the Zulu question for ever, for as long as Cetewayo is allowed to keep a standing army . . . we shall never get on.'

October 8th: 'The kaffirs here are getting worse and worse to deal with, they think the whites are frightened and are therefore as insolent as they can be.' [Charles had recently had a row with some Natal Zulus living near 'Vaalkop', who allowed their grazing cattle to stray on to his land in spite of repeated warnings.]

The Zulus who were his tenants on 'Vaalkop' and 'Howard' were of course an asset, as they paid him an annual rent of 10/– to £1 per hut, and were obliged to supply labour whenever he wanted it; farm-labourers' pay was 15/– per month for a man and 8/– to 10/– a month for a boy. The hut rents did not bring in much, but the labour was worth a great deal to him and he had done well lately:

November 4th: 'There is a good deal of money coming in just now. We have sold our oxen, for which my share is £30, and a butcher is taking 80 of our wethers at 22/6d each . . . we have just sent the wool into Pietermaritzburg, for which I expect my share will be about £30, and I have an offer of 25/– a muid for mealies, of which I have 15 muids to sell, so that my finances are pretty flourishing.'

Farming matters had diverted Charles's thoughts from the coming war with Cetewayo, but David was watching events in Zululand closely; he had decided he would delay his return to Scotland and take part in the scrap, and had had an interview with Sir Bartle Frere, to whom he presented a letter of introduction:

November 10th: 'They are thinking of raising some native levies if there is a row with the Zulus, and have offered me a captain's commission in them if they are raised, which I have accepted. The pay is 15/– a day, and a horse, £273 a year if it lasts so long, which I don't expect. Sir Bartle was very pleasant, I am not bound in any way, for I asked that particularly, but can resign my commission at any time . . . this will prevent my coming home on the *25th* of this month as I intended to do.'

He gave details of the native levies:

'They are to raise seven regiments of a thousand men each, ten companies with six commissioned and six N.C. officers (whites) to each, one man in every four is to have a rifle, the rest assegais.'

David received news of his appointment on *November 21st* as a captain in the 1st Battalion, 1st Regiment, Native Contingent, and left at once for the army camp at Pietermaritzburg. As a parting present for his nieces he bought a heifer with a calf named *Bansela* (Gift) from 'Lynedoch', the cow for Effie and the calf for May; the animals would form the nucleus of a herd for each little girl. Farmers' daughters in South Africa usually had their own stock, which formed their dowry when they married.

Charles went down to Pietermaritzburg early in *December*, to fetch an immigrant named Arnott who was to help him and Jim King on 'Gowrie'. While he was in town he saw a vast concentration of waggons and oxen at the Army camp, and told his mother in his next letter:

'The Imperial Government will have a nice little bill to pay here. They are buying everything at famine prices [oxen worth £7 or £8 the previous year were now selling at £18] . . . The

Zulu affair is a most serious thing, and I wish it were well over. If the first battle is not won, it will make our own kaffirs very dangerous, and what to do with wife and children is awful to think of.' [He had an extra reason for anxiety now, as Margaret was pregnant again.]

Charles was not afraid for David's safety, and did not think he would be detained long by the war:

'The Imperial Government is making great preparations and I think there is little fear of anything going wrong.'

Like many other people, Charles very much under-estimated the Zulus. There was a terrible shock in store for him.

———————

Sir Bartle Frere hurled his challenge at Cetewayo early in *December*. Charles noted in his diary:

December 20th: 'All the country in excitement about the ulti-matum which was sent to the Zulus . . . I think he [Cetewayo] will give in.'

David, writing home, said:

'The Government sent an ultimatum to Cetewayo on Satur-day [*December 11th*], what it is nobody knows, but it is thought the terms are harder than he will care to agree to.' [The most important requirement was the break-up of the Zulu military machine, a condition which Cetewayo was very unlikely to accept. Thirty days was allowed for his answer.]

Charles had said, as far back as *March*, that he hoped the Zulu king would not give in, as he believed he would easily be defeated. His views had not changed, but the local Zulus did not share his optimism:

'The kaffirs here are in a great fright, they say we do not know what the Zulu nation is, and that we shall be eaten up' [i.e. wiped out; the Zulus were not cannibals!] The blacks in Natal knew from experience how dangerous the warriors from across the Tugela could be, as their grandparents had barely survived Shaka Zulu's depredations in the *1820's*. The country had been almost depopulated, its inhabitants either murdered or carried off into Zululand.

Long before the British ultimatum expired, the troops

commanded by Lord Chelmsford, (about 6,600 whites and three regiments of Natal Native levies), moved into position along the Zululand border in three columns. The first column, under Colonel Pearson, was to be based at the mouth of the Tugela river, and the main column accompanied by Chelmsford at Helpmekaar. The third, commanded by Colonel (later, General) Evelyn Wood, was to be based at Utrecht; its officers included a certain Colonel (later, General) Redvers Buller V.C., whose name was destined to be linked with Ladysmith's twenty years later. David Smythe's battalion was with the first column. He wrote from Pietermaritzburg:

December 22nd: 'We have been expecting to leave here for the last week, but I think that without doubt we shall be off tomorrow morning. We have been waiting for tents to come, but as they have not turned up yet we shall go off without them. It will be a funny way of spending Christmas, won't it? . . . Everybody thinks there is very little doubt Cetewayo will fight, even if he does not we are to occupy the country. They say that afterwards we are to go up to Sekukuni's country in the Transvaal in order to quiet him with a little persuasive eloquence . . . Our column consists of three battalions of natives, a thousand men in each, and five troops of horse, also native horse (50 men each) and a rocket battery . . . they are sending out 2,000 more men from Home, and they are expected in a week or a fortnight . . . What would you like me to bring you from Zululand? One of their regiments wears long white ostrich feathers, if we come across them I will bring you some . . .'

Cetewayo's warriors were magnificently-built young men, brave, loyal and utterly ruthless in battle. A warrior in full war panoply was a splendidly barbaric sight, grasping in his right hand his broad-bladed stabbing assegai and in his left his huge ox-hide shield. Below his armpits he wore a short garment made of strips of skin and ox-tails, and a kilt of ox-tails hung from his waist. A fringe of hair was fastened round the calf of each leg, and long, waving plumes were attached to the 'ring' circling his head. When he moved in to attack his enemies he uttered a deep-throated chant which was even more terrifying than the wild war-cry of a Highlander. At the time of the Zulu War some, (though by no means all) of Cetewayo's men were armed

90

with guns, but they were not good shots and were more dangerous using traditional weapons.

Cetewayo rejected Sir Bartle Frere's terms – as had been expected – and prepared to fight. Charles told his mother:

January 19th, 1879: 'War with the Zulus has begun, and the first engagement taken place with no loss on our side. I hear from David nearly every week. He is not across the Tugela yet, but I suppose soon will be. He is in excellent health and likes it if the weather were not so bad . . . wet weather must make a tent very uncomfortable . . . The war of course is the absorbing topic, the reinforcements from Home have arrived but the cavalry which were most wanted have not been sent. Infantry regiments are of little use in a war of this sort, and all the cavalry we have are Colonial Volunteers and a few of the infantry mounted. The Volunteers are the very men for the work, but there are so few of them, not more than 500 altogether, although that I think is not bad for a small colony like this with a scattered population.

'I am glad to see the Native Contingent behaved very well in their first engagement, though I think it was a mistake calling them out at all to fight, but I suppose the authorities could not help it as they could not get more men from Home. It will be a bad job for the Colony if the troops should get a reverse, but all the arrangements seem to be very well made . . . The demand for transport for the troops is enormous, they are offering £3 a day for waggons for Zululand, if I had not so many ties I should be off.'

Three days after he had written this letter came the report of an appalling military setback in Zululand:

January 25th: 'Jim [King] brought news of the total defeat and slaughter of a large number of regulars, Volunteers and natives by the Zulus, and the taking of their camp.' [This was the Isandhlwana disaster, in which 858 whites and 471 native levies were massacred. The British main column had crossed the Buffalo River, advanced to Isandhlwana and camped there; on *January 22nd* Lord Chelmsford and Colonel Glyn had moved out of camp with a large force, and the Zulus had seized their chance to fall upon the remaining troops, who were unprepared for attack, and annihilated them.]

91

Charles wrote at once to Methven to say that David was safe:

January 26th: 'As you will have seen by telegram, very bad news has just come from the Zulu country. Jim King was in town with the waggon and returned yesterday bringing the news, and very sad it is. The Volunteers were all Pietermaritzburg people, so you can think what a state the people were in there . . . the only men who are known to have escaped out of a force of over 1,000 men are two officers of the Native Contingent who cut their way through and brought the news to Pietermaritzburg. The camp waggons, the cannon and a Rocket battery were taken by the Zulus, and we are anxiously waiting for more news. We hope that some may have escaped by cutting their way to the General's column, but anyhow it is a most awful disaster. How thankful we may be that David was not there!'

The triumphant Zulus had immediately attacked Rorke's Drift, where four thousand of their warriors were beaten off with great gallantry by a party of some hundred British soldiers, many of them sick men, commanded by Lieuts. Chard and Bromhead.

The Isandhlwana massacre caused a panic in Natal:

January 30th: 'There is an awful scare through the country. All the farmers within thirty miles of the border have gone into *laager* [armed camp]. We are fortifying a house on the main road about eight miles from this, [probably at Curry's Post] 'and if there is any danger we shall move there. We shall be about twenty-five men, so if they do not come too strong we shall be able to do very well . . . we have no regular post now, as there are no kaffir runners to be got, which is an awful nuisance just when we want to hear all the news.'

Letter, February 24th: 'I expect you will have heard now of the heavy loss we have suffered in Zululand, as they sent a steamer express from the Cape to St. Vincent to telegraph for reinforcements. [Cable communication between Britain and the Cape was not established until *1880*] . . . David is all right . . . I heard from him . . . he is in an entrenched camp on this side of the Tugela . . .

'The sorrow and alarm throughout the Colony is dreadful, the men killed at Isandhlwana were massacred in the most brutal manner, the camp stripped of everything and burnt, and sad to say the General on his return could not stop to give the poor fellows burial as his communications were cut off and he had little ammunition left . . . The general column of which this was a part has retreated to Natal. Colonel Evelyn Wood has fallen back upon Utrecht, and Colonel Pearson (the coast column) has made a camp at Eshowe, 36 miles in the Zulu country, with 1,300 men . . . he is now left with a month's provisions and his communications cut off, so that unless strong reinforcements arrive or they can make up another column to open them again he will be obliged to retreat, which will be disastrous as the Zulus will swarm down upon him if he leaves the camp. [Pearson was not relieved until *April 4th.*] It seems the military officers very much underrated the strength and courage of the Zulus, who have been drilled and disciplined for years, and the young men have every inducement to fight as Cetewayo does not allow them to marry . . . unless they have distinguished themselves by killing people.'

The closing paragraph of his letter cannot have brought his family in Scotland much comfort:

'I hope the Zulus will not come our length, and I do not think there is much chance now as there is a good guard at most points of the Tugela, and as long as the rain continues they can only cross at certain points, *but of course when the river gets low they can cross at any point* . . . Now one feels the responsibilities of a family – how I wish all the row was over!'

The Zulu success at Isandhlwana and the retreat of the British troops had far-reaching and sinister results, for happenings in Zululand were being watched from other parts of South Africa, not least from the Transvaal where many of the Boers hankered to regain their independence. These people now began to say openly, 'If the Zulus can defeat the British, so can we!' Charles heard something of this:

February 28th, 1879: 'The Boers in the Transvaal are talking of driving the English out of Pretoria and setting up their own government again, but I think it will be only talk.'

Lord Chelmsford could do nothing to retrieve the situation in Zululand until he had more troops at his command, and fortunately for Natal Cetewayo did not attack again. During this lull in the fighting Charles heard from his old friend, the Hon. Guy Dawnay; he had returned to South Africa and wrote asking for horses, but Charles had to tell him that all had been sold at the start of the war. The two men did not meet during this visit, or ever again.

Once the British reinforcements had arrived, events moved swiftly:

March 26th: 'The relief column to Colonel Pearson is to start directly, and about time.'

April 6th: 'We have just heard today of the relief of Eshowe ... and Colonel Wood's big fight at Kambula [this was a victory for the British, as was the battle of Gingindhlovu on *April 3rd*] ... everybody here hopes that Sir Bartle Frere will not be blamed at home for beginning the war, as it has certainly been the salvation of South Africa ... from what we know now of the Zulus they might have swept Natal towns and all without the least resistance.'

For the next few weeks Charles was engrossed in home affairs, for Margaret's third baby was due very soon. He fetched Mrs. Biggs, the midwife, from town early in *May*, and on the *18th* his first son, David William, was born at 'Gowrie'.

The child's birth coincided with the return to the farm of Charles's brother David, who was suffering from dysentery and had resigned his commission. He stayed only a few days and then left on the *22nd* for Durban, en route to Scotland. David had had a very dull war, but at any rate was unhurt. A year after his arrival at Methven he rejoined the British Army and was gazetted captain in the 3rd Battalion, the Black Watch.

By the end of *May, 1879,* the British forces in Zululand were nearing Cetewayo's capital, Ulundi, the place where the last great battle of the Zulu War was to be fought. The advance was marred by a tragic incident which Charles mentioned in his diary:

June 4th: 'News of the death of the Prince Imperial.'

The young prince Louis Napoleon, son of the exiled Emperor Napoleon III of France and the Empress Eugénie, had persuaded Queen Victoria to allow him to take part in the campaign in South Africa and was accompanying the cavalry on the day he died. His patrol was ambushed, his horse 'Fate' broke away, and he found himself alone and wounded; he was killed fighting bravely, pierced by the enemy's assegais. His death was a disaster which, as Disraeli said, 'settled the fate of a great European dynasty', for he had been the hope of the Bonapartist party in France.

The news of the Prince Imperial's death plunged Natal into a gloom all the deeper because the Colony was in the throes of a slump:

June 6th: 'I wish the war would come to an end, as everything is so unsettled and prices are fearful. The Government has issued an order pressing waggons and oxen, but people who have only one waggon and span are of course exempt.'

Charles had another grievance: he had just discovered that the projected trans-Natal railway-line would cut through the middle of 'Gowrie' and spoil the farm; railway surveyors were already camped nearby, pegging out the route for the track.

The climax of the Zulu War came on *July 4th, 1879,* when Lord Chelmsford's victory at Ulundi put an end not only to the threat to Natal but to the old Zulu order itself. Ulundi was a classic battle of its period, the troops marching to the fray with bands playing and colours flying. They formed into a densely-packed square to meet the enemy attack, and the Zulus came at them fiercely and courageously, only to be mown down in their hundreds by musket fire. When all was over, Cetewayo had fled and the battlefield was strewn with the bodies of his tribesmen.

CHAPTER SEVEN

IN *December, 1879,* Charles Smythe made a very important decision. He had heard that the Natal Colonisation Company had a farm named 'Eberberg' for sale, and because it adjoined part of the land he owned already he made up his mind to buy it. This was the farm which he re-named 'Strathearn', and on which he built a house for himself and Margaret and their children; it was a home that they all came to love deeply and which has been the family's headquarters and meeting-place for nearly a hundred years. Today the old iron-roofed bungalow standing among the trees Charles planted is a memorial to his vision and energy, for he planned it, quarried stones for its foundations and made many of its bricks with his own hands.

He could not really afford to buy 'Eberberg' in *1879,* even at 10/6d an acre which was what the owners were asking, but some careful calculation showed him that in the long run it would be worth while raising the money somehow, even if he had to sell part of 'Vaalkop' and borrow from the bank and from Mr. King. He had discovered that for only £150 more than it would have cost him to enclose his 3,000-acre farm 'Howard' and maintain the fence, he could have a 7,700-acre block – 'Eberberg' and most of 'Vaalkop' combined – nearly two sides of which had a natural boundary in the Mooi River. Fencing had become essential – lines of narrow iron posts with barbed wire strung between them were changing the face of the Natal countryside – but it was expensive to install and to keep in repair. 'A good long river frontage' would be a tremendous asset. 'Eberberg' cost Charles £1,675 when all expenses had been paid, and he put down a further £40 for a plot in Nottingham (a township only in name) which gave him the right to cut firewood on the 25,000-acre town common; his own farms were all grass with hardly a tree anywhere.

Writing in *February, 1880,* to tell his father about the purchase of 'Eberberg', Charles said:

'I realise I have employed nearly all the money I can expect from you, but as my income from my stock comes to at least £300 a year and my expenditure is not more than £100 I shall hope to be able every year to buy more stock.'

He added, 'I have not done badly for the three years I have been at farming', and he knew William Smythe would agree.

With several farms of his own to develop and 'Gowrie' to run, Charles had almost more work that he could cope with; but busy as he was he always found time to spare for his children, for he was a devoted father. He had already begun to make a companion of Effie, and used to lift her on to a pony's back and take her with him on a leading-rein when he rode down to 'Lynedoch'.

Margaret had two Zulu lads to help her with Effie, May and David now, and the noise in the small farmhouse was deafening at times, especially when young animals had to be brought indoors as well. Charles, much amused, told his mother in one of his letters:

'You may imagine the row in the kitchen on a wet day, with three children, two nurse boys and four or five sick lambs; children, boys and lambs all yelling at once!'

In *April, 1880*, a fourth child was born, a premature daughter who arrived weeks before Margaret's midwife was due at 'Gowrie'. Charles was out in the fields one morning when an agitated servant came running to him with a message, and he rushed back to the house to find his wife already in labour. The next few hours were worse than anything he had ever experienced, for there was no-one to deliver the baby or tell him what to do, and his man Arnott, who had ridden hell-for-leather to fetch a neighbour's wife, returned to say she had refused to come. He was sent off again to get Mrs. King, as there was no doctor anywhere in the district, not even in Howick. The infant was born at one o'clock, a tiny child but fortunately strong enough to survive. She was given the names Margaret (Meta) Grace, after her mother and aunt.

Now that his family of children had increased, and with his partnership with Jim King coming to an end in three years' time, Charles realised he must go ahead at once with his plans

98

for 'Eberberg'. He would begin building there as soon as he could, so that there would be a home to move into when he had to leave 'Gowrie'. Riding over his newly-acquired land one day he had come across what seemed to him an ideal position for a farmhouse: it was a piece of level ground below which the hillside sloped fifty feet to a marshy valley through which a stream meandered for two miles to meet the Mooi; behind the site rose a steep little hill from whose summit he could see the blue ramparts of the Drakensberg. He had shown Margaret the spot, and she liked it as much as he did.

Charles decided to build a large cow-byre at 'Eberberg' before he put up a dwelling there, and work began in *July, 1880*. He had come to an arrangement with an elderly man named Gold, who contracted to erect the byre for 2/9d a yard if the stone was supplied. The building was to be big enough to hold sixty cows, and when finished would be 'the best of its kind in Natal'. By *August* the foundations had been laid, but progress was slow because there was only Gold, Arnott, a Scotsman named Duff and one Zulu to provide the labour. Charles rode over from 'Gowrie' as often as he could, (the distance was about three miles), to quarry stone and transport it to the site. Quarrying was back-breaking work, and as he sweated at it in the sun he thought with irritation of his Zulu tenants idling away their time in the kraals while he struggled to keep Gold supplied with building material. He would give a lot to have a dozen men regularly in his employ! But most Zulus could still afford to be independent and would not come forward unless their mealie crops failed or they wanted money to buy more stock.

He felt that his tenants had an unfair advantage over him, for they were making use of his land and giving little in return: 'From one kraal . . . I get one boy at 11/- a month, he pays me £4 a year and for that runs 70 head of cattle, 200 goats and 25 horses and gets firewood for four huts. Another kaffir has a waggon and oxen on the roads, nearly as much stock, five huts, and pays £5 a year.'

A few months earlier he had tried to force the Zulus to provide him with labourers by giving them the option of paying higher rents or supplying more help on the land:

June 22nd: 'Have been having great *indaba* [talk] with the kaffirs, and am going up to Estcourt with them next Monday to have a contract properly made out before the magistrate. Every hut that gives no work is to pay £4. Every hut that gives one man for six months £2, and every hut that gives two for 6 months, £1. Any giving 4 for 6 months is rent free. I pay them from 7/– to 15/– a month.'

Such contracts were not really much use, because the Zulus being illiterate did not understand them or realise they were meant to be binding. Several headmen moved their kraals as a result of the new ruling, and built huts on Crown land where they had only the annual 14/– hut tax to pay. The other men elected to stay, but Charles was little better off for farm help than he had been before and finally made an application for Indian indentured labourers when some should be available.

If Charles's attitude towards the Zulus seems unsympathetic it is only fair to remember the predicament he and the other white farmers were in; in the *1880's* nearly all farm work had to be done by hand, as there were very few mechanical aids to make up for the shortage of manpower. (Charles had a primitive hay-cutting machine, but there was no workshop nearer than Pietermaritzburg to repair it when it broke down, and as he said, in words that have a familiar ring, 'Unless you are there yourself they never do it properly'). He and his tenants were the victims of a thoroughly bad system under which both sides were insecure: the farmer because he never knew from month to month how many helpers he could count on, and the Zulus because they did not own the land they lived on and could be uprooted and told to move at short notice. The British Government should not have allowed such a situation to come about.

In *October, 1880,* Charles was so short of labour that he noted in despair that his seed-potatoes were spoiling in the loft for want of being planted, and he had only three farm hands to milk thirty-three cows and had been obliged to rope in his wife to assist:

'Madge has to turn to help them, or we should never get through in the mornings.'

Margaret was already making sixty pounds of butter a week, and caring for four children under four years old! But she was as good at milking cows as she was at most other farm chores, and cheerfully took on this job in addition to her usual work.

She and her husband led lives of almost incessant toil in these early years of their marriage, and on the rare occasions when they were invited to a party at a neighbour's farm Charles usually went alone because she could not leave her babies. When he took the waggon into town he seized the chance of going to the theatre if he could, but this sort of treat did not come Margaret's way and her only recreation was riding about the farm or visiting her parents at 'Lynedoch'. In the evenings she made or mended clothes while Charles read the local newspapers or the periodicals his relations sent out from Scotland.

It was not until *November, 1880,* that word came of the arrival of the Indian labourers Charles was expecting. He went down to Durban to collect them, accompanied by Bob King who had applied for several Indians for 'Lynedoch'. The two men signed the necessary papers at the Protector of Immigrants' office at the Point.

November 29th: 'I got six men and two women, but I got the Protector to let me leave a man and wife behind, as the man was so ill he could not walk and I should never have got him home. The next day was the opening of the railway to Pietermaritzburg and . . . great rejoicings there, so Bob and another man . . . asked me to bring up their coolies for them as there was only a special train run on Friday. This left thirty in my charge, but I left them at the depot till Thursday and then took them to Durban and clothed them [the men arrived wearing the Hindu *dhoti* or loincloth, and had to be provided with a coat and pair of trousers each; their wives continued to dress in the *sari*]. I got them into a truck and up to Pietermaritzburg at 7 o'clock at night. [They went on from there by ox-waggon.] I think they will be all right in a month or two, but they are not much use at present . . . it is very difficult not being able to understand a word they say.' [They spoke Tamil or Telegu.]

Charles found the Indians' food his biggest problem:

'They have to get rations of rice, *dohl* [a foodstuff rather like dried peas], salt fish, mealies, etc., and they will not cook together, each man has to have his separate pot, and if one dies

101

on your hands without medical attention you are heavily fined.'
[There was a doctor stationed at Howick now, and he agreed
to attend Charles's coolies at a guinea a visit if called to 'Gowrie'.]

The indentured labourers were quick to learn and settled
down well, all except one who was lazy as well as very dirty;
Charles dipped him, clothes and all, in McDougal's Mixture to
kill the vermin he was harbouring.

In the New Year Charles read in the newspapers that the
rebellion which had long been simmering in the Transvaal had
finally broken out. The first shot in this struggle for independence
had been fired at Potchefstroom on *December 16th*:

January 8th, 1881: 'The year here has had a bad beginning
in the unfortunate rebellion of the Dutch. I am afraid it will
be a long and bitter struggle, and the harm it will do will last
to another generation. If the Dutch stick together and the
English Government insist on keeping the country they will
find it a very different thing from the Zulu War, as the Dutch
are all well mounted on horses thoroughly trained to shooting,
and are splendid shots.'

He felt a certain amount of sympathy for the Boers:

'There is no doubt they have much to complain of. All sorts
of promises were made to them when the country was taken
over, and they never have been fulfilled. The Governor,
Lanyon, [Sir Owen Lanyon] was a very injudicious man who
took no trouble to conciliate them, and filled up all the
Government places with men either from Home, (who knew
nothing of the Dutch ways or language), or men of an unenviable
notoriety here who thought of nothing but screwing as much
out of the Dutch as they could. How far the rebellion may
spread we cannot yet tell – there are hundreds in Natal connected
with those Dutch by close ties of blood, and thousands in the
Free State; if these do not offer help openly they will at all
events hinder the Imperial authorities as much as possible by
refusing to sell oxen or waggons or produce. What they will do
for transport I cannot think, as during the Zulu War it was
drawn both from the Transvaal and Free State, and our trans-

port has already been drawn upon by the Cape Colony for the Basuto War [the so-called 'Gun War' which broke out when an attempt was made to disarm the Lesotho tribesmen] ... fighting now seems to be the normal state of things.'

January 21st, 1881: 'There is nothing new from the Transvaal. Colley [General Sir George Pomeroy Colley] is at Newcastle with about 1,500 men, but whether he intends to try and relieve Pretoria with them or wait for reinforcements we do not know. They have tried a sally at Pretoria, but were beaten back. I should like the Dutch to get a good thrashing, and then they should give them what they want, viz. a government of their own choosing, only allowing the Imperial Government the control of the natives, if it is so fond of them ... There is a great demand for horses already.'

The war pushed up food prices: the cost of flour, rice and mealies had soared now that there were so many British troops in Natal. Charles wished the British Government would send out some store ships. He had no time for the men in power in Britain, and commented:

'Of course the Dutch were to blame for taking up arms, but still I think if our rulers had had the real interests of this vast country at heart they would have been able to have smoothed things over. What we want in South Africa now is peace. What chance is there of the country being opened up, or of any capital being invested here, when we are constantly at war? We shall beat the Dutch ultimately, but with what a loss to ourselves and them. The greater part of them will trek further inland [into the territory which later became Rhodesia] and the Transvaal will be left a comparative desert, and what chance have we of attracting immigration to fill it up? It is all very sad.'

The Boers did not get the thrashing he had hoped for; on the contrary, General Joubert repulsed the British troops at Laing's Nek and Ingogo in northern Natal, before they had even crossed the border. In *February* came news of the rout of the troops at Majuba and the death of General Colley, and this prompted the Liberal Ministry in Britain, led by William Ewart Gladstone, to seek an armistice with the rebels.

Loyalists all over South Africa felt humiliated by the British

Government's act. Charles wrote to his parents in disgust:

February 28th: 'Everybody is very angry here at the peace that has been made with the Boers, I did not think that even a Liberal Government could have done such a thing. If it were not that I have a very low opinion of Colonial talent in the way of self-government, I think it would be the best thing for Natal to follow the example of the Transvaal and separate itself from the risk of being ruled by the originators of such a cowardly policy. The best of it is, they talk of Natal having to pay for the damage done to property during the war, as if we had anything to do with the affair. They have made us pay £25,000 for the Zulu War, which we have to raise by a loan, and because we submitted to that they think they will give us a little more to pay. It is a pity the Crown colonies have not a right to return some members to Parliament [i.e. in Britain] there would not be much chance of any Liberals getting in.'

Charles's profound dislike of liberalism very likely dated from this time. Gladstone's surrender to the Boers left a legacy of bitterness which affected many of the British settlers in Natal, and this strengthened the hand of those who were pressing for Responsible government for the Colony.

In July, 1881, The Pretoria Convention was signed, giving the Transvaal its independence, and British troops evacuated the country. Lord Carnarvon's dream of a Confederation of South African states was dead.

───────────

During all these months of war Charles's builders on 'Eberberg' had been plodding on day after day, and the large cow-byre was slowly nearing completion. Long before its corrugated-iron roof was on Charles had begun work on the homestead, making bricks, arranging for Charlies Speirs to supply him with timber, and calculating the cost of the doors, windowglass and other items which he would have to buy in Pietermaritzburg. The family's need of a larger house than the one on 'Gowrie' was more urgent than ever now, for Margaret had presented him with a fifth child and second son, John Oswald:

April 19th, 1881: 'Madge was taken ill at tea time, and a son

104

was born at 8 ... the children are delighted with their new brother.'

Charles was delighted with the baby too, but Effie remained his favourite. He had horrified Margaret a month or two before by taking the little girl with him, (although she was not yet four years old), when he trekked in to town by ox-waggon to deliver a load of butter and fetch stores:

'Started for Pietermaritzburg the other day ... at the last moment carried off Effie with me, much against her mother's will. However, she made out on the journey capitally. She was extremely good, not a bit frightened, though the roads were something fearful.'

He left her at a friend's house while he was busy in town, and had her photographed before they returned home.

Once the summer rains were over Charles threw all his energy into making bricks for the house on 'Eberberg'. 60,000 would be needed, 35,000 of them kiln-fired bricks for the outer walls (14 inches thick) which would take the full force of the weather. The interior walls could be built of 'green' bricks hardened in the sun. To heat the kilns he required at least six waggonloads of firewood, and all this timber must be cut in a patch of forest three miles away and brought to the farm.

By the beginning of *May* only 25,000 bricks had been made, and Charles began to doubt if the house would be finished even by the end of the year. The amount of work he faced was staggering:

'Sand for mortar has to be dug and driven, say 30 cartloads. Stone for the foundation to be quarried and driven, say 60 loads. About 40 more loads of stone to be quarried and driven to finish the byre. All this to be carried on as well as the ordinary work here, such as forage to be cut and stacked, mealies to pick and dry within the next three months.' [Arnott had been recalled from 'Eberberg', and he and one Zulu labourer were the only farm hands on 'Gowrie' as the Indians were all needed at the house site. The Zulu had to carry food supplies to the builders three times a week, and this took him half a day.]

Charles told his parents, almost despairingly:

'You can really have no idea how much has to be done ... I get quite hopeless when I think of it and remember that this

105

is only the house and byre. There are kraals [for animals] and fences to be made before the stock can be taken over . . . Luckily, I have not got to drive the timber, as Charlie Speirs is to deliver it for me. It will be 18 loads of yellow-wood.'

May 11th: 'Jim came up in the morning and we rode over to 'Eberberg' and marked out where the house is to be and took the levels.'

May 22nd: 'I have been over at "Eberberg" every day for the last fortnight, quarrying stone for the foundations of the house and have a good lot quarried and carted. The brickmaking is getting on slowly. About 40,000 made now. The building, putting in the foundation, the verandah of hammer-dressed whinstone, brickwork, plastering, laying the verandah and dairy with cement, is to cost £150, making with the bricks £210 for the building of the house, exclusive of iron roofing and carpentry.'

Charles had estimated that the house would cost him £600 to £700, and intended to raise the money on mortgage for five years, hoping to get it for 7%. But the final cost was £1,100, which was £400 more than he had expected. Fortunately for him, William Smythe came to the rescue. Charles sent his father a sketch of the proposed building, which was to contain five bedrooms, a sitting-room, dining-room, kitchen and dairy, all at ground-floor level, the whole to be surrounded by a six-foot-wide verandah. There was to be a long passage separating front rooms from back – an unusual feature for a farmhouse of that period. Because of the slightly sloping position of the site the verandah would be some four feet above the ground on the side of the house overlooking the little valley, although level with it on the kitchen side.

Just when Charles was at his busiest in early *July* he had to stop work and hurry down to Durban to meet two farm hands, Malloch and Fly, who had come out from Scotland under an immigration scheme and were to be bound to him for three years. With them came a woman named Susannah Hamilton, whom his mother had engaged to help with the children. The arrival of these three at 'Gowrie' put a great strain on Margaret as she now had a large party to feed at the farmhouse in addition to three builders at 'Eberberg'.

August 1st: 'I got my men [Malloch and Fly] shifted to the new place . . . we then got started to wood-cutting for firewood for the kiln, and got it all cut and driven in 10 days, which was quicker than I expected. I was very glad when it was done, as it was very hard upon the oxen there being 12 waggon loads and it was a good 2 miles, partly uphill . . . I am glad to say the brickmaking is finished at last.'

At this point things began to go wrong:

August 21st: 'The rain came on unexpectedly in the middle of the night and destroyed about 8,000 of my unburnt bricks, so I have to begin making some more.'

This winter rain was a calamity, and it was followed by two days of such cold weather that four cows and two yearlings died of exposure. This was not the end of Charles's troubles, for Susannah Hamilton, who was to have taken over some of Margaret's work, injured her foot and had to be taken to hospital in Pietermaritzburg, and when she returned she handed in her notice. She departed owing him £26.

For the next few weeks Charles was in a state of acute anxiety, fearful that more rain would fall; the builders had almost finished the internal as well as the outer walls of the house, and green bricks standing quite unprotected would dissolve into mud in a heavy downpour.

September 29th: 'The house is getting on rapidly and is within two foot of the top now. I think in another fortnight we will be ready for the roof.' [Would the rain hold off until then?]

By *November 13th* the carpenters from Pietermaritzburg had arrived at 'Eberberg' and got the woodwork for the farmhouse roof ready, and the corrugated-iron was put on a week later. Charles sighed with relief as he watched the last sheet fastened down; the worst was over now, and he could pay old Gold and send him off. He would fetch the ceiling-boards and other materials for finishing the interior when he went in to town to deliver his wool clip.

Just then the weather broke, and as a result the journey to and from Pietermaritzburg was a nightmare:

November 13th: 'The first day out one [waggon] upset with the wool. Luckily nothing broke, but I had to unload and set it up and then get the wool in again in pouring rain. These great wool bales are not easily moved about. Rain poured all night, but the other waggon was tented so I managed to keep dry. Got 9¼d. lb. for the wool, the highest we have ever got; came to £132. I had one waggon loaded with ceiling boards, doors, etc. and the other with iron, cement and groceries, and left Pietermaritzburg on Saturday afternoon but only got as far as the top of the [Town] hill when it came on to rain again. Sunday I got as far as Lions River when again it rained and I did not get back here till 8 o'clock on Monday night. Got all the stuff over to the new place next day. The house has got its first coat of plaster. Malloch has been building a cattle kraal.'

The state of the waggon road made Charles angry; why didn't the authorities put British troops in Natal on the job of making roads and building railways? His opinion of the Gladstone Ministry had not improved, and he wrote:

'Our Legislative Council is sitting just now, but I cannot see that they do much good, the Home Govt. makes them pass just what they like – and the Home Govt. knows just as much about how to rule South Africa as I do about ruling China!'

By Christmas time the house was nearly ready, and Margaret and the children went to stay at 'Lynedoch' while Charles moved the furniture from the old home to the new. His partnership with Jim King had come to an end now, their stock had been divided, and Jim was to take over 'Gowrie'.

On *January 21st, 1882*, he wrote, triumphantly:

'Here we are all safely transplanted to our new abode . . . I brought Madge and the children over on *9th January* . . . the cattle and sheep came over with us, so it was quite a patriarchal flitting. The children are delighted with the new house, the long passage is a fine thing for them, and the verandah all round.'

There was still a lot of painting and papering to be done, and the carpenters were busy on the interior fittings, working with the yellow-wood timber which Charlie Speirs had cut in the indigenous forests of the Dargle; this fine wood was plentiful in the *1880's*, though it is very rare today. Charles and Margaret had only enough furniture to fill their dining-room and bed-rooms, and the sitting-room was likely to stand empty for a year or two, but they were very happy to be settled in the house at last. Charles told the family at Methven Castle, 'I think this will be a very nice place when we have had a little time here'.

He had asked his parents to suggest a Scottish name for the farm, as the Dutch 'Eberberg' did not appeal to him. After a good deal of thought he had chosen 'Strathearn' because of its link with his family's history; it was 'by the banks of Earn' that the lovely Euphemia Murray had lived. Charles still felt the pull of the Highlands, and was not yet aware of the spell South Africa had cast upon him – but in time his love for South Africa would wean him away from the old allegiance.

CHAPTER EIGHT

CHARLES HAD GREAT PLANS for 'Strathearn'. When he and Margaret first moved over there the farmhouse and its byre and cattle-kraal stood bleak and exposed on open grassland where there was 'no wood, not a shrub within three miles,' but already in his mind's eye he saw plantations of pines and oaks springing up, giving shade in summer and protection in winter, and he visualised an orchard of apple, plum and peach trees on the slopes of the hill above the little marshy valley. The 'swamp' itself, ('splendid land', he called it), was to be drained by means of a ditch down each side and would be an ideal place for growing forage. Later on, when he had time, he would lay out lawns and flowerbeds around the homestead.

His mother, writing from Methven, wanted to know how he managed for water at 'Strathearn', and he told her:

'The water is not brought to the house, but I think can be by a ditch about a mile and a half [long]. The kitchen-coolie carries the water from the spring about a hundred yards below the house, and I have guttering along one side of the roof, which fills three barrels when there is a shower. If I find I cannot lead the water to the house in an open ditch I shall build an underground tank and gutter the whole roof and the byre, which will keep us in water all the year round, as they do in Durban.'

He had ideas for improved farming methods, now that he had Malloch and Fly to help him:

'I am anxious to start working horses instead of oxen, as they could get through the work much better now that I have white men who could work them.'

Malloch was breaking in four farm horses to harness, and Charles was going to set him ploughing with a pair of them instead of with a span of oxen as was the custom in South Africa. A horse-drawn hoe would also be very useful, and save hoeing by hand. Charles was very glad to have Malloch working for

111

him now that Arnott had left, for the man was invaluable.

The Indian indentured labourers were well worth their pay, too. Their only vice was a weakness for smoking *dagga* (wild hemp), as a result of which one of them had gone blind one day when out herding sheep and had been found staggering about helplessly while the sheep mingled with the 'Lynedoch' flock! It was three days before the man's sight returned. Another Indian had become temporarily insane through *dagga*-smoking, and Charles had to watch him closely and lock him in his hut at night to prevent his wandering off into the veld.

For a time Charles had two foreigners – a Norwegian and an American, probably runaway sailors – working for him; he gave them 1/6d an hour and their food, and put them to digging a big ditch six feet wide and four feet deep through the swamp.

By *July, 1882*, the railway from Pietermaritzburg had been completed as far as Caversham, and the contractors had begun extending the line northwards and building the station which was to be known as 'Nottingham Road':

July 12th: 'The railway has at last been commenced, and there is a large staff of men on "Gowrie" busy putting up buildings and beginning the earthworks. The station is to be just at the crossing of the road to Fort Nottingham, about two miles from "Strathearn".' [It would be very handy, and put up the value of his land, too.]

Charles took the opportunity of earning some extra money by helping with the construction work:

July 23rd: 'I have been working over at the railway camp all this week, I contracted to drive stone for them at 2/6d per load, so put on both the carts, Malloch driving one and I the other, and have managed to knock out £3 a day which is a very welcome addition to my finances. I shall go on again whenever they have enough stone quarried to keep us going ... hard work, but pays well.' In *October* he wrote, 'I am supplying the railway camp twice a week with sheep, butter and milk.'

The only sad event in what was turning out to be a particularly successful year for Charles and Margaret was the death on *August 7th*, a month after it was born, of their sixth child, a boy they had named Victor Murray. The baby was buried at the foot of the Paddock Hill behind the farmhouse, Charles making the tiny coffin himself with the help of Bob King.

Infant deaths were so common in the *1880's*, nearly every family expecting to lose at least one baby, that the young couple accepted their loss calmly, as being the Lord's Will, and by *December* were making plans for the usual festivities at Christmas and New Year.

December 24th, 1882: 'Mother's packet of Christmas cards arrived all right, much to Effie's delight, so pretty they are . . . We are going for a picnic tomorrow over to a waterfall upon the Mooi River in the waggon . . . the children are looking forward to it. We are to have two fowls, a tongue, a plum pudding and a cake. The four men who are stone-walling [i.e. building dry-stone walls to enclose part of the land near the house] are going away for three days, which will be a relief to Madge.'

On New Year's Day the Smythe and Speirs families were to join the Kings for a party at 'Lynedoch'.

Charles's brother David had sent a sum of money as his Christmas gift that year, and Charles told him in a letter of thanks:

'I shall buy two heifers, one for David and one for Meta. Effie is getting quite rich now, she has 8 head of cattle consisting of 3 cows, 3 calves, one yearling and one 2 years old. Unfortunately all her young beasts are oxen, but I think she has a very good start in life.'

He was already planning for the children's future.

That letter to David might easily have been the last Charles ever wrote, for a few days later he had a miraculous escape from death during a thunderstorm. He and a Zulu shepherd had been out looking at the sheep when a vivid flash of lightning struck the earth between them:

'It just felt like a bullet striking me on the back of the head – and I could hardly keep my feet for a minute or two, however neither the kaffir nor I were any the worse except a tremendous headache for an hour or two after.'

Malloch narrowly missed being killed while driving a load of stone across the farmyard in a horse-drawn sledge: a flash of lightning blasted a duck within five feet of him and hurled him bodily to the ground. One of his arms was temporarily paralysed.

The storms were unusually severe that summer, and on *February 10th, 1883*, one of them brought disaster to 'Strathearn'. Charles, still very shaken, wrote to his mother next day to tell her the distressing news:

'You will be sorry to hear that a hail storm came on yesterday afternoon, which in half an hour entirely destroyed my whole year's work. You cannot imagine the destruction – nobody would believe it unless they saw it. Not a growing thing has escaped. The mealies are bare stalks, with here and there a cob chewed as if a beast had been eating it. The turnips which we had just finished thinning, there is not a trace of – pumpkins, beans, buckwheat, in a word everything utterly destroyed. All my young trees, pines of different sorts that I had got from Pietermaritzburg Botanical Gardens, peaches, apples, peeled and smashed, it is too disheartening. The hailstones were not so big as they were the first year I was at "Gowrie", and did not pierce the iron roofing, but there was such a hurricane of wind the roof was taken off the coolies' house and carried about 200 yards. Luckily none of the animals was hurt as far as I know yet ... I shall try putting in some turnips and cabbages for the cows, but I am afraid it is too late as we shall have the frost in another month or two ... we had the best crops in the district.'

A few days after this catastrophe came a message from 'Lynedoch' to say that old Mr. King had been thrown out of his trap and badly injured. Margaret rushed off at once to nurse him, (she had a competent Scottish girl named Mary Niven to help her and look after the children now), and was away three days. On her return she found her husband, Fly and two Indians hard at work clipping the sheep, and was obliged to give them a hand as Charles was so short of labour; Malloch and the other men were busy stacking hay for use as winter fodder. 'Hay will be the only thing we have to depend on for the beasts this year,' Charles wrote, despondently.

The year had begun very badly, and the outlook appeared to him to be gloomy not only at 'Strathearn' but over the whole of Natal:

'Things are not very flourishing in the Colony just now. I suppose it is the reaction after the Zulu and Transvaal wars, and there is a good deal of uncertainty as to the results of

114

Cetewayo's restoration. I think it would have been better if they had given him his kingdom back entire or not at all.' [After the war of *1879* Zululand had been divided among thirteen chieftains, but these had fought amongst themselves and the British Government had recalled Cetewayo from exile, though as ruler over a kingdom reduced in size.]

The shock of losing his crops in the hailstorm, and the cumulative effects of two years' overwork, had lowered Charles's spirits and left him in need of a break. He decided to pay a brief visit to Scotland, and sailed from Durban on *April 25th* for East London where he transferred to the mailship *Kinfauns Castle* for the voyage to Southampton. Towards the end of *May* he arrived at Methven and was reunited with the family he had not seen for eight years.

He did not meet his friend Frank Rhodes during this visit to the United Kingdom, for they had quite lost touch. Frank was serving with the Royal Dragoons in Ireland, and was at the start of a very successful military career. Cecil had taken his degree and no longer travelled back and forth between Oxford and Kimberley; he was a member of the Cape Parliament now, and had founded the great De Beers Mining Company.

While Charles was in Scotland Margaret took charge of 'Strathearn', but there was little work to do on the farm in winter, and she had the able Malloch, Fly and Mary Niven to help her. Two months after her husband had left her she had found she was pregnant again.

She had one or two scares while Charles was away, the first when the children lit a fire under her bed and nearly set the house alight! Margaret was not easily frightened, but the smell of burning terrified her. Her second scare came one night when she woke to hear soft footsteps in the passage and then saw her bedroom door opening and a figure approaching her; for a moment she froze with fear, but the unwelcome visitor uttered a plaintive cry, '*Memsahib, memsahib!* Too much sore tooth got-it. Tooth he go peep! peep! peep!' It was one of the coolie's wives, her hand to an aching jaw, come to ask for a pain-killer!

Margaret was the sort of person to whom others turned naturally for help, confident that she would give it gladly. She had been known to miss an outing she had been looking forward

115

to for weeks, rather than disappoint someone who was in trouble and needed her. Many a time she was sent for in the middle of the night to attend neighbours' wives in childbirth. She did not confine her kindness to white people, but visited the local Zulu kraals if there was sickness there.

Charles missed her very much while he was away – perhaps he had not realised until then how much he loved her. They had never been separated before, and he was accustomed to discuss everything with her and often to rely on her judgment, especially in farming matters. He returned to Natal in *August* and was very happy to be back; 'Strathearn' had wholly replaced Methven as 'home' now.

August 25th: 'Found the children much grown, and Oswald, who could not say a word when I left, talking quite plainly a mixture of coolie [Tamil] and English.'

In no time he was up to his eyes in work again, for September brought spring and the lambing season, and Nature as usual had a challenge for him. He wrote on *September 23rd:*

'We are very much troubled with the vultures, and I am obliged to send Fly out all day with my gun to frighten them away. Whenever they see a ewe lambing they sit round and try to get the young lamb. They get worse every year, we used hardly to be bothered with them.'

On *January 3rd, 1884,* Margaret's seventh baby, Elizabeth Camilla, was born. She arrived prematurely, just as Meta had done four years before, and again Mrs. King had to be sent for in a hurry to help her daughter. Margaret had an easy time, so the midwife who was to have come out from Pietermaritzburg was put off. Charles sent Fly to Estcourt to register the infant's birth.

Camilla was weaned early, and as soon as she was old enough to be left in Mary's care her mother began to go about and enjoy herself a little; in *April* she and Charles went to a party at 'Fordoun', and a few days afterwards they rode to the Speirs's home at the Dargle, Margaret mounted on the mare she had named 'Vixen'. In *May* Charles broke the news that he had

116

arranged a very special treat for her: they were to travel down to Pietermaritzburg by railway on the *26th*, spend a few days there, and then go on to Durban. Margaret was as thrilled as a child at the thought.

The journey had an uncomfortable start, as they had to travel from Caversham to Lidgetton (the railhead) in a platelayer's truck and then wait in bitter cold and rain from ten o'clock in the morning until four in the afternoon for their train. It was Margaret's first trip to Pietermaritzburg since Effie's birth in *1877*, but for old Mr. and Mrs. King who went with them the occasion was even more extraordinary – 'They had never been there since they landed thirty-five years ago!,' Charles noted in his diary, 'And things are rather changed since that.'

When the Kings trekked to Caversham in *1849* from Durban the Natal capital had been a village of thatched cottages, but it was now a large town, (by the standards of the *1880's*), with busy streets full of horse-drawn carriages and Cape carts; only the tented waggons in the market square looked the same, each with its span of sixteen oxen, its little *voorloper* to lead them and its driver with his long whip. The couple were quite bewildered by the noise and the crowds as Charles guided them to their hotel. He wrote afterwards:

'I think they were very much pleased with their trip, but would not stop more than one night as the minister was coming [to Lynedoch] on Sunday to hold sacrament.'

Three days later he and Margaret went down to Durban, booked in at the Royal Hotel, and took a ride to the Point to see the docks and the shipping in the Bay; next morning they went shopping, and left for Pietermaritzburg in the afternoon. They returned home by a contractor's train on *May 31st*. Margaret had never had a real holiday before.

The following month she and her husband gave their first party at 'Strathearn'. It was 'rather an undertaking', as Charles said, as fifty guests had been invited. He was afraid there would be 'a great scarcity of young ladies', which would spoil the dancing, but the men found plenty of partners after all:

June 15th, 1884: 'The guests [thirty-five came] began arriving about four o'clock, some in waggons, some on horseback. We gave the ladies our bedroom and the children's room to dress in. The children were moved into the small bedroom next Malloch and Fly's room, where they slept with their two cousins from 'Lynedoch'. The gentlemen dressed in the new stone storehouse, which is between the byre and the house.

We had tea at 6, at two long tables – planks on trestles – in the dining-room, and then began dancing in the sitting-room at 7.30. The spare room where I write was turned into a smoking-room, and refreshments in the kitchen. Danced till 1, and then had supper in the dining-room. Fowls, ducks, beef, ham, bacon, pork, trifles, custards, jellies, pineapples, oranges, etc. Danced again till daylight at 6.30. Then they went and changed, and were all off by 7.30. We then had all the house to sort.'

Margaret had prepared the refreshments herself, except for some shortbread, a cake and some pastry from 'Lynedoch', 'and the only appliance', Charles said proudly, 'one small stove'.

The Smythes were not the only party-givers at 'Strathearn' that winter:

July 6th: 'My coolies are giving a grand entertainment to all their friends today, they have been cooking day and night the last two nights, a whole sack of flour has been made into *chupatties* which are things like scones fried in melted butter. The children have been much occupied with the preparations, they are to be entertained too. I hope it will not make them sick, they are to have all sorts of messes.'

In *September* the three eldest children started lessons with a Miss Bell, the first in a succession of governesses; Effie was seven years old now, May six and David five. Their education was going to be a problem, as Charles realised, because there was no school in the district and the farm was so far from town that governesses would not want to stay there long. David soon found he did not care for sums and pot-hooks, as his father noticed:

'He prefers being allowed to drive the oxen or sent to turn beasts. He can very nearly crack the waggon whip – which is not at all an easily acquired art.'

Margaret taught the children to ride, and began taking them out on horseback as often as she could. Charles described one of these rides in a letter to his mother in *April, 1885:*

'I wish you could have seen the turnout yesterday . . . Effie on the horse I bought for the children, Violet Manisty [a

118

thirteen-year-old friend] on the horse I usually ride, May perched on the top of a great big mare, sixteen hands high, who usually works the plough . . . Madge was in charge on her own filly, which she broke in in the spring. The children all on men's saddles as we only possess one side-saddle. They went down to the river and back, about four miles, May in front the whole way, armed with a mealie stalk with which to beat her enormous steed whenever anybody else came near her. This was her first ride – except when the horses are going up or down to the plough, when there are usually two on each horse. I am glad to say they do not lack confidence on horseback, which they certainly do not take from their father, who never gets on a horse's back unless he is obliged.'

One of the hazards of riding in Natal was the fact that the countryside was pitted with antbear holes. Antbears were seldom seen, and Charles had been very interested when he managed to unearth one:

'I never saw one before, nor did Madge, it is like a pig in the body but a curious head and no teeth. I went down at night to the potatoes, as there had been a porcupine doing a lot of damage among them, and the dog took up the scent of the beast and we chased it to a hole and then got spades and dug it out. It dug faster than we could, but I sunk a hole in front of it and then we got hold of its tail and tied a riem to it and tried to pull it out, but it has most extraordinary strength and I had to shoot it at last before we could get it out. We have been eating it, but it is not very good. I got the porcupine . . . by setting a gun for it – it is splendid eating.'

The children had a very happy existence, spending all their time out of doors when their lessons and household chores were done, and running barefoot in summer because Charles thought it 'much more healthy for them than going about with wet boots'. They joined in the farm work eagerly as soon as they were old enough, learning to care for the stock just as Margaret had done when she was young, and were on the friendliest terms with the labourers and their families; all of them became as fluent in Zulu and Tamil as they were in English. Margaret taught her daughters to cook and sew, make butter and jam, cure bacon and preserve fruit, and the elder

119

girls were put in charge of the babies after Mary Niven left, early in *1887*, to marry Fly. Charles must often have reflected on how different his youngsters' upbringing was from his own childhood in the nurseries of Methven Castle.

The Smythes' life at 'Strathearn' – during those years when the children were growing up and before other interests obliged Charles to be often away from home – was family life at its very best. Close links of affection and loyalty were forged then, which later sorrows and separations could never break. At the back of this feeling for unity was the clan spirit which was an inheritance from generations of Highland forebears.

Like most Victorian settlers in Natal Charles and Margaret observed Sundays rather solemnly, putting a ban on unnecessary work and noisy games. In the morning everyone – including the white farm hands but not of course the Indians, who were Hindus – assembled in the dining-room for a religious service; Charles had written in *1882*, soon after moving to 'Strathearn':

'On Sundays, directly after breakfast, I read psalms, lessons, epistle and gospel, and Church prayers.'

The handyman, Deacon, who did the plastering and papering of the house, was a great asset at these services – 'he was in the choir in some very high church in England, and he leads the singing . . . Malloch is also a very good singer, but he does not know the English chants, so we have two Scotch psalms for his benefit.'

Early in *1885* some of the farmers in the Nottingham Road district erected a wood-and-iron church near the station, and Charles began taking his family over there in their waggon whenever a minister could come to hold a service. The Presbyterian minister came fairly often, but there were very few Anglican services because of a shortage of clergy. Margaret gave a silver Communion plate, and regularly organised lunches and concerts in aid of church funds.

The Smythes had no close neighbours – the Natal Midlands were still only sparsely populated – but other farmers and their wives sometimes rode over for the day to visit them, and now and then their Speirs relations would arrive en masse or friends from Durban or Pietermaritzburg come to stay for a week or two. Margaret was very hospitable, and Charles a delightful host. At Christmas and New Year there were lively parties at 'Lynedoch', as Mr. and Mrs. King loved having their grand-children under their roof. Charles regretted that his parents had never seen Effie and her brothers and sisters; his mother had long ago become reconciled to his marriage, and was generous in her gifts of clothes, toys and books for them. There was always tremendous excitement when 'the box from Scot-land', packed with presents, was opened at 'Strathearn'.

———

When the Smythes linked hands with their relatives at 'Lynedoch' to sing 'Auld Lang Syne' at midnight on *December 31st, 1885,* they had no idea that the year ahead was going to be one of the most momentous in the history of South Africa. Yet *1886* is remembered today for the discovery of the immensely rich Witwatersrand goldmines in the Transvaal, a discovery which led to the founding of the great city of Johannesburg and eventually to the transformation of South Africa from a poor agricultural to a prosperous industrial country.

News of the opening of the mines did not break until the middle of *1886,* but was all the more welcome when it did because Natal's economy, like the Cape's and the Boer republics', was in a bad way. In *February* Charles had complained that there was no demand for anything: 'Mealies which are usually £1 per sack at this time of year are only 6/–', he wrote. He and the Kings had held a joint cattle sale at Nottingham Road station, (the local Farmers' Association had not yet been founded), and had had to accept very low prices for their beasts. To make matters worse there had been an appalling epidemic of horse-sickness in the district, in which more than three thousand horses died in three months, May's mare among them. The disease had been almost unknown at that altitude.

Charles had found one thing at least to be thankful for at the beginning of *1886,* and this was the great improvement in communications in Natal. He had written to his mother:

January 3rd: 'At last the railway is open and we have a daily post within three miles, and I shall be able to get anything we want from Pietermaritzburg at once. You cannot imagine what an advantage it will be. A train comes here at 9, getting to Durban at 6 – distance 111 miles – no great speed, of course, but what an advantage over the old style!'

There were more ships calling at Durban harbour now:

March 7th: 'An opposition line of steamers have started, and freight has fallen from 55/– to 15/– per ton in the last two months.'

The price of many imported goods including barbed fencing wire had dropped sharply, and Charles found, 'I can put up ... a good fence for £70 per mile, which is very cheap compared to what it used to be.'

The finding of gold on the Witwatersrand was announced in *July,* and caused a sensation:

July 18th: 'There is great excitement in the Colony about the Transvaal goldfields, some of the reefs are turning out very rich and companies are being floated all over the place – it is all reef as yet, no new alluvial having been found. One company which was formed six months ago with £1 shares is now selling at £46. It will do a great deal of good to the Colony if they continue to turn out well.'

September 19th: 'Still great excitement about the gold-fields, and lots of people are leaving and going up there, and there is every sign of more prosperous times. I am not at all inclined to speculate myself, and I think those who stop behind will probably do better than those who go.'

Charles remembered how he had wasted time, money and energy trying to make a fortune at gold-digging in *1874,* and he did not want to repeat his mistake. In any case, he was committed to farming, and was planting trees on a big scale now that spring had come. He had bought a lot of seedlings in Pietermaritzburg: a thousand young pines, (not the Scotch pine but the fast-growing and luxuriant *pinus insignis*), and a great many fruit trees as well. Most of the pines were set around or near the homestead, and on a gentle slope to the west of the house Charles put a double avenue of them which in time came to be called 'The Cathedral' because of its magnificence. He planted oaks and cypress, black wattle and the beautiful Australian blue gum, and his weeping-willows were already doing well in the swamp.

The plantations were often threatened by grass-fires in the dry season; it frequently happened that Margaret saw flames approaching the young trees – while her husband was at the far end of the farm, battling to save his grazing land – and ran out with water only just in time.

For once Charles was not short of labour at 'Strathearn'; he had taken on more Indians to replace those whose indenture period had expired in November, and several Zulus were working for him as well. Each of the Indians who left had three choices open to him: he could accept a passage to British India, elect to stay in Natal and take up a plot of land on the coast, or contract to serve for a further period of five years, not necessarily with the same employer. Charles's labourers departed for Durban to get their 'free' papers, but to his surprise the two best workers among them soon returned and asked him to take them on again. He wrote:

'One of them is one I had to flog two or three times, very severely, which shows that if you treat them justly and only flog them when they really deserve it, they think none the worse of you.'

[Corporal punishment was the rule in the 1880's, and it was the accepted thing for farmers to assert their authority with the aid of a *sjambok*, a whip made of rhino hide. But by the end of the century a noticeable change of attitude had begun to come about: the black man was less submissive, the white less arrogant, than before.]

Charles had lost his two white assistants, Malloch and Fly, but the handyman named Deacon was back; he had been 'tutoring' in a Boer household near Harrismith since he left 'Strathearn', and was 'full of amazing accounts' of the life he led there. The backveld Boers found it so difficult to get teachers for their children that they tended to take almost anyone as *meester* (tutor), but the man was often expected to help on the land and generally make himself useful in addition to holding school; he got very little pay and usually slept in an out-house. The character 'Bonaparte Blenkins' in Olive Schreiner's 'The Story of An African Farm' is a caricature of a typical *meester*.

The Boers were not very popular with the British in Natal in *1886*, as farmers from the Transvaal were interfering in Zulu politics. Lukas Meyer and others had supported Dinizulu, eldest son of King Cetewayo, (whose reign had not lasted long after his restoration, and who was now dead), and helped him to triumph over his powerful rival, Chief Zibebu. In return Dinizulu allowed the Boers to declare a large part of north-western Zululand a Boer republic and claim the rest of his territory as being under their protection.

Charles thought that the new Lieut. Governor of Natal, Sir Arthur Havelock, had handled the affair very badly:

October 31st: 'Although Havelock has been receiving deputations from the Boers and the Zulus he refuses to give the Legislative Council any information as to what is going on, which, as we are the people most interested in the settlement, is hardly fair. The result is, the Council is adjourned in order to lay the subject before the Secretary for the Colonies.'

The British Government decided to recognise the 'New Republic', but with reduced boundaries, and the Boers dropped their claim to a protectorate over Dinizulu's country. The Natal settlers saw this as another cowardly retreat on Britain's part:

November 21st: 'The recent settlement in regard to Zululand has given much dissatisfaction here. The whole arrangement was made between the Governor and the Dutch, without our Legislative Council being consulted the least in the matter ... to allow a few Dutch filibusters to have the best half of the country and practically drive out the Zulus was a scandalous shame, and though I have always been against Responsible Government for Natal I think we shall be driven to it.'

During the same month, *November, 1886,* Charles's family was increased by the birth of another son, Mungo Charles. Margaret had now had eight children in nine and a half years, and as a result had suffered much from tooth decay. A dentist in Pietermaritzburg had extracted twenty-six of her teeth under chloroform, but in those days dentures could not be fitted immediately and for three months she had had to live on slops.

Charles had the new baby inoculated against smallpox, early in the New Year:

January 3rd, 1887: 'Grace's baby had just been vaccinated, so we got the doctor to send some lymph from it last week when it was ready, and we vaccinated Cammy [Camilla] and

Mungo. Mungo didn't take, so I have just been vaccinating him again from Cammy, also two coolie babies and Madge, who had not been done since she was little. I am glad to have got it done with such good lymph, as I do not think the doctors are very careful here who they get it from.' [In the *1880's* vaccination could be performed by anyone. Supplies of vaccine were received in South Africa periodically from London, but as there was no means of cold-storage the arm-to-arm method had to be used, with lymph transferred directly from a successfully-inoculated patient to the next in need. It was not until *1893* that smallpox vaccine was manufactured in Cape Town.]

When Mr. Burgess, the vicar of Howick, came to 'Strathearn' to christen Mungo, Charles discussed church affairs with him and heard some astonishing things:

'The English church in Maritzburg is in a very bad way, they seem to get hold of most extraordinary men. The Dean of what used to be Colenso's church [Bishop Colenso had died in 1883] was had up in the police court the other day for assaulting one of the church wardens at a vestry meeting, but it seemed it was a regular free fight, so he got off . . .

'Bishop Macrorie was sued by one of his clergyman for his salary, which the bishop had refused to pay him on account of his consigning some of his parishioners to the Place of Perdition in the language of a bargee!'

As usual, Charles was taking note of what was happening beyond Natal's borders:

March, 1887: 'Lots of people still going to the goldfields from here . . . but very little gold coming down.'

He thought many of the companies that had been formed were likely to smash soon. (Cecil Rhodes's Goldfields Company, founded that year, was one which survived). But he was very wide of the mark when he wrote, 'One good alluvial field would be worth more than all their reefs for attracting population,' for people were flocking to Johannesburg from all parts of South Africa, Britain and Europe, and the tented camp was already developing into a town.

The Zululand question had been settled for the time being, and he was relieved to hear that that country was safe from further Boer encroachment:

125

May 29th, 1887: 'The British have at last annexed the remaining portion of the Zulu country, after having allowed the Boers to seize upon all the best of it. I am very glad they have secured what they have, as under proper government it will be an outlet for our rapidly increasing native population, which is our great difficulty.' [White magistrates had supplanted the chiefs as the most powerful men in the various districts of Zululand.]

The subject of Responsible Government for Natal was interesting Charles more than ever before, and he was still against it although admitting that those who advocated it had a strong case:

'Our Legislative Council is to meet again in June, and I think it is very likely it will be dissolved and a fresh election take place on the question of Responsible Government. I think myself that we are not fit for it, as we have not enough independent men [i.e. men of independent means, as members were not paid] to carry it on, the last session proves that if the elective members will only stick together they can prevent the Executive from doing anything very foolish, but there is a very strong feeling in favour of it, principally men who have but a small stake in the Colony.

'It is a pity we have such an unpopular man for a Governor, a man who does really do and say the most foolish things. [Charles thought Sir Arthur Havelock 'most pigheaded'.] The fact that the Government estimates for last year, as regards our financial position have been proved utterly wrong, and the estimates of the elective members quite right, is apt to make a great many people think that we could manage things better if left to ourselves.'

CHAPTER NINE

IN *June, 1887,* Charles took Effie, May, David and their three eldest Speirs cousins to Pietermaritzburg for the celebrations held in honour of Queen Victoria's Golden Jubilee; the Queen had reigned for fifty years, and there were public festivities in every part of the British Empire. 'Effie and May are to have their new frocks, and chip straw hats trimmed with blue ribbon to match their frocks,' he had written a day or two before they set off. The party travelled to town in the luggage van of the train, as all the coaches were full, and Charles admitted afterwards that he had found the excited children 'rather a handful' but added, 'we got on all right'.

July 10th: 'There were beautiful fireworks [in the Market Square] finishing with a portrait of the Queen; a review of troops, volunteers and mounted kaffirs, and a big kaffir dance [a Zulu tribal dance in full regalia, with sticks and shields] . . . We went in on Monday, and returned on Thursday.' [He left the children with friends one evening, and went to see the Gilbert and Sullivan opera 'Ruddigore'.] 'Then we had all the Speirs family here on our return, for a week, so we had a houseful with thirteen children, but they all enjoyed it. I exhibited the magic lantern [which his brother had sent from Scotland] which worked capitally and was a great success . . . I never saw one throw clearer pictures, there was one of Perth which was most interesting, and Red Riding Hood was much appreciated.'

Margaret had not been able to go because she could not leave the younger children. She had a ninth child on *August 28th*, a seven-months baby whose unexpected arrival caused a family crisis as there was no nurse in the house. Charles wrote:

'Madge was ill through the night, and another son was born at 7 a.m. Sent a boy over to "Lynedoch", and Mrs. King came over about three.'

He handed the new-born infant to ten-year-old Effie to wash, a horrid experience for the little girl which she was still able to recall vividly in old age seventy years later. A nurse from Pietermaritzburg was sent for, but she did not come until the *30th*.

Sept. 10th: 'Madge and the baby [Edric Murray] are getting on all right . . . Miss Adamson [the governess] has been very good and helpful, she and Effie have done all the housework. Effie is quite capable of doing it all herself, only it is rather much to do it all as well as lessons. The bread-baking alone for such a lot makes a great deal of work, and the dairy also . . . The only part I have to do is the churning and making up the butter, which is a job I do dislike as I cannot smoke at all during the time I am at it, and it takes me half a day, and when I complain I am told it is very good for me!'

Perhaps Margaret was not sorry for him to find out how much she normally had to do.

Edric's birth had been registered at Estcourt and should have been followed by a certificate showing that he had been successfully vaccinated, as this was now compulsory. But a year later Charles wrote, on *September 30th:*

'Was summoned and had to go to Estcourt for not having vaccinated Edric, and was fined 1/–. I have never had a good chance of getting lymph for him, or I would have had it done.'

Edric was the last of Margaret's children whom old Mrs. King was to see, for she died after a brief attack of dysentery at *Christmas time, 1887*. Margaret spent a fortnight at 'Lynedoch', nursing her mother, and was heartbroken at her loss. Mrs. King, who was seventy-four, had carried on her usual work almost to the last and in the week before being taken ill had made no less than 102 pounds of butter.

'I wonder how old Mr. King and Miss Ellis will manage without her,' said Charles.

He had had to take over the hated dairy work again while Margaret was away, but the elder girls, Meta in particular, had coped wonderfully well with the babies. 'Meta is such a capital nurse, far better than Effie or May,' he noted.

Each of the girls was quite different from the others in personality; Cammy was the one who amused him most, and he told his mother that when he and Margaret had been discussing a mysterious rash Mungo had developed, she had suddenly piped up with, 'Do you not think it is lung-sickness, Mama?' 'This of course, from our always being afraid of lung-sickness when a beast is ill!'

In *March, 1888*, Charles became aware of a battle to come between Natal, Cape Colony and the two Boer republics over the question of Customs duties, a problem which had only arisen since the extension of the railways.

March 18th: 'We are going to have a great political struggle on the subject of joining a Customs Union with the Cape, by which our Customs duties will be raised from 7% to 12%, and the only people who will profit are the coast sugar growers, who will get sugar into the Cape 7% cheaper. Our revenue is in a most flourishing condition by our low tariff, we have drawn all the goldfields trade from the Cape – [trade] which has given so much employment to our railway [Natal Government Railways] that it is now a paying concern, and why the Government should want to force on this union I cannot think, except that Downing St. has a Utopian scheme of a united South Africa, which they will never get us to swallow until it suits ourselves.'

There was a marked divergence of interests: Cape Colony, whose railway-lines were approaching the Orange Free State from several directions, desired to continue these lines through both republics and secure free trade throughout South Africa. President Kruger, on the other hand, wanted to keep the Transvaal entirely independent and was pressing for the completion of his Delagoa Bay track; he was determined, too, not to allow Cecil Rhodes's proposed Cape-to-Cairo railway to pass through the Transvaal, (the line to the north was eventually built through Botswana), and tried to get President Brand to support him by keeping the Cape lines out of the Free State. Brand refused to ally himself with Kruger, but Natal found it in her interest to work with the Transvaal against the Cape.

May 27th: 'We are extending the Natal railway to the borders of the Transvaal [it had already reached Ladysmith] and as long as the Delagoa Bay railway is unfinished we are pretty sure to do well, as we get the whole trade of the goldfields . . . I think there is no doubt now that the goldfields will steadily increase in population, and although the Transvaal tax everything we send up in the shape of produce most enormously, still as the population increases it is sure to give us a market. The Cape has been trying to bind us into a Customs union with the help of the Imperial Government, but I do not think they will manage it as we have nothing to gain, and our goldfields trade to lose by it.' [The Cape and the Orange Free State joined the Customs union after discussing it at a special conference, but the Natal delegates refused to join as the Colony would have had to raise her rates to 20%.]

Charles had expressed his views on Customs tariffs at a meeting at Nottingham Road in *March*, and had been applauded; the local people respected him for his grasp of affairs, keen interest in Natal's progress and success as a farmer. Although he was only thirty-six he was recognised as a leading figure in his district, as he found to his surprise when the following letter reached him:

'Colonial Secretary's Office,
Natal.
May 21st, 1888.

'C. J. Smythe, Esq.,
"Strathearn".

'My dear Sir,
'I am desired to inform you that, in compliance with a request made to the Governor for the appointment of a Justice of the Peace in the District of Nottingham, His Excellency proposes to confer upon you a Commission of the Peace, and I am to enquire whether you are willing to place your services at the disposal of the Government by accepting such commission.

'I am, my dear Sir,
Yours faithfully,
C. Bird.
Assistant Colonial Secretary.'

Charles wrote to his parents on *June 2nd:*

'I have just been created a J.P. for the Colony, and was in Pietermaritzburg yesterday being sworn in. There was a petition got up some time ago to have a J.P. created in this district, but I do not know why the Government picked on me.'

He was pleased to have been chosen, and although he did not realise it the appointment was a milestone in his life: in holding public office for the first time he was at the start of a new career.

The following month events in Zululand attracted his attention, and he had cutting words to say about what he considered to be Britain's mishandling of the current problem:

July 8th: 'Here we are again with another Zulu war on hand for no earthly reason but that there is mismanagement, and they appear to be going to work again with a handful of troops as if they have gained no experience from the last war. I should not be a bit surprised if they had another Isandhlwana, and there will be lots of troops sent out and money wasted like water. However, it is no business of ours – we offered to take over the Zulu country and annex it to Natal, but the Imperial authorities would not have it, so they must pay for their own bungling. It has done me some good indirectly, as I have sold three horses for the soldiers at good prices.' [The Zulus had rebelled, mainly because they were dissatisfied at the white magistrates having greater powers than their chiefs. The revolt was put down, and Chief Dinizulu was tried, found guilty of treason, and sentenced to ten years' imprisonment on the island of St. Helena. Zululand was not formally joined to Natal until *1897.*]

The year turned out a very sad one for Margaret, beginning as it did with the death in childbirth of Mary Fly (Niven) the girl who had worked for her at "Strathearn". Mary and her husband had been living on a farm near the Smythes' ever since their marriage. Margaret had helped to nurse the girl in her illness, and was upset at its tragic outcome. Bob King made a coffin, and he and Charles took it to the farm on a cart and brought the body back to Nottingham Road churchyard for burial; afterwards poor Fly took the baby to town to be cared for, but soon it too was dead.

In *October* seventy-seven-year-old Mr. John King fell seriously

131

ill, and Margaret was called to 'Lynedoch' to look after him. Her sister Grace was pregnant and could not help, and the elderly Miss Elizabeth Ellis was unwell and could do little. Margaret spent six weeks caring for her father:

'It is hard upon Madge,' Charles commented, 'But I suppose it is her duty.'

While she was away the children were laid up with influenza, and he had a painful abscess on his hand. Eventually a nurse was found for Mr. King, but he was too ill to recover and died on *January 12th, 1889*.

'He was a good friend to me,' Charles wrote, remembering the help and invaluable advice his father-in-law had given him in his early years at 'Gowrie'.

With thoughts of illness in mind, expecially since his mother had just written to tell him that a Scottish relative was suffering from cancer, Charles wrote to tell her of a South African herbal remedy he had heard of:

'There is a plant which grows in the Transvaal that the Dutch make an ointment of, which is said to be a certain cure. I have seen a Dutchman at Estcourt, he had a cancer on his cheek and this ointment entirely cured him. I have got some of the seeds of the plant and will try to get some of the ointment and send it to you [he was unsuccessful]. There was a great deal in the newspapers here about it at the time of the Emperor Frederick's illness [father of the German Kaiser, Wilhelm II] and I believe some was sent to Germany, but I never heard more about it.'

The Witwatersrand gold-mines still dominated the news, and Charles commented on *March 17th, 1889*, that Natal was being 'depopulated by the rush to the goldfields'. A man who had been working for Charlie Speirs had gone to the Rand and after only five months there had returned with nearly £5,000. He brought £130 in cash, and 170 shares worth 28/- each, the proceeds of claims he had pegged out.

The gold rush was the indirect cause of Miss Adamson's departure from 'Strathearn'; the governess threw up her post in *April, 1889*, and joined her brother in Johannesburg. The rush to the mines affected the labour market in Natal considerably, and Charles found that Zulus were going in crowds to the

9. Charles Smythe (*Local History Museum, Durban*)

10. Margaret Smythe in 1890

11. Effie, age four

12. Mungo (left) and Edric, who became the father of the South African V.C., Lieut Quentin Smythe

Rand, 'where they get very high wages, but a lot of them die because of bad sanitation'; conditions in the black shantytowns which had sprung up were appalling. The scarcity of farm hands led to his having to apply in *November* for more indentured coolies. 'Does it not seem a shame,' he grumbled, 'With the country swarming with natives that we should have to send to India for labour!'

In spite of a shortage Natal's economy was flourishing:

'We have a surplus of half a million' [pounds] he wrote. The Customs duties had been reduced to 5%, the free list increased, and Natal had offered to build a railway-line for the Orange Free State, from Ladysmith to Harrismith via Van Reenen's Pass. The 'railway war' with the other states was as fierce as ever:

June 9th, 1889: 'The feeling is very bitter just now, and the people who will profit by our quarrels are the Dutch republic.' [the Transvaal.]

On the domestic front Charles was waging a war of his own against rats and mice, which had become a plague in the farmhouse since the death of the family's pet cats. A cat was borrowed and shut up in Charles and Margaret's bedroom, 'as the rats have taken to play games in our beds, which is more than I can stand.' The creatures had the impudence to run along the passage with mealie grains which they stored in his spare boots, and had actually tweaked Margaret's curls as she lay in bed. It was high time to get some more cats for 'Strathearn'.

In *January* of the following year, *1890,* Mrs. William Smythe of Methven Castle received letters from her grandchildren in Natal which amused her very much. Her eldest grandson wrote: 'My dear Grandmama,

'I am going to write to you for the first time. We have killed the porcupine at last, but there is another at the potatoes you have to keep out of their road or else you would get a prick from them and their quills are very poisonous Papa has finished clipping his sheep now. Excuse bad writing. I am milking seven cows now night and morning. Goodbye with love and kisses from

'David Smythe.'

Nine-year-old Meta's letter read:
'My dear Grandmama,

'Thank you very much for all the nice things you sent us. I hope that you are all well. Graham is going to be christened soon by Mr. Burgess. [Graham Haldane, born in *October, 1889,* was the latest addition to the family.] Papa is dipping the sheep, to Mungo's and Edric's delight. I have 4 heifers and one ox. It will soon be the holidays again. We have 13 cats and 13 pet lambs. Elsie is the favourite. David is milking nicely now. Goodbye with love and many kisses. From your loving little grandchild,

'Meta Smythe.'
'P.S. Wishing you a happy New Year.'

The New Year was not a happy one for the 'Strathearn' family, for the three-month-old baby, Graham, had died of bronchitis:

January 1st, 1890: 'Poor Madge feels it very much, but the other children being ill [they had bronchitis and coughs] has given her so much to do that there has not been much time to mourn.'

January 5th: 'It has been a weary time with them all more or less ill, and being so unaccustomed to having any of them ill, and losing the Baby, has made us more anxious.'

Charles buried his infant son beside Victor's little grave at the foot of Paddock Hill.

He tried to divert Margaret's thoughts from the tragedy by carrying her off with him to agricultural shows at Pietermaritzburg and Estcourt, and once they went to a ball at Nottingham Road:

'She loves dancing, and very seldom has an opportunity,' he told his mother.

Margaret began to attend meetings of the newly-formed Rifle Association, of which he was president, and to his delight proved a very good shot. He hoped there would be some fishing for them both in the future, too, as the Government had imported trout and was stocking some of the rivers and mountain streams. He had had no chance of enjoying this sport since he was last in Scotland:

'500 youngsters have been put in the Mooi River about a

mile below "Strathearn", so we are looking forward to some trout-fishing in the course of two or three years.'

August of that year brought a renewal of the controversy over Responsible Government for Natal:

August 4th: 'We are on the eve of new elections, the Council having been dissolved after passing a motion by a majority of 2 votes in favour of Responsible Government, so the coming elections are to turn on that question, and we are going to try hard and get anti-Responsible men in . . . I do not believe in Responsible Government a bit, we are so few whites and such a large native population.'

Like many other people in Natal, Charles wanted to be sure of the protection of British troops in the event of a Zulu rising; fear of the Zulus was always at the back of their minds.

October 26th, 1890: 'The elections have gone against us, the Responsibles having got a majority of 4 seats. We can only hope now that they will fall out over the conditions in which Home Government will grant Responsible Government.'

About this time one of Charles's Scottish cousins, Bertie Boyle, a member of a titled family, enquired what openings he could expect to find in Natal if he decided to come out to the Colony. Charles thought Bertie not at all the right type for colonial life, and could not resist having a little fun at his expense when he wrote:

'There is no demand for unskilled labour, but what about the Mounted Police? There are lots of nice young fellows in it, 6/- a day and find your horse and rations, there is not much money to be made in it, but it is a good way of seeing the country, and if smart and *steady* you are sure to rise. Then there is the railway, clerks get a good pay at first, £8.–10. a month, but living is dear. There is also the chance of occupying Crown lands for speculators who must have men to occupy them – but that is a rough, lonely life. Then there is the Chartered Company in Mashonaland – if I was going out again, that is what I should try for . . . I believe they are giving out farms there now, on conditions of occupation. The best way would be to join the Pioneer Force and then you could find out what is going on.'

Bertie changed his mind about coming to South Africa.

The Chartered Company which Charles mentioned in his

135

letter had been founded in *1889* by Cecil Rhodes, who was by this time a man of immense wealth and influence. He had secured a mining, trading and administrative charter over King Lobengula's domain in what is today Rhodesia, and in *1890* he sent his British South Africa Company pioneers to occupy the north-eastern region; the men were to receive a 3,000-acre farm there apiece.

Charles had another appeal early in *1891*, this time from a young Scot named Kenneth Soutar who had begun training as a doctor but found the work too harrowing. Charles made it clear that he would not take Soutar on as a pupil-assistant unless he paid a premium of £50 for his first year at the farm and £25 for the second:

'A young fellow coming out here, however willing . . . is really no use until he has learnt colonial ways, and it makes a lot of extra work in the house and Madge has about as much as she can do already. It is different here to what it is in the purely white colonies [such as Australia and Canada], we have the raw labour here and it is only skilled men that there is a demand for.'

He remembered what a difficult time he had had himself until he met Mr. King.

Young Soutar arranged to come, arrived in *May, 1891*, and was at once put to brickmaking as Charles was building an additional wing to his farmhouse; 'Strathearn' was uncomfortably crowded, for Margaret's aunt, the eighty-year-old Miss Elizabeth Ellis, had come to live there and was occupying a room in which several of the children had previously slept. Miss Ellis had brought some treasured pieces of furniture with her, including a camp-bed and folding table given her by Colonel Boys of the 45th Regiment, whose housekeeper she had been when he was acting Lieut. Governor in Pietermaritzburg; the colonel had used this bed and table throughout the Peninsular War!

On *August 2nd, 1891*, Margaret gave birth to her eleventh child, a son who was to be christened Patrick Evelyn. Mungo, now four years old, was tremendously excited at the news of the baby's arrival, and rushed off to ask his father what it was to be called. Charles told him 'Pat', but as the family had a pony of that name, as well as one called 'Nightcap', the little boy became thoroughly confused. He astonished the other children by announcing, 'Papa says our new brother's name is *Nightcap* Smythe!'

Charles had almost more work than he could cope with during the second half of *1891*, for the extension to the house – a long passage with bedrooms either side and a large schoolroom at the end – occupied much of his time. He was busy with church affairs, too, and was Nottingham Road's delegate to the council which met to discuss the appointment of a new bishop for Natal. Ken Soutar did his best to help him on the farm, but still needed constant supervision. To cap all, an unexpected swarm of locusts – a plague rarely seen before in the Colony – descended on 'Strathearn' in the spring:

October 4th: 'They settled in the fields below the house, myriads of them, about two inches long, the ground was quite brown with them. Luckily there was some dry grass about and we all went down and ... fired the grass and they went off, disappearing on the horizon like an enormous cloud of dust .. I never saw anything like it, and the sort of helpless sensation one had when they were getting up around you is indescribable ... we have plagues enough in Natal without them.'

The problem of his children's education was giving Charles a good deal of anxiety, as the two eldest boys were getting too old for a governess:

'I wish they would start a school at the station [i.e. at Nottingham Road village] and then they would be able to ride over there ever day, but I fear there are too few children about for it to answer.'

May wrote to her grandmother in *November:*

'Last *September* we all [she meant the six eldest children] went over to the station, and were examined by the Suprentend-ant of Education, we all passed and Papa got £12 to help pay for our Education, and will be going again some time next *September*.' [In the districts where there were no free schools the Government gave the fathers of successful candidates £2 per child per year towards the cost of a tutor's or governess's salary.]

The young Smythes spent nearly six hours a day at their lessons, as May's letter tells:

'We go out for a ride every day it is fine, after we come out of school, which is from 9 o'clock to half-past 12, and from ½ past 2 to quarter to 5.'

Charles had suddenly realised that his family was growing up. In *April* Effie and May (a month off fourteen and thirteen respectively) had been bridesmaids at the wedding of his former assistant, Malloch, and had stayed on for the evening reception which followed. They had danced from 8 p.m. until daylight, when they rode home with their father. The two young girls had looked very charming in their frocks of cream India muslin with cardinal red sashes, and had been 'in great request' as partners. 'It made one feel very old,' Charles commented. (He was thirty-nine.)

The children's schoolroom was ready for them by the end of the year, and on *February 1st, 1892*, they started work there under a new governess. Sitting at the big table in this room with its long windows either end looking on to the garden, eight-year-old Camilla wrote to tell her grandmother the latest news of the farm; there had been an unusually large number of cobras and puffadders about that season, and one of them had given her a great fright:

' "Strathearn",

April 16th, 1892.

'My dear Grandmama,

'I was walking up the paddock hill and, I saw a snake it was a very bad one I called Papa and Mr. Soutar to come and kill it Papa ran with the crowbar Mr. Soutar with two stones, and the snake ran under a big stone but Papa took the crowbar and rolled the stone over, and killed the snake. Mungo and Edric told me to thank you for the nice book you sent them. Goodbye love and kisses from your loving little granddaughter,

'Cammy Smythe.'

'P.S. I was very fritend of the snake.'

The cost of adding a new wing to the house, and the extensive fencing of land which Charles had undertaken during the last few years at £40 per mile had strained his resources and left him often very short of hard cash, and in *June* he reviewed his position carefully:

138

'The dairy [profits] just about keeps the house in groceries and draperies,' he noted. He had about a thousand sheep, 'which are the best-paying stock there is, if the kaffirs did not steal them so; as it is, they bring in about £150 a year.' Then there were 150 head of cattle, 'which bring in, besides the dairy, about £100 a year, and 58 head of horses which . . . may be put down at £50 a year.

'I have let part of the farm to Malloch at £30 a year, and the kaffirs on the place pay £25 a year and provide a certain number of boys for work.'

He was hopeful for the future, as land was increasing in value all the time in the Nottingham Road district:

'I believe that my land, with improvements on it, should fetch close upon £10,000. The boys will still have a fair-sized farm each when it is divided among them, but my difficulty is to make provision for the girls [in those days there was, of course, no question of their going out to work]. Under my Will they have this house and about 100 acres of land around it as long as they remain unmarried, and they have some stock of their own.'

He had ambitious plans for his son Oswald, then eleven years old:

'I shall try and get Oswald into a lawyer's office when he is old enough. He is an extremely sharp boy at his lessons, and has plenty of confidence in himself.'

David, on the other hand, was cut out to be a farmer.

If Charles was fairly happy about his own financial state, he was less certain of his country's position:

June 7th, 1892: 'I think there is likely to be a hard time for the Colony the next year or two. The refusal of the Transvaal to allow us to continue our railway to the goldfields, while they have allowed the Cape to continue theirs, will deprive us of the carrying traffic we have always had, and as the local traffic is not enough to make our railway pay we shall either have, to lower our Customs duties for goods and transit, and so do away with that source of revenue, or face direct taxation, which is sure to fall upon land. [There was no income-tax in Natal then.] It is a pity, though we did not think so at the time, that we did not join the Cape Customs Union instead of cutting each other's throats by carrying at a loss for the benefit of the Trans-vaal Dutchmen.' [The Cape's railway-line from Kimberley reached Johannesburg that same year. Natal was later allowed to extend hers, and it reached the Rand in *1895*, a year after the completion of Kruger's Pretoria-to-Delagoa line.]

The Responsible Government controversy in Natal was still going on; self-government was to be granted – that was certain – but Britain had not yet decided what form the Colony's new constitution was to take. Charles considered that the pro-Responsible Government party had 'all the cleverest and most unscrupulous men on their side', and he feared they would win again at the elections to be held in October, 'though a great deal depends on the Dutch vote in the northern counties'. He told his mother:

September 4th: 'I was at a political meeting at Howick on Thursday, and the Responsibles had their great gun there, a Mr. [later, Sir] Harry Escombe, as well as their candidate, and our man never showed up . . . there is a strong feeling against absentee landlords and land-owning companies, and if the Responsibles win they promise to tax all land held by absentees, so as to force them to sell.'

He was glad to turn from politics to the affairs of the popular Nottingham Road Rifle Association. He had given a gold medal as first prize in the ladies' shooting competition, and was delighted when Margaret won it with 20 points out of a possible 25, defeating Miss Hutchinson, the Karkloof champion. Effie had been third, and May fifth so, as he said, 'the Smythe family rather scored, out of eight competitors.' In the *September* competition May, who was only fourteen, tied with Miss Hutchinson and then beat her in the shoot-off, to everyone's amazement:

'How May kept steady I do not know, as it is a most trying thing to shoot under such conditions – I do not think she can have any nerves!'

About this time a series of balls were held at Nottingham Road to raise money to pay off the debt on the new wood-and-iron village hall. Charles described the ball which he and his eldest daughters attended in *August* as 'a very smart affair', with music provided by two military bands, one from a Hussars regiment and the other from the York and Lancaster Regiment, both then stationed in Natal. Margaret helped organise the supper, but could not join in the dancing because her twelfth child was expected in two months' time. The baby, a son who was given the names Rowan Montrose, was born on *October 11th.*

Three weeks before the baby's arrival Charles had received news by cable that his father had died in Scotland on *September 17th.* On hearing when the funeral was to be, he had immediately wired to his mother, 'We shall follow you in the service at 3.30 p.m., which will correspond with 1.30 your time.' So, while William Smythe was laid to rest in a churchyard six thousand miles away, Charles gathered his wife and children around him in the dining-room at 'Strathearn' and read aloud the 'Order for the Burial of the Dead' from the Anglican prayerbook. He felt his bereavement very deeply.

When *Christmas* came round he was in no mood for the usual party and picnic, and Margaret, who had barely recovered from Rowan's birth, was worn out after nursing old Miss Ellis, who had been ill. 'She is a great handful when laid up, and requires constant attendance,' Charles told his mother. In the same letter, written in *December, 1892,* he made a biting comment about Cecil Rhodes, who was then visiting England:

'I see Mr. Rhodes has been talking very big about the Chartered Company at Home. I should be very sorry to hold any shares in it. He is a man who has got on very well – you know he is a brother of that Herbert Rhodes I came out with when I came here first.'

Charles was still feeling morose in *January, 1893,* as the latest political developments in Natal had exasperated him:

'Just think how annoying – after having . . . defeated the Responsible Government party . . . by 14 to 10, two of the county elections (this one and Newcastle division) have been declared null and void owing to mistakes of the polling officers, and new elections are to be held . . . As each county returns two members, and our man only got in by 6 votes here and 3 in Newcastle, it will be a very close thing.'

There was a long delay in announcing the result of this second election, as the messenger bringing in ballot papers from an outlying polling-station accidentally dropped the box in the water while he was trying to cross a flooded river, and they were reduced to pulp! The pro-Responsible party thought they had a majority on the intact papers and applied to the Supreme Court to compel the election officer to make a return in their favour, but the Court declined to interfere and so did the Governor.

A decision was reached after a great deal of wrangling, and Charles was displeased to hear that the Opposition group he supported had lost. There was nothing for it now but to accept defeat gracefully; at any rate, the long-drawn-out struggle was finally over. Natal's status had changed, and she had reached a new and important stage in her history. His fervent hope was that the right men would be found to lead her people wisely in the years ahead.

CHAPTER TEN

BEFORE *1893* THE THOUGHT of taking up politics had never occurred to Charles; he believed that his life's work was on the land, and he expected to be a farmer for the rest of his days – certainly until his sons were old enough to take charge of his stock. But in *June, 1893,* he suddenly found himself being propelled towards a political career almost against his will, and was so surprised by this turn of events that he hardly knew how to deal with it:

June 4th: 'I hear there is a requisition going round for signature for me to stand for Member of the Legislative Assembly at the next election which will take place in *September* under the new form of Government. I cannot say that I have any ambition to become a legislator, and I was astonished when I heard about it – I am no speaker, nor have I money to stand in a contested election – I suppose if I get a strong requisition I shall have to stand, but if they can get a better man I shall withdraw with the greatest pleasure. I hoped they would have put in James King [his brother-in-law] who knows far more about the Colony and Colonial politics than I do, but they say he would not have as good a chance as I would. I really do not know what I shall do as yet.'

A great many people in the district signed the petition asking him to stand for Parliament, and he was persuaded to put his name forward as a candidate:

July 17th: 'I am now in the middle of an election contest, much against my will, but as I had consented to stand I cannot very well draw back now. My opponents are Morton, a very wealthy farmer near Howick ... then there is a missionary, Scott ... then there is Peckham, a farmer at the other end of the district, who I do not think has much chance. Lastly comes the man I am really fighting, and that is Yonge [Cecil A. Yonge], a lawyer from Pietermaritzburg, who used to be a

143

farmer here and represented this division for three years but turned his coat on the Responsible Government question and has been beaten twice at elections since. He is a fluent, plausible speaker, experienced in electioneering...James King has retired from the contest, which is a pity as I believe him to be the best man of the lot of us ... there are then five candidates for two seats ... To nobody's astonishment more than my own, my speeches have hitherto gone off well.'

Polling in Charles's division (the Lions River division of Pietermaritzburg county) was to take place on *September 19th*. On *August 6th* he wrote:

'I am busy electioneering still. We are now come down to three candidates for the two seats – Yonge, Morton and myself. They say that I will be first, and that the fight will be between Morton and Yonge, but I think myself that Yonge is sure to get in, as he is working very hard, and should I get in I should really prefer him as a colleague to Morton.'

He told himself that he wouldn't care much if he were not elected:

'It will be a nuisance having to be away from home, and the expenses will mount up to something.' [The fact that members received no salaries had had to be taken into consideration.]

In *September* he went to visit voters in New Hanover, a part of his constituency in which there was a large German settler community.

September 17th: 'I have been down here all this last week, electioneering. It is a part of the division quite different from ours, being occupied almost entirely by small German farmers who are about a third of the whole voting strength. But the other candidates have been down before, making a house-to-house visit, a thing I do not approve of. Mr. Woodhouse, my election agent, came down with me, and we have had a hard time of it, a week of harder riding than I have had for a long time ...

'I never thought my German would be of use to me [he had not spoken the language since he was a student in Germany in *1870*] and thought I had long forgotten it, but it has come back to me wonderfully this week and proved of great use as many of the Germans cannot talk English much and are delighted when I can speak to them in German. One old chap I "had" beautifully. We had a German with us, showing the way and introducing us to the people – when we came to this house the two were talking together and the old chap said he thought if I was a farmer I could not be educated enough to get into the Council, so I just said to him, in German, that I might be more educated than I appeared! You should have seen his face, it was most amusing . . . These Germans are a queer lot they do not take newspapers, and are ready to believe anything. It is a nuisance having to be away from home just now, as the sheep are lambing and the cattle are very thin, some dying'.

Interest in the elections was intense in Charles's own district, and the excitement increased daily as polling day, *September 19th,* drew near. The results were announced on the *20th,* and he reported:

'I was head of the poll with 241 votes, Yonge next with 230, and Morton 192.'

Thirty or forty of his supporters had gathered outside the post office at Nottingham Road station to await the telegram giving the results:

'The stationmaster ascended the signal post with the telegram, and there read out the numbers, and I was at once seized and carried off in triumph. There were only three men in the whole Nottingham Road district who did not vote for me . . . there was no question of political faith about the election, but simply personal popularity, as the country is not yet divided into parties. Jim King has succeeded in getting in for the next division, Umgeni.'

Charles travelled down to Pietermaritzburg on *October 18th,* to be sworn in as a member of the Legislative Assembly, and afterwards attended a meeting of members to discuss the choice of a Speaker; when the House met, Henry Ellerton Stainbank was elected for the position. The House then adjourned.

When Parliament was formally opened by the Lieut. Governor, Sir Walter Hely-Hutchinson, a few days later, Effie and May Smythe were among the guests who watched the ceremony in the crowded Town Hall. The girls were chaperoned by Mrs. James King:

'I thought it was a pity they should not go and see their father in the role of a legislator for his country,' Charles said.

145

Margaret was not able to be present as she could not leave her houseful of children and the ailing Miss Ellis.

Parliament was prorogued on *October 26th*, and would not be summoned until *March, 1894*, when the regular session was due to begin. Under Responsible Government Natal now had an Upper House or Legislative Council and a Lower House or Legislative Assembly. The eleven members of the Upper House were chosen by the Governor and the Ministers, and to qualify must be men thirty years old or over, have lived in the Colony for ten years or more, and own land worth at least £500. They were appointed for ten years. The Lower House consisted of 37 members chosen by the electorate at the general elections to be held every four years. The combined consent of the Queen and of both Houses was necessary before any measure became law, and in this way Britain retained ultimate control over the Colony's legislature.

The Lieut. Governor appointed the Ministers: the men who made up Natal's first Ministry were Sir John Robinson (Prime Minister and Colonial Secretary); Mr. (later, Sir) Harry Escombe (Attorney-General); Mr. (later, Sir) George Sutton (Colonial Treasurer); Mr. (later, Sir) Frederick Moor (Secretary for Native Affairs); and Mr. T. K. Murray (Minister of Lands and Works).

Charles had had plenty to think of apart from electioneering, that year. He had bought another 1,350 acres of land about ten miles from 'Strathearn' in *August, 1892*, named the farm 'Steybraes', and had recently put Ken Soutar on it to run sheep. Soutar lived in a makeshift house on the property, and spent his week-ends at 'Strathearn'.

Charles was still active in Anglican church affairs, and attended Church Council meetings in Durban and Pietermaritzburg. 'One perquisite of an M.L.A. is that I get a free pass over the railway whenever I travel,' he noted; he never tried to acquire 'perks' for members of his family, for he was scrupulously honest.

What little leisure time he had was spent in helping to run the newly-formed Polo Club at Nottingham Road, (he had been elected President), and he attended every shooting match organised by the local Rifle Association.

146

However busy he was, he kept up a regular correspondence with his relations overseas and was eager to hear their news. 'I see Elgin has been appointed Viceroy of India,' he wrote in *October, 1893*. [His first-cousin-once-removed, the 9th Earl of Elgin, was Viceroy from *1894* until *1899*; the Earl's father, the 8th Earl, had been Governor-General of Canada and introduced the system of Responsible Government there.] The following month Charles noted with pleasure that his brother David had been promoted Lieut.-Colonel, the 3rd Battalion, The Black Watch.

Events in Rhodesia attracted his attention:

November 26th: 'Everybody is very pleased here at the Chartered Company having been so successful in their expedition against the Matabele, though I am afraid it will not do our trade here much good, as most of their stuff goes through from the Cape.' [There was a serious rebellion of the Matabele in *1893*, which was put down by the British South Africa Company's troops and police. King Lobengula fled, and died not long afterwards.]

In the New Year a new governess was installed in the 'Strathearn' schoolroom – the same Miss Wilson who about thirty years before had taught Margaret and her sister at 'Lynedoch'! Charles considered her too elderly and too expensive, (she would not come under £60 a year, having had £100 in her last place, he complained), but good governesses were hard to find. Encouraged by his wife, Miss Wilson started giving all her eight pupils piano lessons:

'The piano begins at 6 a.m. and with the exception of mealtime and school hours does not stop till 6.30 at night, even David is learning,' wrote the long-suffering father. 'But worst of all, my two companions, Mungo and Edric, have been snatched away to be put through the mill. Our civilisation is a mistake – when our children are just at the nicest age, and beginning to be useful and intelligent, they are taken away to be ground down to a uniform pattern, to say nothing of the chance of ruining their health by a confinement that is not natural.'

Life on the farm was never without incident, and early in March came a day of drama which no-one in the house would ever forget:

147

'We got a dreadful scare on Tuesday. About midday Oswald [then aged thirteen] came running in and said he had been bitten by a snake on the foot – that he was running down barefoot to the orchard for a peach before going into school again, and he felt something prick his foot, and looked down and saw a big snake going off. I ran out to try and get the snake, to find out whether it was poisonous or not, but could not see it, but one of the dogs began barking at the stone wall about ten yards from where Oswald had been bitten, and in the direction the snake had gone. I left two kaffirs to watch the wall, and went in to see how Oswald was.'

Charles found that Margaret had acted promptly; she had been mending sheets when her son rushed in, and had torn off a strip of linen and tied it as tightly as she could round his leg below the knee. She then sucked about a cupful of blood out of the places where the two fangs had penetrated, bathed the wounds to make them bleed freely, and applied poultices of bread-and-milk and carbolic acid. When sucking out the poison she had rinsed her mouth each time with gin, as there was nothing more suitable handy. Charles continues the story:

'I had sent a kaffir off for the doctor [a Dr. Wylie had a practice at Nottingham Road now] as we were certain by this time that it was a poisonous snake from the way his foot was swelling. The kaffirs shouted they saw the snake in the wall, and I went out and shot at a piece of it I saw through an opening in the stones – we then pulled the wall down and I found an enormous puff-adder, the largest I have ever seen. I thought when I saw it the boy would be sure to die, as it is the most venomous snake we have, and the kaffirs all said there was no chance for him. The doctor came in about two hours, by which time the leg was so swollen you would have thought the skin would have burst, however it never got above the tying at the knee, and though the doctor injected permanganate of potash into about a dozen places in the foot, and strychnine into his arm, I do not think it did any good – he said himself that sucking the wounds had saved the boy. The leg was very painful that night, but the swelling gradually went away and he is now nearly all right again.'

As mother of a large family Margaret had to be able to cope

13. Loyal Zulu, scouting for the British (*Illustrated London News*, 1879)

14. 'Lynedoch' waggon about to start for town

15. Charles Smythe as Speaker of Legislative Assembly of Natal

with any emergency. Only a few days before Oswald was bitten she had had to make preparations for an operation to be performed in the house, as Drs. Wylie and Campbell were coming to remove 'a swelling on one of Effie's breasts, about the size of a walnut.' [Fortunately, the cyst was a harmless one.]

In *April, 1894,* Charles took a room in Pietermaritzburg in readiness for the opening of the Parliamentary session; he planned to return to 'Strathearn' every week-end. An invitation to dine with the Lieut. Governor at Government House caused him some anxiety, because he was afraid that the cut of his twenty-three-year-old dress suit might be unfashionable.

The Lower House met in their new neo-classical Legislative Assembly Building in Longmarket Street, the most imposing edifice in the Natal capital:

April 21st: 'The Government have published a lot of Bills they are to bring forward, but the great question of the session will be upon railway affairs, which are not in a satisfactory state. Then the harbour works [at Durban] is another great question; for all the money that has been spent upon them, the bar still seems to behave in a most erratic manner and I think the whole question will have to be referred to some of the authorities in engineering at Home.'

Charles had been down to inspect the harbour mouth; it was obvious to him that Durban would never become a major port while the sand bar prevented large ships from entering the Bay. Innumerable experiments had already been made by Messrs. Milne, Vetch and others to increase the depth, but to no avail. In time dredging and the narrowing of the entrance channel would do the trick; by *1898* the depth of water over the bar was more than 18 feet, and from then on Durban swiftly developed into one of the most important ports in the world.

He managed to combine politics and farming very neatly:

May 13th: 'I have been down in Pietermaritzburg the last three weeks ... tomorrow is an offday, being Whit Monday, which I will devote to killing and salting down an ox for home consumption ... in the Queen's Birthday week I hope to get my hay dried ... the Parliamentary work goes on pretty smoothly, there is no regular opposition yet, so the Government get through pretty much their own way.'

The sittings were over by *July 5th*, and he left for home; the Legislative Assembly would not be meeting again for nine months. His summing-up was:

'I got on pretty well, on the whole, but I do not care much about it, and unless it gets more interesting I do not think I shall stand again. It costs more than I can well afford, though I try to do it as cheaply as I can.'

He naturally had no idea that the passing of one of the Bills presented that session was to have far-reaching consequences not so much for Natal as for millions of people in another part of the world. This particular Bill was a measure brought in to disenfranchise the Indians in the Colony, many of whom had qualified for the vote. The new law was bitterly resented by the Indian community, and led by a young lawyer later known as the famous 'Mahatma' Gandhi they resisted it to the full. The Bill had the direct effect of launching Gandhi on a political career which eventually brought about Britain's loss of her vast Indian Empire.

The Asians – first introduced into Natal in *1860* – had increased in numbers so rapidly that by *1894* they were causing the white settlers anxiety. The whites realised that if Indians were allowed on the common roll they would soon gain complete control of the Colony's legislature. This possibility ought, of course, to have been foreseen by the British Government and by the colonists themselves when the question of importing Asian labour was discussed in the late *1850's*; Indians were clever and hard-working, and could compete with the whites and the Zulus in every sphere. But lack of wise forethought was something which had bedevilled Natal's affairs from the start.

Mohandas Gandhi had come to South Africa from India in *1893* on business pertaining to a client's lawsuit, and when that matter was settled he was asked to stay on in Durban and contest the Disenfranchisement Bill. He organised a committee, interviewed officials, (he found a friend and ally in Harry Escombe), and presented an unsuccessful petition to the Legislative Assembly in *June, 1894*. In *August* he helped to found the Natal

150

Indian Congress of which he was chief executive officer, secretary and treasurer, and in order to earn a living while he carried on the fight he became an advocate of the Supreme Court of Natal and began to practise in Durban. The unassuming young lawyer had suddenly emerged as an outstanding political leader.

The nine months between Charles's first Parliamentary session and the next passed uneventfully at 'Strathearn'. Effie and May were allowed to drop lessons at the end of *1894*, as their father said, 'They will be far better employed in housekeeping and sewing.' Effie, at seventeen, was looking very grown up:

'Effie is now going about with her hair up, and long skirts, it makes such a difference, I keep taking her for Madge.'

She (and May) took part in a crazy cricket match at Nottingham Road, 'eleven ladies against eleven gentlemen with broomsticks,' and she made the top score.

Charles had found a new governess for Meta, Cammy, Mungo and Edric, and sent David and Oswald to a private day-school which had recently been opened in the village.

In *February, 1895*, the family circle was enlarged by the arrival of Charles's brother Frank, who had been in business in Scotland but had lost his job and was posing rather a problem to his relations there. Charles had good-naturedly agreed to have him, 'I feel that living out here I have not borne my share of the family's worries and troubles,' he told his mother. He regretted his kindness very much, later on.

The Natal Parliament was opened on *April 25th*, and then adjourned until the *29th* when work would begin in earnest. Charles wrote:

'I think the Ministry will have more opposition this year than last. I should be sorry to see them turned out, though I cannot agree with them in everything.'

May 19th: 'We have no sittings on Friday mornings this year in the Assembly, so I generally manage to get up by the midnight train on Thursday night and walk from the station, getting home about four o'clock ... I think the present Ministry is

151

pretty safe for this year, and there is to be no fresh taxation . . . We hope for great things from the extension of the railway to Johannesburg, which ought to be open by the end of the year.'

His being an M.L.A. brought Effie the chance to mix with Pietermaritzburg society. She had 'come out' officially at a dance at Nottingham Road, and on *June 6th* attended the Governor's Ball in the capital, chaperoned by her mother:

'The Town Hall was very nicely decorated, and there was a very good supper. All the military officers and Volunteers in full uniform, which made it very gay. The Governor and Lady Hely-Hutchinson came punctually at 9.30 and stood on a dais at one corner, and everybody walked past them and shook hands, rather a trying process for them as there were about 600 people. Then dancing began, and supper at 12, and all over by 2.30 . . . Effie danced most of the dances.'

The Legislative Assembly session ended on *August 8th*, and Charles reported back to his constituents:

September 8th: 'Had a most enthusiastic reception at Dargle. They passed a vote of confidence in me, and asked my colleague to resign. [Yonge was unpopular because he had voted with the Government on a matter concerning Durban harbour.] There is to be a meeting at Nottingham Road next Saturday, when I expect the result will be somewhat similar.'

October 5th: 'Political meeting at Nottingham Road about the refusal of the Home Government to allow the Indian Franchise Bill . . . passed resolution in favour of refusing franchise to Indians.'

November 10th: 'Farmers' Association meeting at Howick on the coolie franchise question – but as we were all unanimous on that subject the meeting was very tame.' [Gandhi's efforts to resist the Bill had been partly successful; he had appealed to the Viceroy of India, (Charles's relative, Lord Elgin), and the Secretary of State for the Colonies, and as a result the British Government had refused to allow the Natal legislators to disenfranchise Indians already on the electoral roll. The Natal Government had, however, managed to resist the enrolment of any more Indians.]

The completion of the Durban to Johannesburg railway-line had brought Charles an enjoyable jaunt:

October 24th: 'We had a very nice trip to Heidelberg in the Transvaal to witness the linking of the last rail of the Charlestown – Johannesburg line. There were about fifteen of us went up, and the eating was excellent, and what was better, the whole thing did not cost anything – all supplied by Government. It is twenty-four years since I was at Heidelberg – things are rather changed since then. I could have bought any farm about there then for £300 or £400, now they are worth £100,000. It is curious to see the lines of conical white beacons marking out the gold claims for miles and miles. Of course the Heidelberg claims are only newly taken up, and there are only a few established mines there.

'When I last passed through the country where we went in the train, the buck (wildebeest, springbok and blesbok) were in thousands as far as one could see – now there is not one left. It is galling to think that Gladstone let that country of untold riches be alienated from the British Empire without a struggle, and we shall never get it back now, for there are too many mixed nationalities there now to consent to come under British rule. I have got on a sore subject . . .'

November 10th: 'The Johannesburg railway is to be open for passenger traffic next week – hundreds of our natives will be going up when it is opened, and although they get very high wages it does them a great deal of harm as they learn lots of bad habits, besides the Colony losing their labour. I am afraid it will lead to trouble in the end.'

Charles was holding political 'report back' meetings until well into December:

December 1st: 'I have to go to two political meetings next Saturday among my German constituents. I go to Pietermaritzburg by night train on Friday, leave 5.30 a.m. [Saturday], I drive 4 hours, address a meeting at 9.30 a.m., then drive 2 hours, address another at 2.30, and if possible back to Pietermaritzburg 4 hours and home by midnight train, reaching home 2.30 a.m. I am sorry for the horses [he sometimes did fifty miles with the same pair] but they are hired, and the latter part depends upon the weather. If it comes on wet I shall not start for Pietermaritzburg. The burning questions are labour supply and the Indian franchise.'

153

He was very tired by the time Christmas came. Margaret was even more weary, for she had had to cope with sickness in the family ever since *July*, while of course carrying on her dairy work as usual. First, everyone had had influenza, then in *October* nine of the ten children were in bed with measles; Miss Ellis, meanwhile, was growing more and more feeble and needing a lot of attention. In *December* Charles wrote:

'Effie and Meta have both been laid up with something very like enteric fever ... Effie was very bad indeed ... she was in bed for more than a fortnight ... they are both reduced to shadows. You may imagine what work it has been for Madge, the constant nursing.'

To lighten Margaret's dairy work he bought a cream-separator which would separate 45 gallons an hour; at £23 it was 'an expensive luxury', but would save her a great deal of labour. She was pregnant again, expecting another baby in *March*.

The year *1895* had not been a particularly happy one for Natal or for the folk at 'Strathearn', and everyone would be glad when the last few days of *December* had slipped away. But *December* did not end quietly, for something happened on the *29th* which electrified South Africa and caused profound shock in Britain when it became known: it was the irresponsible 'Jameson Raid', which was to have grave consequences.

Cecil Rhodes's friend and lieutenant, Dr. Leander Starr Jameson, had ridden across the border from Botswana with a band of five hundred troopers, with the aim of supporting a rising by the *Uitlanders* (foreigners) of the Witwatersrand against President Kruger's government. Rhodes, then Prime Minister of Cape Colony, had been deeply involved in the plot to launch the raid and the *Uitlander* revolution which was intended to follow. He had been frustrated in his efforts to entice the Transvaal into a railway and Customs union with the Cape and Natal, which he hoped would be a first step towards some sort of political union under the Crown; when his attempts failed, he gave secret support to the *Uitlander's* Reform Com-

154

mittee. The Boers had known about the plot for months, and had been watching the raiders' movements closely. They pounced upon Jameson and his men at Krugersdorp on *January 2nd, 1896*, and forced them to surrender.

Charles Smythe was as startled by the news as everyone else in Natal:

January 12th, 1896: 'The New Year has opened very badly for South Africa, with this wretched business in the Transvaal, and the dreadful accident which happened on the Natal railway [there had been a serious accident at Glencoe, in which forty people had been killed and many injured] . . . the excitement about the Transvaal affairs has been intense. The Boers have been so provokingly in the right all through, and the English so entirely and utterly in the wrong that my sympathy has to give way to my sense of justice. It is all too provoking to say any more about.'

It is not really surprising that Charles sympathised with the Boers rather than with the *Uitlanders*, (who had a number of genuine grievances), because the Boers were in the same position as the Natal colonists; like the Natalians, they had allowed a huge influx of aliens into their country and were now in danger of losing their own identity and being swamped by people whose ways were, in their opinion, inferior to theirs.

February 22nd: 'I hope Jameson will be punished, though I have no doubt he was only the tool, but the ill-feeling that has been caused by his action between Dutch and English, not only in the Transvaal but in Natal and the Cape, will take years to die away.' [Jameson had been handed over to the British Government for trial, and was sentenced to imprisonment with hard labour. Rhodes accepted responsibility for the Raid, and resigned from the Premiership of the Cape. The four leaders of the Reform Committee were condemned to death by Kruger, but the sentences were commuted to fines of £25,000 each, which Rhodes paid.]

Charles had been astounded to find that one of the Reform Committee leaders was Frank Rhodes. Frank had left the Army in *1894*, with the rank of colonel, after having served with distinction in Egypt and the Sudan; he had acted as military secretary to the Governor of Bombay, and subsequently

155

accompanied Sir Gerald Portal on his arduous journey to Uganda. On leaving the army he went to Rhodesia, where he deputised as Administrator for Dr. Jameson, and from there he moved to Johannesburg and became involved in the Reform Movement. He had been in the Raid plot up to the hilt, and had actually obtained the concession from two African chiefs for the piece of land on Botswana's eastern border which was to serve as Jameson's jumping-off place. At the last minute, realising that the Raid was bound to fail, Colonel Rhodes had tried desperately to stop Jameson, but in vain.

When the four leaders were set free, Charles told his mother:

June 14th: 'There was great rejoicing in Pietermaritzburg at the release of the Reform prisoners at Pretoria. I daresay you remember I came out here with Frank Rhodes when I first came to Natal, then he went home and joined the army and I went to see him at the barracks [in Edinburgh] when I was home in '73, but have not seen him since.'

Frank went to Rhodesia after his release, and took part in the fighting against the Matabele rebels in *1896*. In *1897* he attended the Inquiry into the Raid which was held in London, and his honesty and truthfulness made a very good impression. All the same, he was stripped of his Army rank when he was found guilty of treason.

Some of the settlers in Natal and the Cape had formed a South African League to uphold British supremacy and had urged the British Government to intervene directly in Transvaal affairs, but Charles was strongly opposed to action of this sort:

'I do hope Mr. Chamberlain [Joseph Chamberlain, the Colonial Secretary] will not be led away by the jingo section, but will trust to time and patience to settle matters. Anything like war with the Transvaal would mean ruin to Natal, and so far the Dutch have only acted within their rights.'

Margaret had given birth to her thirteenth child on *March 6th, 1896*. She had hoped for a girl, but a boy – her ninth – arrived instead; he was christened Keith fforester. With a wife, eleven children, his brother Frank and old Miss Ellis to provide for,

156

Charles was finding his finances strained and was obliged to cut down expenses in every possible way; he had sent Oswald as a boarder to Maritzburg College, but this meant that he could not afford to take on more Indians when the other indentured labourers left, and he had had to get rid of the governess and put Effie to teach Meta, Cammy, Mungo and Edric in her place. His daughters had to make do on a very small allowance:

'I give £2 a month each, and they have to clothe themselves and pay for anything they want.'

May 'came out' at a dance in *June*:

'May is now in long dresses, with her hair up. She is rather pretty, and most amusing.'

David was helping his father on the farm now; it was a bad year for farmers in Natal, as a locust invasion had done immense damage in the late summer. In *February* Charles had written:

'The locusts, alas, are still with us . . . the Government have been doing what they can by buying the eggs and appointing district locust officers who have power to turn out the natives to destroy them, but I am afraid that without the aid of nature all that are destroyed are but as a drop in the ocean, and the expense already amounts to about £7,000. The oats are what they are fondest of, and there will hardly be a straw of forage thoughout the Colony . . . I see nothing to stop the locusts increasing till winter comes. It is a very dry season, too, which favours them.'

But a far more terrible plague – the dreaded rinderpest – was on the way:

April 12th: 'There is a great alarm about the rinderpest, which after decimating the cattle in Central Africa for the last three years has crossed the Zambesi and broken out in Mashonaland and Bechuanaland [Botswana]. The Cape and Transvaal governments are trying to stamp it out, but I am afraid they will not manage it, and if it comes here the effects will be most disastrous . . . we are stopping all transport cattle at the border, and I hope may be able to keep it out.' [The disease had swept down Africa from Somaliland, and Africans had already lost thousands of head of cattle.]

August 23rd: 'Rinderpest is still spreading in the Transvaal, and our Government are putting up a double fence all along the border. All cattle found between the fences are to be at once destroyed – I trust we may be successful in keeping it out.'

Parliament had opened on *April 8th*, and the question of Indian franchise overshadowed all other subjects:

'The Home Government vetoed the Bill we passed two years ago to prevent the Indians obtaining the franchise, and now the Ministry have brought in another Bill, which I do not like much, giving the Government power to give the vote to such Indians as they may think fit, which seems rather a tall order.' [Gandhi, continuing the struggle, left for India in *June* to rally the active support of the Indian National Congress. He intended to bring his wife and two sons back with him when he returned in a few months' time, as he had taken a house for them in Durban.]

What with political and farming problems Charles had a great deal on his mind in *1896*, and the running of the Nottingham Road Rifle Association took up much of his limited leisure time:

July 12th: 'We are arming the Rifle Association here with new rifles taking the Lee-Metford ammunition, and revising the rules, which has entailed a good deal of bother on me as President, and I am very doubtful if the new ammunition is as good for native warfare as the old Martini-Henry, but as the Government has adopted the Metford we are bound to follow suit.'

He approved of the fact that elementary military training in Natal schools was compulsory, and attended a parade held at the cadet corps' camp in the capital in *1896:*

'There was a grand turnout of all the cadets from the different schools in the Colony . . . they mustered in Pietermaritzburg all in uniform, about 1,200, and had three days' drilling and a review by the Governor. It was a great time for them.'

Charles was pleased that his son David had joined the Volunteers as a part-time soldier, and said:

'It will do him good to be drilled a bit, and mix with other lads . . . most of the young fellows in the district belong to the Natal Carbineers.'

He had no plans for any of his seven sons to make soldiering his profession as his eldest brother had done; it was out of the question, anyway, because a British Army officer of that day needed a comfortable private income to supplement his pay. But even if he could have afforded it, Charles would have hated to send any of his boys overseas. He wanted his children near him. He believed his sons' place was in Natal – that was where their future lay; if they were ever called upon to fight, let it be in defence of the Colony.

CHAPTER ELEVEN

'CECIL RHODES IS receiving ovations everywhere on his way to England, but for all that I do not believe much in the value of Rhodesia at present.'

So wrote Charles in his diary on *January 1st, 1897*. Rhodes's prestige had been dramatically restored by the courage he had shown, during the Matabele rising, in going unarmed into the Matopo Hills with only a few companions to make peace with the rebels; as a result he was fêted all the way down from Rhodesia to Cape Town, when he left for London to face the Inquiry into the Raid and into the administration of his Chartered Company.

He was not the only celebrity to attract the crowds that month, for Ghandi had a noisy reception – though of a very different sort – when he arrived in Durban from India on the *13th*:

January 21st: 'Durban has been getting up a demonstration against the Indian immigrants, who are coming in large numbers, and the Assembly is to meet at the beginning of March as a result, and try and pass some laws to check the immigration, but it is a very difficult matter to deal with.'

When Gandhi's ship, the *S.S. Courland*, tied up at the wharf a mob of hotheads calling themselves the 'Colonial Patriotic Union' had tried to prevent him and the other Indians on board from disembarking. Mr. Harry Escombe addressed the angry demonstrators, told them that what they were doing was illegal, and persuaded them to disperse. Unfortunately for Gandhi, he was recognised while on his way to a friend's house, and a crowd gathered and attacked him; he was rescued by Mrs. Alexander, the wife of Durban's Superintendent of Police. The hotheads threatened to burn down his friend's home, but with Superintendent Alexander's help he escaped from there in disguise and took refuge in the police station. The

161

storm eventually blew over and Gandhi settled down in Durban with his wife and sons and carried on his legal practice. The British Colonial Secretary demanded an explanation of the *Courland* incident, but Ghandi refused to prosecute his assailants.

When Natal's Legislative Assembly met in *March* the subject of the Indians and the problem they presented was very much to the fore; not only were too many entering the Colony, but they were putting white shopkeepers out of business:

April 2nd: 'I have been down in Pietermaritzburg at the Assembly the last two weeks . . . things are going pretty smoothly as yet, but there is some very drastic legislation with regard to Indian immigration and trading which will need careful handling.'

Charles had seconded the reply to the Governor's speech at the opening of the Assembly, and been 'received with great applause' when he appeared in the House wearing his kilt of Murray tartan. On *March 23rd* he had attended the laying of the foundation stone of the new Colonial Office buildings in Pietermaritzburg. There had been changes in the Ministry this session, which was the last session before a general election was held, and Mr. Escombe had succeeded Sir John Robinson as Premier. Charles was sorry Sir John had retired:

'He will be a loss in the Assembly, as he was generally liked and has had great experience, having been a member since *1863*.' [He had come to Natal as a child of eleven with his settler parents, at about the same time as John and Janet King landed.]

The Colony's economic position was the subject of much discussion in Parliament:

'Our revenue has increased enormously, owing to the Transvaal trade, but our expenditure has also increased, and with times being so bad in the Transvaal we can hardly expect to do so well this year. Our railways have earned 11% on their capital cost, which is pretty good for a Government railway, but were it not for the Transvaal trade the railway would not have paid working expenses, and yet there are people who wish us to quarrel with the Transvaal. I trust Mr. Chamberlain will not be led by the extremists to do anything that will endanger

162

peace, as the general opinion of South Africa is certainly in favour of leaving things alone and trusting to time to do away with the ill-feeling which has been intensified by the Jameson Raid.'

But Chamberlain could not help becoming involved in Transvaal affairs, for in *mid-April* President Kruger presented Britain with a vast bill of costs for the Raid, one item of which was a million pounds for 'moral and intellectual damages'! In reply Chamberlain protested against Kruger's alleged breach of the London Convention ratified by Britain and the Boer republic in *1884*. To show the Boers she would stand no nonsense, Britain sent a naval squadron to Delagoa Bay:

May 16th: 'There was great excitement when the fleet anchored off Durban on its way to Delagoa Bay, and there is no doubt it had a good effect on the Transvaal. I think things will all quiet down if the Boers are left alone, but to fight them would be madness. The newspapers are no guide to public opinion, and if England attacks the Transvaal except as a very last resource she will have the Free State, half the Cape Colony and a quarter of Natal against her. However, I think things will go all right.'

While this exchange between Kruger and Chamberlain was taking place, preparations were going ahead all over the British Empire for the celebration of Queen Victoria's Diamond Jubilee in *June*. Charles told his mother about some of Natal's plans:

'Two out of David's troop [of the Natal Carbineers] have been picked to go Home for the Jubilee celebrations. There are fifteen going altogether, and a team of shottists. £3,500 the Colony is to pay for this little trip . . . our Prime Minister, Escombe, goes Home also, and though he has his faults politically, he will compare favourably with any of the Colonial Prime Ministers.'

Natal's own celebrations began in *May, 1897*, as Charles's diary tells:

May 20th: 'Went up with deputation of whole House to Government House to present address to the Queen on the 60th year of her reign. House then prorogued.'

May 24th: 'To Pietermaritzburg with Effie and May for ball

at Government House in honour of the Diamond Jubilee.'
[The Governor's electric lights – an innovation at the time –
failed for three hours during the evening, but dancing went on
by candlelight.]

June 6th: 'The girls went to another dance last week, about
9 miles from here ['Strathearn']. Left at 4, danced all night,
and got back here at 9.30 a.m. half frozen, and that is what they
call pleasure! . . . I hope David will soon be able to undertake
escorting his sisters about, without it being necessary for me
to go.'

[Charles had a fifth daughter now, a baby girl born in *April*
and christened Cecilia Iris. She was destined to be the last of
Charles's and Margaret's children.]

June 20th: 'The date of the Queen's accession sixty years ago.
Sunday service at Nottingham Road church . . . pulpit draped
with Union Jack . . . sang "God Save the Queen".'

The Colony had given itself up to festivity and thanksgiving
while the celebrations lasted, but by *August* there was little to
rejoice over as the dreaded rinderpest plague had reached Natal
at last. About £8,000 per month had been spent on guarding
the frontiers, and a thousand men were on patrol with powers
to shoot any animal that crossed, but all to no avail. Charles
had been written in *May*:

'The reports about the various preventatives are so conflicting
that it is impossible to say whether they are of any use or not.
There is no doubt the German specialist, de Koch [Robert
Koch] was too sanguine and announced that he had found a
preventative before it was fully tried.'

August 10th: 'Rinderpest is breaking out all over the place . . .
the nearest to "Strathearn" on one side is about 12 miles, the
other about 17. Two days ago the Government issued a proclamation forbidding all movement of stock except horses, mules
and donkeys. This does not affect us so much as we are near
the railway, but I do not know what the unfortunate people
will do who live nowhere near a railway [and depended on
ox-waggon transport.] We hope to minimise the number of
deaths by inoculating, and if we could keep clear for another
month, when there would be a bite of grass, we might get off
with a 20% loss, but I am afraid if we get it now we shall lose

164

very heavily. The interest in the elections [due to take place shortly] has been superseded by the rinderpest, but we have got five of our meetings over up at this end of the division . . . everybody says that I am quite safe, and therein lies my danger, as the contest for the second seat between Greene and Peckham will be very keen.'

Charles had lost his best election-agent in *June*, as one of the other candidates had offered the man an £100 fee, which was much more than Charles could afford:

'If the thing costs me more than £50 altogether I shall leave it alone, as I consider if I give my time to the Colony it is quite enough without being out of pocket over it.'

When the election results were announced, he was head of the poll for Lions River division.

By the end of *October* rinderpest was playing havoc with the Colony's stock:

October 29th: 'Things are still pretty bad with the cattle, they keep on sickening, but we are getting a good percentage through now. I hope to save nearly half. The loss to the Colony will be enormous, as the natives are saving very few. One of the kraals in this place has lost 35 out of 36, another lost his all (16), and now they are dying at all the other kraals.' [The epidemic was a calamity for the Zulus, as for the tribesmen in most other parts of South Africa.]

Writing about Parliamentary matters, Charles said,

'Things political have had a turn over. Mr. Escombe resigned when three of his ministers lost their seats. Mr. [later Sir] Henry Binns, a retired sugar planter, is now Prime Minister.'

He had heard some very interesting news concerning himself:

'There is a rumour that I am to be asked to be Speaker, but I am not very keen on the job as one's constituents do not like their member not being on the floor. Another thing, I have had very little experience, and though of course it is an honour there is a good deal of expense attached and the salary is very small, only £400 a year. I hope they will find somebody else before Parliament meets about the *18th*' [*November*].

A few weeks later, rumour had given place to fact:

November 24th: 'Meeting of members at 9.30 in the reading room. Winter [Mr. H. D. Winter] proposed, and Jim King

165

seconded me as Speaker. No other nominations. Tailor waiting, who measured me for robes.'

At twelve noon the Assembly met, and Charles was officially nominated by Mr. Winter before the House, Mr. Henry Binns seconding and Mr. Escombe approving the appointment:

'I thanked them, then went up to the dais with Winter and Binns, who with an assistant got me robed and I then returned thanks to the Assembly and took the Chair . . . there was a slight difficulty in getting me into the robes, as my predecessor was a very short man, and the attendant who was assisting me was also a short man, and could hardly manage to tie the bands . . . at the back of my neck.'

Later on Charles was escorted to Government House, where the Lieut. Governor received him.

'Next day was the formal opening of Parliament, and at a quarter to twelve I went into the Assembly in full dress, and preceded by the Serjeant-at-Arms and followed by all the members marched across to the Town Hall where the Governor read his speech and handed me a copy. Then we marched back to the Assembly where prayers were read by me, minutes read and confirmed, notices given, and then we adjourned. My full dress consists of dress shoes with cut steel buckles, black silk stockings, black broadcloth knee breeches, black coat (court cut), heavy silk gown with a small boy to carry the train on State occasions, at other times the train is looped up. An ordinary silk hat completes the costume, a wig not being considered necessary . . . I am assured I looked most dignified!'

Charles had come a long way since he first became an M.L.A. only four years before. Mr. Winter in nominating him described him as able and painstaking, and Mr. Escombe, referring to his cultured background, called him 'one of this Parliament's most learned men'. 'The Natal Mercury' said, on *November 25th, 1897*:

'That he will endeavour to be a fair, impartial, and reliable Speaker we have no doubt at all, and with the support of the House, which will be readily accorded to him, we trust he will find his tenure of office a pleasant one . . . we congratulate Mr. Speaker on his election.'

On *December 18th* Charles wrote:

'Parliament has adjourned till *January 4th*. We should have been finished altogether, as we have annexed Zululand, which was the business for which we were called [Zululand had been formally joined to Natal], but the farmers brought pressure to bear on the Government to tax Australian frozen meat, and ... are making such a fuss about it that they thought it better to adjourn for a bit. I have got on satisfactorily in my new position, though it is rather slow.'

January 6th, 1898: 'The Session began again on the *4th*, and we are now busy wrangling as to whether Australian frozen meat is to have a tax of 2d per pound on it. The farmers of course are in favour and the towns against, so there is a pretty little squabble on. For myself, being now removed from the stormy level of the floor to the serene altitude of the Chair (with a big C) I get very tired of it, especially in this awfully hot weather.

'My duties consist of walking in solemn procession into the Assembly as the clock strikes the hour, with the Serjeant-at-Arms in front of me and the clerks behind. Ascending the dais, I bow solemnly first to the right then to the left. The clerk at the table calls "Prayers!", and I read the prayer for Parliament and the Lord's Prayer, then take my seat and business begins. I have to keep order, settle any points that arise, and if in doubt wade through volumes till I find precedents. There is one good thing, my power is supreme, and whether I am right or wrong as long as I stick to it they have to do as I tell them and accept my ruling. When the House is not in session I have to come down about once a week and look after things and sign papers. Altogether, my duties are more ornamental than useful.'

Parliamentary business in *1898* was concerned mainly with Durban harbour matters and the question of Natal's joining the Customs union – both hoary issues but which aroused strong feelings; the Colony eventually entered into a Customs union with the Cape and the Orange Free State. In *July* the Pietermaritzburg Town Hall, where Natal's Legislative Council had its rooms, was burnt down and Charles had to find the members a meeting-place in the Legislative Assembly Building.

On the social side he had a busy time:

May 28th: 'We have not been sitting this week, as it was the festive week in Pietermaritzburg. Review, Agricultural Show, Races, etc. I went to a dinner at Government House on the

167

Queen's birthday, and on Thursday May, Meta and I went to a small dance there and met Royalty in the shape of [Prince] Alexander of Teck, who is in the Hussars.' [Prince Alexander was the brother of Princess May, who later became Queen Mary. In *1904* he married Queen Victoria's granddaughter, Princess Alice, and from *1923* to *1931* as Earl of Athlone he was an extremely popular Governor-General of South Africa.]

On *June 8th* Charles gave an official dinner to the Lieut. Governor, the judges, and both Houses of Parliament:

'Sixty-one people altogether, and it cost me the sum of £81, which I rather thought rather wasted, the principal items being champagne and cigars.'

Charles did not neglect his home and family; he made some necessary alterations to the house at 'Strathearn', building on a large new kitchen and a pantry and converting the old ones into bedrooms. The pines surrounding the house were stately trees now, and the air was filled all day long with the cooing of the African doves which nested in their branches. The tall pines were a favourite roosting-place, too, for hadedah ibis – noisy birds that flew off at dawn and returned at sunset with wild cries which echoed down the sky. 'Strathearn' meant more than ever to Charles since he had heard in *March, 1897*, that his family in Scotland had left Methven Castle for good and had let the place to tenants; this news had upset him, for he loved his boyhood home deeply and liked to know it was still there to return to, if only on a visit; the Highlands seemed to have retreated one step further into the mists of the past. His brother David, who was nearly forty-eight, had retired from the Army early in *1897*, and in *August, 1898*, announced that he was getting married, rather to Charles's surprise. Frank Smythe was still living at 'Strathearn' and was a great trial to Margaret as he had begun drinking heavily and was very unruly. It was as well that her other burden – the nursing of her aunt, Miss Ellis – had been removed by the old lady's death at the end of *1896*, for she could not have coped with both. Eighty-five-year-old Miss Ellis had been a difficult patient, and obstinate to the last: when the doctor suggested she take a nip of brandy she had refused flatly, saying she was afraid the habit might grow on her!

168

By the beginning of *1899* the threat of war between Britain and the Transvaal was looming darkly over South Africa, but there was still hope that open conflict might be avoided. Charles noted:

'Negotiations . . . being carried on between the Imperial and Transvaal governments for the purpose of improving the condition of the *Uitlander* population.'

At the end of *May* Lord Milner, (the British High Commissioner), met President Kruger and demanded that he give the vote to all *Uitlanders* who had lived in the republic for at least five years, but Kruger refused and the talks broke off. In *August* the Transvaal's State Attorney, Jan Christiaan Smuts, (soon to be known as 'General' and years later as 'Field-Marshal' Smuts) declared that the demands Milner had made in May would be acceptable provided Britain dropped her claim to suzerainty over the Transvaal. Chamberlain rejected this condition, maintaining that Britain had a duty to protect British *Uitlanders* from oppression. Some historians believe today that Milner and Chamberlain jointly carried Britain into war with the Boers; Milner is said to have blocked the moderating forces inside South Africa and presented the Colonial Secretary with arguments for intervention, and the latter to have persuaded a reluctant British Cabinet that the use of force was necessary. But the blame for the situation was not all on Britain's side; Kruger's intransigence had been one of the chief contributing factors.

The British troops stationed in Natal at the start of *1899* were mostly in camp at Ladysmith, where an epidemic had recently caused many deaths among them; the Army of those days knew little about hygiene. Some of the men were sent south to recuperate at Nottingham Road, (which was higher and healthier), as Charles told his mother when he wrote to her on *March 4th:*

'Three batteries of artillery have arrived . . . from Ladysmith as the men were so bad with enteric up there and they think the change will do them good. The tenant of 'Gowrie' is making a good thing of it, as he gets 4/– per horse, per month, and there are over a thousand horses now in camp. I have not met any of the officers yet, but I suppose I shall have to call.'

169

British regulars were not the only soldiers camped in the district at that time, for the Natal Carbineers were there as well:

March 24th: 'The Volunteer encampment began on Sunday so I expect the house will be pretty full tomorrow night. The [annual] camp was to have been at Ladysmith, but enteric fever has been so bad there . . . that it has been changed to Balgowan, the next station to this.'

The village suddenly became very gay with all these young men about, and there were dances, polo matches and concerts. Effie, May and Meta were determined not to miss the fun, however bad the weather:

'May, Meta and David have just started [on horseback] for a concert at Nottingham Road. It is a thick, wet mist and cold wind, and I congratulate myself that I can stop comfortably at home and be represented by proxy.'

In *May* the Natal Parliamentary session began, and Charles plunged into work again:

May 26th: 'We duly opened Parliament . . . and things have gone smoothly as yet . . . I had to go . . . to the official [Queen's] birthday dinner on the *24th* and had a fairly good dinner but as it was a dreadfully cold night and I was in my knee breeches and silk stockings I felt chilly about my legs before it was over.'

June, 1899, brought him a change of post and unexpected promotion; the Prime Minister, Sir Henry Binns, had died, and the new Premier, Lieut. Colonel (later, Sir) Albert Hime, invited Charles to join the Ministry. He was offered the position of Colonial Secretary. At the same time Mr. (later, Sir) Frederick Moor was invited to become Secretary for Native Affairs.

Charles Smythe and Frederick Moor were friends and had the same views on political matters. Before agreeing to serve they had a serious talk and came to the conclusion that Hime's offer had presented them with a chance to strike a blow (so to speak) in the cause of peace: they would insist on certain conditions being met before they accepted office. On *June 9th* the two men had a long interview with Colonel Hime and told him what these conditions were:

'We gave him our definite answer that we would not join unless Ministers consented that a despatch should be sent to

170

the High Commissioner, stating that this Colony claimed the right to be heard before any hostilities took place between England and the Transvaal.'

The Prime Minister told them he must have time to consider this stipulation, and would give them an answer at six o'clock that evening.

'When he came, he read out a paper by which Ministers agreed to write to the High Commissioner at once, that in their opinion before any steps were taken that are likely to cause hostilities with the Transvaal, they claim as a right to be consulted in the matter. That in the event of the High Commissioner's reply not proving satisfactory, Ministers agree to bring before Parliament, and support in the House, a resolution on the above lines during the present session. This was the wording as much as Moor and I could remember it. On these terms Moor and I agreed to join. Hime then arranged for a meeting of the Executive Council at Government House at 9, where we attended and were sworn in by the Governor.'

After this Charles left for home, looking in en route at a dance going on in the hall at Nottingham Road, where he broke the news of his appointment and was warmly congratulated.

A few days later he told his mother:

June 15th: 'Alas! it is no longer "Mr. Speaker" who writes to you, but the "Hon. C. J. Smythe . . . Her Majesty's trusty and well beloved servant, Colonial Secretary of Her Colony of Natal," as I am termed in the letter of appointment. Force of circumstances and a sense of duty compelled me to give up my comfortable billet and take a prominent part in the government of the Colony. Had it not been for the crisis through which we are passing with regard to the Transvaal, and in which I thought that the moderate counsels of my colleague Moor and myself might tend to peace, I should never have thought of joining the Ministry. I believe that what we have done and the stand we have compelled the Government to take have already done good.'

His letter continues:

'You may be interested in the personalities of the Ministry: the Premier and Minister of Land and Works is Colonel Hime, who for many years under the old form of government was

Colonial Engineer. Then there is Mr. Bale Q.C., Attorney-General, Colonial born and lived most of his life in Pietermaritzburg though educated in England. Moor, Secretary for Native Affairs, Colonial born farmer but made a good deal of money at the Diamond Fields. Mr. [later, Sir] William Arbuckle, Treasurer, Scotchman, used to be in business in Durban, but now a farmer. Winter, Colonial born farmer, Minister of Agriculture, and myself, six in all. I find an immense quantity of work to do, as my predecessor was Sir H. Binns who died a fortnight ago and had been unable to attend to work for a long time.' [It will be noticed that four of the six Cabinet members were farmers; Natal was then a mainly agricultural country, with very few industries.]

Charles broke off his letter at this point, but finished it next day:

'I forgot to say that my new position carries a salary of £800 per annum, but as I shall have to be in town the whole year now instead of just when the session is on, I do not gain very much that way. I intend to go home on Friday nights and return by midday on Monday, but it will break up my home life a good deal. There is, of course, always the chance of being turned out by another Ministry. I think my constituents are pleased at my taking office, as they had a sort of idea that their interests were not able to be sufficiently represented when I was Speaker. The family, however, do not share their views and think that Mr. Speaker was a more imposing person than the Colonial Secretary.'

He certainly had his hands full now:

July 28th: 'The departments under my office are Posts and Telegraphs, Audit, Emigration, hospitals and asylums, Magistrates, Railway and Harbour, involving an expenditure of £250,000. In addition to these any matter which does not exactly belong to any dept. is handed on to me, and all communications to the Government have to come through this office. I have also to deal with such subjects as leprosy, bubonic plague, etc. and shall soon be an expert in matters relating to quarantine . . . I am getting accustomed to the working of my office, and have a very good staff of clerks.'

All this time the fear of war had been steadily increasing:

172

August 19th: 'Things are not looking well in the Transvaal, and I am afraid we may still be driven to war. The position is most unsatisfactory as there is no trade doing, and I am afraid our revenue will suffer heavily.'

As though there were not troubles enough, Natal was in serious danger of being infected with bubonic plague from across the Mozambique border:

September 9th [a Saturday]: 'I was not able to get home last night as I usually do, as I had some pressing work this morning. We are threatened with bubonic plague from Delagoa Bay, where there is no doubt they [the Portuguese] have it though they refuse to give us official information of it. I do not think it will ever take hold much in this country ... but it is best to be prepared.'

Referring to the approaching war, Charles wrote:

'I am afraid the Imperial Government does not realise what they are entering upon ... we can only hope that war may be avoided, as every white life lost means one less to maintain order among the native population.' [His old dread of attack by the Zulus had never quite left him.]

He had only one thing to rejoice over in these last few weeks before the outbreak of the South African War: Oswald had passed his matriculation examination and been proposed as a candidate attorney:

'He has to serve his four years' articles beginning at £48 and rising £12 per annum and will then, if he passes his final exam, be a full-blown lawyer.'

Charles added, 'Board and lodging in digs costs £7 a month.'

The two sides – British and Boers – were now drifting very rapidly into a state of armed conflict:

September 25th: 'Heard that troops had been marched forward from Ladysmith to Glencoe and Dundee.' [The troops, about four thousand in number, were under the command of General Penn-Symons.]

September 28th: 'Heard oxen were being commandeered [by the military]. Went up to Hime's house at night, and decided to call out the Volunteers.'

173

October 5th (letter):

'So critical did the situation appear last Thursday that we decided on calling out the Volunteers to assist the Imperial troops. The order was given on Friday, and by Sunday morning the greater part were mobilized, though many had to ride a very long way to get out to their corps. The enthusiasm they showed and speed with which they turned out were most gratifying.' [All over Natal young men – including David Smythe – had donned their uniforms, saddled their horses, seized carbines and equipment, and galloped off to their troop headquarters.]

Charles still believed that the worst would not happen, and that a show of force on the part of the British could save the day. He said:

'Now that the [British] troops from India have begun to arrive, I hope that the most acute stage has passed, and if the Boer leaders can only keep their men in hand I believe there is a chance of peace still. Our position as a colony is most unsatisfactory, whatever happens we are not likely to gain anything, and the loss entailed by the stoppage of our trade and the expense we are being put to in connection with defence is most serious. In all the negotiations that have taken place we have never been consulted [this was a very sore point], but with blind loyalty we sacrifice our revenue and probably the lives of our children for Imperial ideas . . .

'David is with his troop, scouting somewhere on the Free State border. Oswald is in his office, I refused to let him join the Volunteers.'

His hopes of peace were not fulfilled. Kruger, wishing to strike before Britain had time to divert any more troop reinforcements to South Africa, sent the British Government an ultimatum which expired on *October 11th*. Hostilities had begun.

Charles and the other members of the Natal Cabinet soon found themselves relegated to the rôle of onlookers while the soldiers went ahead with their plan of campaign, for their advice was brushed aside. It was galling to have to confess, on *October 26th*:

'In the face of the awful crisis through which we are passing most of the ordinary business is at a standstill, and martial law having been proclaimed reduces our position to more or less of advisers. Unfortunately, the military [i.e. the British Army officers] as usual prefer their own ideas to those of people who are much better acquainted with local matters and conditions than they can possibly be. The forward move to Glencoe from Ladysmith was made in direct opposition to the advice of Ministers, though the Governor [Hely-Hutchinson] advised it; the unfortunate General Penn-Symons has now paid the penalty for it, as we have just received news of his death from his wound [at the battle of Elandslaagte]. From what I saw of him he seemed such a cautious man that I cannot understand his sanctioning the move, which was at once condemned by General White [General Sir George White, British commander in Natal] on his arrival, but it was too late then to withdraw. The remainder of the troops from Glencoe have just arrived in Ladysmith, which relieves one from the anxiety of the last three days as we were afraid they would be attacked on the march, but the moral effect of leaving camp-baggage and wounded behind is very bad.'

The Boers had taken the offensive, and had poured into northern Natal at the start of the war. They were all mounted men, expert horsemen and superb shots, organised in commandos which were extremely mobile; they had the advantage of being armed with German Mauser rifles, which the Transvaal government had been importing in large quantities since the Jameson Raid, and which were superior to the British Lee-Enfield rifle.

Charles felt very bitter about Natal's involvement in the war:

'One cannot help feeling that the Imperial Government have treated us very badly. The inhabitants of Newcastle and Dundee and all the English farmers north of Ladysmith are ruined. Our towns are crowded with refugees of every sort and colour. Our Volunteers are being shot down, and all because in spite of our warnings the Imperial Government persisted in a policy which, whether right or wrong, they were not ready to back up with sufficient force.'

He had had a letter from David, but was anxious about him:

'David was at Ladysmith from *October 2nd* to *October 20th*, he with the rest of his troop was out at Bester's, watching the Free

State border [the Free State Boers were expected to come down Van Reenen's Pass]. They [the Natal Carbineers] had no tents, nor had they their clothes off them for that time. Their food was what is known as "bully beef" and ship biscuits, and during the last week it rained nearly every night. However, he does not seem to mind, and says he is quite well. On the *20th* the Boers attacked them, and they maintained a running fight from kopje to kopje from noon till two in the morning when they got into Ladysmith. On *Thursday 24th* his corps . . . were at the battle of Tinta Inyoni, and as I see one of his troop was killed and several wounded I expect he had a hot time of it, though I have not heard from him. I was at the office at 9 p.m. that night, waiting for news, and it was rather trying standing at the telephone, hearing the names.'

Charles was not seeing much of Margaret and the children at 'Strathearn':

October 26th: 'I have only been able to get home at 8 p.m. on Saturday night and leave at noon on Sunday, for the last two weeks. Madge has got the sheep shorn and the wool to the station, so that will be so much saved if the Dutch come. She will not leave the farm, she says the children are better there than in town, and does not believe the Dutch will molest them personally, but I am afraid it will break her heart if they raid the stock.

'I went to see Cammy at her school yesterday. [Camilla was at a private boarding-school in Pietermaritzburg.] She was in a great way about the war, as they do not see any papers and hear all sorts of rumours.'

Margaret's decision to stick it out on the farm was a brave one, for Ken Soutar could not be there all the time and Mungo, the eldest of the boys still at home, was barely thirteen. Her three eldest daughters, Effie (aged 22), May (21) and Meta (19) were attractive girls who were in a way more of a responsibility when the country was so unquiet than were the younger children. She had a lot of extra stock to care for, because Charles had taken in beasts belonging to farmers who had managed to get them out of the danger zone.

By the end of *October* Sir George White and the Natal Field Force had taken up a defensive position at Ladysmith; the town

176

was surrounded by the Boers on *November 2nd*, and they settled down to starve the garrison into surrender. The Colony was now in an extremely vulnerable situation; there was little to stop the rest of the Boer horsemen from pouring down on Pietermaritzburg and 'driving the British into the sea at Durban' if they made an all-out effort before more troops arrived from England.

The town of Estcourt was virtually the front line, and the handful of soldiers there had orders to hold out at all costs. But on *November 15th* the officer in command made a fatal mistake: he rashly sent out about a third of his force in an armoured train to reconnoitre towards Ladysmith, and the train was derailed by the Boers and the men taken prisoner after a stiff fight. The engine was freed from the wreckage, thanks to the heroic efforts of a young war-correspondent named Winston Churchill, (who was afterwards captured), and it reached Estcourt safely, crowded with wounded. The ambush took place near a station called Chieveley, about fifty miles north of Nottingham Road.

A few days before this incident Charles had written:

November 10th: 'Things are looking a lot better ... I think now that as long as Ladysmith holds out the Boers will not come farther down. Besides, they have to a certain extent lost their opportunity, as five regiments ought to arrive here by the day after tomorrow, though I am afraid there is no artillery with them, which is the only thing that is any good.'

His optimism was not shared by the British commander in Pietermaritzburg, who was hurriedly fortifying the military camp in the capital; Charles's comment about this was:

'A most useless proceeding, as it is completely commanded by the hills around, whereas if they fortified the hills themselves no-one could come near Maritzburg. The latter is what we have advised, but I suppose they will take their own minds of it and get into the same mess as they are in at Ladysmith where the town and camp are in a hole surrounded by hills on which the Boer artillery is planted.

'We heard from David on *November 1st*, the day before it was invested, but of course not since. He was very well then. One of my nephews, Jim Speirs, joined the Carbineers and got into

Ladysmith by the last train that got in.'

Despite his feeling that the Boers had missed their chance to break through, Charles knew that he might easily be wrong; 'Strathearn' was situated directly in the line of advance, and there would not be much left for his family to live on if commandos began raiding the farm. He decided to take precautions:

'I went home last Saturday night to help Madge to make preparations in case the Boers came. We took up two planks in the sitting-room floor, and stowed away flour, meal, sugar, rice, and all sorts of tinned stuffs, so that if the Boers came and took all the provisions the family might have something to fall back upon. [The space between the floor and the foundations of the house was dry, and made an excellent hiding-place for the food]. Then we buried what spirits there were, not very much, luckily. This was all done between nine at night and one in the morning, with the aid of Soutar and Oswald, for whom I had got leave for a week. [He had chosen to do this job secretly, at dead of night, so that the younger children and the African servants should know nothing about it; it was safer that way.] Sunday morning I got together all my papers, and put them in a box which I left Oswald to bury as I had to leave at two o'clock, so it was a busy time. Madge had buried all the valuables before I came up.'

On his return to town Charles was not wearing a starched shirt as he usually did, but had put on one of the flannel shirts he wore about the farm. He said he would be more comfortable in that, if taken prisoner!

By this time Pietermaritzburg had become a vast casualty-centre:

'The Assembly buildings here are turned into a hospital for the Volunteers, and they are very comfortable there ... they have turned the [Maritzburg] College into a hospital and sent all the boys home. Cammy's school is still going on, I shall send her home if they close it and the railway-line is still open. If not, I shall have to look after her here. It is an anxious, distressing time.'

November 24th: 'We are having a rough time of it ... at present half the Colony is in the hands of the Boers. Our troops hold Ladysmith (isolated), Estcourt (isolated), Mooi River at present open to communication but may be cut off at any moment as the Boers are this side of it. At Nottingham Road there are about 2,000 infantry and more coming, but I see no end to it if this is the British plan of action. The Colony is being swept of stock everywhere . . . I went home last Saturday, returning [to town] on Sunday. The family is to stay on, whatever happens; as far as we can learn, no harm has been done to persons or their property who have remained on their farms.'

With many of the mounted Volunteers besieged in Ladysmith, it had become necessary to call out any available horsemen left in the district to act as scouts:

'On Monday we ordered out all the four Rifle Associations in Lions River district, to assemble at Nottingham Road. A hundred mounted men turned out; Oswald went up from here to turn out with Nottingham Road group.'

At 'Strathearn' Effie and May took turns at Charles's telescope, keeping a sharp look-out for any sign of Boer commandos approaching; from a point near the farm gate they had an unimpeded view, through a gap in the hills, of the countryside to the north. They had already spotted Boer horsemen moving about in the veld. Charles told his mother:

'Effie wrote saying they could see the Boer tents in the distance, near Highlands [beyond Mooi River]. Then we heard all sorts of reports about the Boers being at Impendhle and Howick, but all proved untrue. On Wednesday, 5 p.m. May wrote that they had heard heavy firing up Mooi River way, evidently two big guns and some smaller.' [As there was no telephone at 'Strathearn' Charles had to be content with these notes sent by post, and prayed that the railway-line to town would not be cut.]

May also told him of her mother's kindness to a party of soldiers who had come by the farm:

'We killed a sheep and roasted it for some sixty Thorneycroft's Mounted Infantry, they have just been fed in the schoolroom. Soutar and Nichols have been with them as guides. They had had nothing to eat since last night, and were ravenous.' [Margaret had organised things with her usual efficiency, the men filing through the schoolroom past the table where she and

179

her daughters, serving the meal, heaped their plates with food. Afterwards they gathered on the lawn and gave 'Three Cheers for Mrs. Smythe!' and then sang, 'For She's A Jolly Good Fellow.' Nine weeks later, most of Thorneycroft's men were killed in the appalling slaughter of the battle of Spion Kop.]

Effie had written to her father on *November 23rd*:

'It is really getting worse and worse. Firing started at 5 a.m. this morning up at Mooi River, but has ceased now, 11 a.m. Soutar, Teasdale, Welch [local men] and several others have been at 'Strathearn' and say the Boers have a 40-pounder and have been blazing at the bridge [on the Mooi] and it is supposed if they destroy it they will be all over here in a few minutes.'

Effie amused Charles with her account of Oswald's contribution to the war effort:

'Oswald is acting as orderly to an officer up at the range [i.e. the hills lying between 'Strathearn' and Nottingham Road station]. He calls himself an A.D.C.!'

She went on:

'George Ross has taken command of the Rifle Association, but has neither a sword or revolver. He has just passed 'Strathearn' with a patrol of 22 men with only a stick! If the Boers come across today there is no saying when we shall get into decent working order again, but I have great hopes that they have been driven away from Mooi River. I wish it was all over, fancy, I haven't got the clean clothes put away yet – there seems such a lot to do, and we cannot settle to it . . .'

Effie's letter broke off at that point, as to her astonishment she had just caught sight of her mother coming towards the house accompanied by two rough-looking characters – obviously Boers. Margaret had had rather a frightening experience; she had been alone looking at cattle in a field about a quarter of a mile from the homestead when she became aware of two bearded men with rifles and bandoliers approaching. It was an unpleasant moment, but she waited till they reached her and then calmly asked what they wanted. They replied in broken English that they wished to know where the nearest British camp was. She suspected that these were scouts sent ahead by some raiding commondo, and thought that at any minute the rest might arrive.

180

She described the whereabouts of the British camp, and to her immense relief the men said they were glad it was so near as they wanted to give themselves up! They were deserters, who had slipped out of a Boer *laager* on foot, unobserved.

Telling his mother the story, Charles ended:

'Madge said, "All right, if you come up to the house there is a patrol there who will take you in." (This was Mr. Soutar and Mr. Welch, who happened to have called at "Strathearn" on their way further on), so she took them up to the house, gave them a square meal which they were much in need of, and Soutar and Welch took their rifles from them and marched them over to the station after being objects of much interest to the whole family. They were Germans, and said they had wanted to escape from the beginning, but never got an opportunity.'

Effie reported what the men had told them:

'They say there are not so very many Boers, they have three 7-pounders, and Joubert [General Joubert, the Boer Commandant-General] is with them. [The news about Joubert was incorrect, as Charles happened to know]. They say the Boers are not looting and do not destroy houses when occupied, and give receipts for anything they take ... I really feel if these are not spies, that the Boers may not get to Nottingham Road yet.'

Charles heard full details of this incident next time he went home. His visits to the farm had become more difficult now, because of the precautions the military were taking against enemy agents:

'I have to get a pass to go up, and then have to have it countersigned by the officer commanding at Nottingham Road in order to obviate being stopped and brought in by the infantry pickets which are between the station and the house.'

November 26th: 'The hundred men of the Rifle Association are all the mounted men there are, [in the Nottingham Road district] and they brought in the good news last night that the Boers were retiring across the Bushman's River and I do not think they are likely to return, so I hope to escape scot free with stock and everything else. They have done most frightful damage to all the places that were left unoccupied, wantonly destroyed everything in the houses and taken all the stock, but when people remained they appear not to have interfered with their houses or themselves, and given them receipts for any stock they took, to be paid at Pretoria after the war!!.' [The farmers were not always let alone by the Boers, as Charles found later; in *January, 1900*, he came across his friend Mitchell Innes, then a refugee, and heard he had been taken prisoner on his farm but had managed to escape.]

The Boers in Natal had been extraordinarily shortsighted in keeping an unnecessarily large force at Ladysmith and in not attempting to strike at Pietermaritzburg and Durban when they had the chance. While they remained inactive General Sir Redvers Buller had landed at Cape Town with his army, had sent columns up each of the Cape trunk lines, and had sailed on to Durban to lead his main column to the relief of the besieged town. After the general's arrival Charles wrote:

December 8th: 'We are expecting a forward movement on Ladysmith about the beginning of the week. I am afraid it will be only after very heavy fighting and much loss of life that Ladysmith will be relieved. The Boers are all on the north side of the Tugela River now, with the exception of a few at Colenso, and I hope that they will not get further down than that again.'

He had heard indirectly that David was still safe and well. Oswald had returned to his work in town, as the Rifle Association men had been allowed to go home once the Boers had retired across the Tugela:

'Oswald did not manage to get within shooting distance . . . though they were pretty near once, when a patrol was following them up as they retired.'

His eighteen-year-old son had done useful work attached to various British officers:

'He had been guide to a colonel one day, whom he described as a grumpy old brute and whose horsemanship he had a very poor opinion of, but was much taken with an artillery officer whom he had been showing over the hills and who was very jolly with him.'

Charles had no great opinion of the British Army officers:

'They are tied up in regulations and afraid to act independently, they will not listen to what we tell them, and by the time they have learnt how to fight the Boers thousands of valuable lives will have been lost.' [How well this comment applied to Buller himself!]

Of the non-commissioned soldiers he said:

'The British troops are as brave as they can be, but infantry is no good here against the Boers, who are all mounted.'

In order to make up for the loss of the mounted Volunteers shut up in Ladysmith, Natal raised a mounted corps called the 'Colonial Scouts', ('500 men in ten days', Charles reported), to try to check commando raids:

'They are nearly all Natal men. This makes 2,000 mounted men and 1,000 infantry raised in Natal in addition to the 2,000 Volunteers that we started with.'

It was a fine effort on the Colony's part, but although proud of his country Charles was heartbroken at the miserable state into which it had fallen since the war began:

'The accounts of the destruction and wanton damage done by the Boers is terrible. Homesteads which men had spent their lives in making comfortable are ruined, and stock driven off. I only hope the Imperial Government will compensate the people. We can do nothing, as a government we are about bankrupt. No trade, no revenue, no railway traffic. The Imperial Government has agreed to lend us £500,000 at 4% to carry on with, as we should not be able to pay salaries next month. I do not know how it is all going to end.'

His gloom increased tenfold during the next few days, the so-called 'Black Week' of the South African War. Between *December 9th* and *15th* General Buller was defeated at Colenso, Lord Methuen at Magersfontein and General Gatacre at Stormberg in the Cape. Casualties were heavy. As a result of these disasters Lord Roberts was despatched to South Africa as Commander-in-Chief, with Lord Kitchener to assist him, for it was evident now that the struggle would be long and difficult; these two giants would succeed where generals of lesser experience had failed.

Towards the end of *December, 1899*, Charles wrote:

'It has been a sad Christmas time, but still I feel thankful to have all the family assembled with the exception of David, and to have the home for them to assemble in. There are so many unfortunate people cut off from their homes and occupations, whose situation is to be deplored.'

He and Margaret had tried to make Christmas Day happy for the children; Ken Soutar and several others had been invited to dinner, and there were games of 'Aunt Sally' in the morning, tennis and rounders in the afternoon, and whist for the grown-ups in the evening. His farm labourers were not forgotten:

'Gave the kaffirs a sheep for Christmas.'

But the family's anxiety about David overshadowed their gaiety:

'The provisions in Ladysmith must be running short, and if they have to fight their way out the loss will be frightful, and there seems to be little chance of relieving them.'

As if things were not bad enough, a drought was threatening Natal:

'If we do not have heavy rains directly, I am afraid we shall have famine among the Zulus to add to our other difficulties.'

After four days at 'Strathearn', which he described as 'the longest time [at home] I have had since I joined the Ministry,' Charles returned to Pietermaritzburg to be faced with the news of the sudden death on *December 27th* of Sir Harry Escombe:

'We have had a great loss to the Colony . . . Escombe was far and away the best political man we had, and though we differed on Colonial political questions such as Free Trade and Franchise, on the greater South African questions he was thoroughly sound. I travelled down in the train with him about three weeks ago, and he quite approved of all we had done and offered his services in any way to assist us. His death was quite unexpected, some heart affection, and his loss at this present crisis is irreparable.'

It was a grim ending to *1899*, the last year of the nineteenth century. The only ray of brightness, though Charles made no mention of it in his diary or letters, was the triumphant return to the Army in Natal of Winston Churchill after an audacious escape from prisoner-of-war camp in Pretoria, a feat which, coming at such a dark hour, caused a sensation and made him a popular hero.

CHAPTER TWELVE

IN *January, 1900*, General Buller made one attempt after another to break the Boer stranglehold on Ladysmith, where the garrison was by now getting very short of food and was suffering grievously from disease. Charles received news of David from time to time, as letters were smuggled in and out of the town by Zulu scouts at considerable risk.

On *January 27th* he wrote in his diary, 'Heard that General Buller had taken Spion Kop and Thaba Nyama on the Ladysmith side of the Tugela,' but next day, 'Got a telegram in the afternoon, saying that our forces were unable to keep their position and had retreated south of the Tugela again.' Hundreds of British soldiers had been killed in the frightful carnage of Spion Kop.

February 9th: 'News of Buller not being able to press his advance across Tugela to Ladysmith at Potgieter's Drift.'

Better news came from the northern Cape:

February 15th: 'Kimberley relieved.'

Cecil Rhodes had been in Kimberley during the siege, and – although Charles did not know it – Frank Rhodes was one of the ten thousand men languishing in Ladysmith. Frank had gone to the Sudan as a war-correspondent in 1898, when Kitchener led his troops up the Nile to capture Khartoum and avenge the murder of General Gordon; he had subsequently been reinstated in rank and restored to the active list of the British Army.

During the siege of Ladysmith Colonel Rhodes served as a Staff Officer (Intelligence Duties), and was mentioned in despatches 'for meritorious services performed'. It is very unlikely that he ever came into contact with the young Volunteer trooper, David Smythe. David was then about the same age as Charles had been when he and Frank first met.

Writing to his mother on *February 16th*, Charles told her:

185

'Still we seem to be as far as ever from the relief of Ladysmith, and it is too sad to see the long lists of deaths from disease there. We heard indirectly that David had been very ill but was better ... The heat has been very trying this last week, there could not be a worse time of year for our troops. I see French [General Sir John French] has gone careering off into the Free State ... it is a wretched dry region up there, and I hope he will not get cut off ...

'The invasion of Zululand [by the Boers] is making things a bit unpleasant there, and is being used by men whom you would think ought to know better as an argument to induce us to arm the Zulus against the Boers. This we steadfastly refuse to do, and though the fate of Natal depended on it I would never consent to it.'

The Africans as a whole took no part in the South African War, though some were employed as scouts or waggon-drivers. The Indians were not involved either, except for the stretcher-bearer corps raised and led by Gandhi, which brought in the wounded from the battlefields. Gandhi had not yet become an apostle of non-violence, and he had a great admiration for the British 'Tommy'. Also, he wanted to prove to the Government that the Natal Indians were as patriotic as the whites. When the fighting in Natal was over he returned to India for a time, but came back before the end of *1902*, moved to Johannesburg, set up a legal practice there, and proceeded to campaign for the rights of Indians in the Transvaal.

Charles was indignant over the internment, on mere suspicion of having assisted the enemy, of Boers living in Natal:

'Another very unpleasant thing is the way the military are dealing with our Dutch farmers. Any trumpery tale is believed, and men are in prison now, and have been since *October*, on most shadowy accusations and without having had a chance of a trial. This sort of thing will lead to great trouble hereafter, and they will not believe that we as a government are powerless to prevent it. However, it is not much use growling. We asked the Home Government in *June* that before any steps were taken calculated to bring on hostilities our opinion should be consulted, and they never took the slightest notice of us, and except when they want us to undertake a responsibility which they are

186

unwilling to undertake themselves, they ignore us.'

The strain under which he had been living for weeks was telling on his nerves, but it was not to last much longer because on *February 28th, 1900*, after heavy fighting, British troops and Colonial Volunteers broke through into Ladysmith and the Boers retreated. *March 2nd* was declared a public holiday in Natal in celebration of the relief of the town.

A few days after the siege ended, David Smythe wrote his father a letter which gave some idea of his experiences:

'I received your letter dated *23rd*, today. We had not been relieved by that time, or even expected to be, as it came like a thunder clap. We were all very sick of talking of being relieved, and even the day that [the relieving force] came in we heard about 12 o'clock that the Boers were in full retreat but said, "We shall believe that when we see it!" At 5 o'clock we were ordered to saddle up, and then there was a rush – we saddled, drew one day's rations, and started off; before we got five hundred yards from the town we were met by the other Carbineers . . . Then we were really happy, we cheered and shouted till we got back to camp in great joy, although we were half starving as horse flesh is not at all satisfying.

'Our rations were: 1 oz. of *bad* mealie meal, $1\frac{1}{2}$ biscuits, 2 cups of tea, 1 oz. sugar, $1\frac{1}{4}$ lbs. horse flesh, per day, and we had to work on that. The work was to clean up the stables and camp, inspection of arms, then take your horse out to grass and cut a heap of grass for him – in the blazing sun, and the Boers firing at you all the time.

'The Boers must have cleared in an awful hurry, they left their tents, as if they were coming back in an hour's time – we went out there on Thursday and found their pots boiling with fire still alight, we loaded ourselves with "grub" and returned to camp. We went out again yesterday with a waggon, we filled it with Boer meal, flour and potatoes and onions, and then the Tommies came so we were ordered to fill a Boer waggon that was left and take all the sacks and put them in one place and guard them all night until our waggons came today . . .

'I got some paper, nibs and ink, with which I am now writing, I will finish this tomorrow as Lights Out has sounded.

'Sunday: I have got a few pieces of shell which will be worth keeping, and send you a postcard of Ladysmith printed during the siege. I hear we are going to leave this place tomorrow ... I hope we are going to get leave to go home and get some decent food, etc. I am in pretty fair health ... They did not get Merlin [his horse] for horse flesh, he is rather thin but is pretty strong ... I was in hospital ten days with fever, but was not very bad. Natal fever [laziness] was a common complaint ... I have never shaved since I left home, and don't intend doing so till I come back. I hope you are all well, and everything doing well. Have you started the hay? I wish I was back, for the kaffirs will humbug the machine.'

Charles was, of course, overjoyed that his son was safe.

March 8th, 1900: 'The good news of the relief of Ladysmith was enthusiastically greeted last week. So many of our relations and friends were shut up there, and disease was playing such havoc, that the news was much more welcome than any of the successes in the Free State, etc.' [Lord Roberts had won a great victory at Paardeberg, had driven the Free Staters back, and entered Bloemfontein.]

Charles had never been a jingo, and despite his anger at the destruction wrought by the Boers in northern Natal he had the wisdom to see that hatred of them was something which must not be fostered. He had the courage of his convictions, but expressing them openly at this time made him unpopular. He told his mother:

'I am rather afraid that we are going to have troubled times in our Cabinet ... the question being the manner in which the Dutch colonists in Natal should be treated ... About two-thirds of Klip River county, two-thirds of Umvoti county, and one third of Weenen county are inhabited by colonists of Dutch extraction, and ... there is no doubt that a large proportion of the Klip River men have given assistance to the invaders. Now Moor and I are of the opinion that those who are caught redhanded assisting the invader should be severely punished, but that we should not go out of our way to work up evidence against men who, though at heart disloyal, were not caught in overt acts of treason. The other four Ministers, headed by Colonel Hime, wish to take the other course, and the press of the Colony together with, I am sorry to say, the Governor,

188

appear to wish that every man of Dutch extraction should be promptly hung, drawn and quartered! In my opinion, if we are to have permanent peace in South Africa, we must conciliate, not persecute, and instead of considering every Dutchman disloyal till he has proved himself loyal, we should consider him loyal till proved disloyal.

'I know I am looked upon with disfavour by the Governor on account of the views I hold, but my stake in this country is not only all that I possess, but the future welfare of my children, and I am not going to be a party to a policy which in my opinion is wrong as regards Natal, and which is fatal (as regards the whole of South Africa) to the future maintenance of peace. I trust wiser counsels will prevail; Lord Roberts's proclamation to the Free State was the act of a statesman who looked to the future.' [Lord Roberts had declared that all Boers who laid down their arms and took an oath of neutrality would not be interned, and would be allowed to return to their homes. Unfortunately, this policy was not as successful as he had hoped, because a large number of those who took the oath were forced by men still active to rejoin their commandos.]

Charles believed his views might lead to his losing his post as Colonial Secretary. He warned his mother:

'It is well, if I should have to resign and probably be branded by the newspapers as a pro-Boer, that you should know the real facts of the case.' [His critics would have been interested to hear of his descent from the Dutch prince, William the Silent, and might have said that it explained his sympathy for the Boers.]

Six months later, writing on the subject of the treatment of the rebels, Charles reported that the Special Court for trying offenders in Natal had finished its first case, one of the worst, and had imposed three years' imprisonment and a fine of £1,500 or two further years in gaol. He thought two years in prison would have been enough, but a heavier fine as the guilty man was very wealthy.

Meanwhile, the Volunteers who had been shut up in Ladysmith had returned to their homes. David turned up unexpectedly on *March 19th*, looking taller and thinner but otherwise all right. Young Jim Speirs, on the other hand, was 'a terrible sight . . . just a skeleton with the skin drawn over it,' as a result of enteric fever. David's leave was short, and on the *26th* he left to rejoin his troop. Soon afterwards the family circle at 'Strathearn' was further depleted by the departure of Mungo and Edric to Michaelhouse, the Natal public school then situated in Pietermaritzburg.

British successes in battle continued: Mafeking was relieved on *May 19th*, and in *June* Lord Roberts entered Pretoria.

June 6th: 'Now that Pretoria is in our hands, the war must surely soon come to an end. The genuine Boer must be as anxious to get back to his family and farm as our people are, and I do not think the foreign element can maintain a guerilla warfare without their assistance. [Charles was wrong, for guerilla warfare was to continue for another two years.] I have a letter from David of the *2nd June*, he says that it is cold, weary work at Mount Prospect, facing the historic Majuba, but he intends to see the thing through now, and if they want volunteers to go up to Pretoria he is going. I wish it was over and he was back at the farm again, as the grass-fire time is coming on, and that is the one thing that really frightens Madge. She and Effie go out with the kaffirs to burn breaks whenever it is a favourable evening, but I expect some night they will let it away and get a proper scare.' [A day of hot winds in *August* caused devastating fires; at Ixopo more than twenty Africans were burnt to death and many more injured, and in Zululand over eighty were killed.]

Parliament had opened on *May 3rd;* Charles had said:

'We do not propose to introduce any legislation beyond what is absolutely necessary, and the main thing will be the passing of the Supply Bill and a Bill to borrow a million in order to go on with public works.'

It was not possible to estimate the coming year's revenue, as everything depended on when the railway to Johannesburg would be open again.

July 6th: 'Our revenue is beginning to look up again, which is a relief as we did not impose any fresh taxation and are dependent entirely on hopes of things booming after the war is over . . . The cost of keeping the Volunteers in the field is a great drain on the Colony, not only their pay which is over

190

£30,000 per month, but the loss through the men being away from their farms and businesses.'

September 6th: 'We are paying 75% of the direct losses sustained by the colonists as passed by the Commission, which money Mr. Chamberlain has promised is to be extracted from the Transvaal and Orange River Colony [the Orange Free State had reverted to its former name], but I am afraid we shall have to wait some time for it. The total amount will probably be a million and a half.'

David returned to 'Strathearn' on *October 9th*, very glad to be able to take up his farming life again. Nottingham Road celebrated the home-coming of the local Volunteers by holding a sports meeting and a banquet at which Charles presided, and he gave a dance which more than a hundred people attended. By this time the war had been declared at an end, as President Kruger had fled South Africa and his government had collapsed, but many highly mobile commandos were still at large under brilliant leaders such as Generals Smuts, Botha, De la Rey and De Wet.

Charles was delighted when he heard that the Conservatives in Britain had won the so-called 'Khaki' election, (Winston Churchill had entered Parliament for the first time, as M.P. for Oldham), but the state of affairs in his own country depressed him:

'Still the fighting and destruction of property goes on, and South Africa starving for money and peace to develop its resources sees the work of years destroyed . . . What I am most afraid of is that the way in which the war is going now may stir up the natives, and if they once get mixed up in it no-one can tell what the result will be.'

General Buller, who had never lost his popularity despite the monumental blunders he had made in the Natal campaign, was leaving for England and Charles took a prominent part in the celebrations held in his honour:

October 23rd: 'Natal has been very enthusiastic over General Buller, and I think the old gentleman must be pleased. I sat next him at dinner at Government House, and he spoke most kindly about Natal. I am very sorry he is going away, as we lose the benefit of his influence at Pretoria, where I am afraid

191

influences are at work in favour of the Cape against Natal. On Wednesday the Corporation gave a lunch to the Volunteers, at which General Buller was present, and afterwards he was presented with an address; the sword and goblet, for which over £1,000 has been collected, he is to receive in England. On Thursday we gave him a dinner at the Club, and he left on Saturday morning receiving an ovation in Durban, where he spent three or four hours before embarking.'

Charles's position brought him into contact that year with other high-ranking British officers, including a Scottish general whom he had known as a schoolboy. He had written in his diary on *May 17th:*

'I was at dinner at Government House last night, and met an old Glenalmond boy in General Wolfe Murray . . . we had a very interesting talk.'

Early in *December* Lord Roberts passed through Natal on his way home:

December 4th: 'May, Meta and David went to Nottingham Road [station] to see Lord Roberts pass at 7.30 a.m.'

Roberts was fêted in Pietermaritzburg, 'but there was not the enthusiasm that there was about Buller, who was more particularly connected with Natal,' Charles reported.

The Smythes, happy to be all together again, had a gay Christmas. There was much to be thankful for, for David was safe, the farm intact, and Edric and Oswald had both recovered from severe attacks of enteric fever. The boys had become infected with the disease in town, but had been nursed back to health at home, by their mother.

January 23rd, 1901: 'Heard that the Queen died at 6.30 last night at Osborne, after a reign of sixty-four years.'

It came as a shock to Charles, as to millions of other people in the British Empire, to be faced with the fact that the Victorian era was over; Her Majesty had been so long on the throne that one could not imagine anyone in her place.

January 26th: 'Telegram from Bird [Natal's Assistant Colonial Secretary] to say King Edward VII was to be proclaimed by the Governor at noon on Monday.'

February 2nd: 'The Bishop of Pretoria held a memorial service at Nottingham Road. Queen Victoria was buried at Frogmore. All public places closed.'

June 21st: 'We are beginning to make preparations for the visit of the Duke and Duchess' [of York, later King George V and Queen Mary] in *August*. Most of the suite are to run up to see the battlefields at Colenso and Ladysmith, which will be a good deal more to their taste than repeating the functions they have had to go through in Australia.'

Charles was having a very busy time in Parliament:

'We have got the estimates passed, close on five millions, which is a lot of money for a country like this.'

In *July* he officially opened the South Coast railway-line connecting Port Shepstone with Durban.

August 12th: 'I went down to Durban with the rest of the Ministry.' [To meet the Royal visitors.]

August 13th: 'Went down to the Point at 9.30 and waited on the wharf for the landing of the Duke and Duchess of York. Drove in the procession through Durban to the Albert Park, where addresses were presented and then to the Royal [Hotel] for lunch and up to Pietermaritzburg by the pilot train preceding the Royal train. Received the party at the station, and then to dinner at Government House, where the Duke and Duchess are.'

August 14th: 'Drove in the procession through Pietermaritzburg and to opening of new Town Hall by the Duke. In the afternoon to the Park with Effie, where there was an inspection of Volunteers and cadets and native chiefs, about fifty. In the evening walked with the girls to the Park to see the fireworks, which were very good. Then to Government House for reception at 9.45. An awful crush. The girls did not go.'

Charles reported later, 'The visit of the Duke and Duchess ... must have cost the country over £30,000 for the three days.'

Saturday, *August 17th*, was a very special day for him and Margaret:

'Our silver wedding. Got a very pretty biscuit box from the family, and salt-cellars from Frank and two butter-knives from the Laidlaws ... Dinner in the evening, at which all the family

193

were present except Oswald, Mungo and Edric.'

The war seemed to have receded into the background, but they were suddenly reminded of it on *September 18th*, when David received an urgent message to turn out for active service with the Carbineers. He rushed off to Greytown to help check a threatened attack by guerillas led by General Louis Botha.

During the month while he was away from home the Natal elections took place and Charles was once again 'head of the poll' for his district.

Charles had been overworked before the elections:

'We have been running the Government with only five ministers [because the Attorney-General had been appointed Chief Justice]. I have been appointed Minister of Education in addition to my other duties, but I hope to be able to shirk it if we return to office, as the colour question lands one in endless trouble. The Government schools are theoretically open to all, but the white objects to his children sitting next to a "nigger" in school, and the unfortunate Minister has to decide what particular shade of coffee and milk is prejudicial to the interests of the school!'

By the beginning of *November, 1901*, Smuts and his guerillas had penetrated deep into Cape Colony:

November 7th: 'I am afraid the Boers are getting many more recruits in Cape Colony than is generally known.'

Charles and his friend, Moor, were still suspect:

'There is a strong opposition being worked up, more especially against Moor, the Minister for Native Affairs, who is accused of being a pro-Boer, which is absolute rubbish, but to call anyone a pro-Boer is sufficient to get up a cry against him ... We have decided to go on without an Attorney-General in the Ministry. It will be awkward, but none of the lawyers who are qualified will give up their practice for a seat in the Ministry [because salaries were so low] and one can hardly blame them.'

The Parliamentary session was over, and Charles was home for Christmas, when his brother Frank was suddenly taken ill; the doctor had warned him that heavy drinking might affect his brain, (he had had a head injury as a child), but he had taken no notice of this advice:

December 21st: 'Frank, who has been very peculiar for some

194

time past, appeared to go out of his senses altogether, and I had to send David for the doctor about midnight. Got him to bed about two, and then sat up till four.'

December 22nd: 'Heard Frank going about at 5.30. Dressed and found him walking about . . . evidently out of his mind. David and I kept watch on him till 2, when we inspanned the cart and took him over to the station. Soutar and I went to town with him.'

Charles had his brother temporarily committed to the asylum, ('he appeared quite well pleased'), a move which brought relief to Margaret and the others at 'Strathearn'. Two days later there was another dramatic incident:

December 24th: 'Rowan was bitten by a snake, probably a night-adder, in the veld. With great presence of mind Mungo took off his belt, tied it round the boy's leg above the knee, and began sucking the wound and spitting out the blood . . . the foot swelled, and was very painful all Christmas Day.'

Fortunately, Rowan soon recovered.

Charles's final entry for the year was:

December 31st: 'The Boer War still continues, although the towns are all in our hands . . . and the railways. A number of people have returned to Johannesburg, and the mines are working, but not to any great extent. The blockhouse system is being extended, with good results.'

Lord Kitchener had had blockhouses built at strategic points, with barbed wire strung between them, as a means of checking guerilla raids. Farmhouses were burnt down wherever they might serve as armouries or sources of information and supply for roving commandos. Boer women and children from the farms were placed in concentration camps for their own safety, but a large number of them died of infectious diseases, (as did many people in the loyalist refugee camps), not through neglect on the part of the military but because the general standard of hygiene in those days was appallingly low. Far more British soldiers died of diseases such as enteric and typhoid fever in the South African War than were killed in battle.

––––––

The fighting ended early in *1902*, the Peace of Vereeniging was signed on *May 31st*, and Lord Milner took charge of affairs in

195

South Africa, combining the offices of High Commissioner and Governor of the Transvaal and Orange River Colony; he was to hold this post until *April, 1905*. A vast reconstruction programme was begun, in which he was ably assisted by a group of clever young men, (including John Buchan, the celebrated author, later Lord Tweedsmuir), who became known as 'Milner's Kindergarten'. Joseph Chamberlain came out to South Africa towards the end of *December, 1902*, and Charles went down to Durban to meet him. In their talks he expressed the need for conciliation, which was Charles's own conviction.

Cecil Rhodes died two months before the Peace of Vereeniging, and was buried in a spot known as 'World's View' in the Matopo Hills in Rhodesia which he had chosen himself. His brother Frank entrusted the grave to the care of the Matabele tribesmen. Frank retired from the Army the following year, and in *September, 1905*, he died of blackwater fever at Cecil's former home 'Groote Schuur' at Rondebosch, Cape Town.

Charles Smythe had a personal bereavement towards the end of *1902*, for on *November 14th* news came from Scotland that his mother was dead. It was a heavy blow, as he and Emily Smythe had been deeply attached to each other and had kept up a regular correspondence ever since he first went out to Natal. His letters to her had all been lovingly copied out, and filled a whole series of hard-backed notebooks.

The following year, *1903*, brought many changes: Camilla, now nineteen, became engaged to a Karkloof farmer, Campbell Shaw; Frank Smythe died; Oswald was admitted as an attorney of the Natal Supreme Court; Patrick (12) and Rowan (11) were sent to boarding-school at Maritzburg College. Finally, just after Christmas, Charles's sister 'Bice' (Beatrice) and cousin Mimi Boyle came out to South Africa on a visit – he had not seen them for twenty years.

Charles's political career had a setback in *August, 1903*:

'The Ministry of which I was Colonial Secretary for four years was defeated in Parliament, and resigned.'

A new Ministry was formed by Mr. (later, Sir) George Sutton, and Charles, out of office, found himself demoted to the rank of member of the Legislative Assembly. But he was a member-with-a-difference, for he retained the right to be

16. Return of Natal Volunteers, 1900

17. Winston Churchill and Lord Elgin (*'Punch' cartoon, April,* 1906)

A PROUD PARENT

18. British Lion (to his cub Natal). "Go it, young 'un. I like to see you fighting your own battles. But, if you want me, I'm here." (*'Punch'*, *May*, 1906)

known as 'The Honourable'; a letter had reached him, which read:

'Prime Minister's Office,
Pietermaritzburg.
November 5th, 1903.

'Sir,

'I have the honour to inform you that His Excellency the Governor has received a notification from the Secretary of State that His Majesty the King has been pleased to approve of the retention by you of the title "Honourable", and that notice to this effect will be published in the "London Gazette".

'I have the honour to be,
Sir,
Your obedient servant,
G. T. Plowman,
Secretary to the Prime Minister.'

The next twelve months passed uneventfully for Charles and his family, apart from David's becoming engaged to a young widow named Fanny McKenzie. May visited Scotland, then went to stay with her Aunt Bice who was now living in the south of France, and Mungo and Edric left school. Charles was anxious about Natal's economic position, and wrote:

'The Colony has been passing through a time of great depression, and money has been very scarce. The revenue is likely to be far short of the estimates.'

The country had not yet recovered from the disastrous effects of the South African War.

CHAPTER THIRTEEN

CHARLES REMAINED IN the political wilderness for nearly two years, but in *1905* he made a spectacular return to public life and in a matter of only a few months reached the apex of his career: in *January* he had held no office, in *May* he became Prime Minister and Colonial Secretary of Natal!

Before the opening of the Parliamentary session which saw the rapid change in his fortunes he had been engrossed in family affairs, for two of his children married, first Camilla and then David. Both weddings took place in the little wood-and-iron church at Nottingham Road.

Charles's description of Cammy's wedding day is a series of bald facts with no elaboration:

January 4th: 'Had cows milked by 6.30 a.m. Started Effie and Cammy in Campbell's [bridegroom's] trap at 8.15, waggon at 8.45 and trap with Joe and Flynn [two horses]. Waggon contained Edric, two blacks, Helen and Janet [cousins], Meta, Madge, three little boys . . . Soutar, Oswald' [Also in the waggon was Charles's and Margaret's fourteenth and last child, Cecilia Iris, the baby of the family.] Cammy dressed in the [village] hall. Kathleen Chadwick, who was bridesmaid, came down by 10 a.m. train and back by 12. I took Cammy up to the church at 10, where Campbell was waiting, and the clergyman married them. Then went to the hall, where there was a table laid with cakes and fruit . . . tea, claret cup, whiskey and soda.'

There was to be no honeymoon, and the young couple left after the reception for Campbell Shaw's farm at Karkloof.

David's wedding on *January 17th* was a quieter affair:

'Sent waggon to the station with the milk and David's things. Drove over to the church with Meta, Oswald, Madge, in carriage [a spider]. Effie, Pat, Rowan, Keith and Iris in milk cart. Mungo and Edric rode.'

199

The service was at 2.30 p.m. 'Only a few people in church, as there were no invitations. David and his wife rode home from the church.' The couple were to live at the farm 'Onverwacht', which was Fanny's for her lifetime. (The marriage was destined to be tragically brief, for she died in childbirth in *October* that same year, and David returned to 'Strathearn'.)

Two months later Charles went down to Pietermaritzburg for the start of the Legislative Assembly session:

'It was very soon evident that the Sutton Ministry could not last, and in the early part of May the whole of the Government party, and with four exceptions the whole of the Opposition, agreed that I should be Prime Minister and form a coalition Ministry. This I did, taking [John G.] Maydon, [Thomas] Watt, and [Walter] Clayton of the latter Ministry, and [Thomas] Hyslop and [Henry] Winter.'

Charles realised that his job as Premier and Colonial Secretary would not be easy because of the widespread economic depression which still gripped Natal:

'There was a big deficit between revenue and expenditure, and we tried to pass various taxing Bills which were thrown out in the Upper House.'

The white colonists protested vigorously when a house tax was suggested, and the Government did not know which way to turn in order to raise revenue; the Treasury was empty, and some means of finding more money was essential.

The problem was solved, so Charles and his Ministers thought, with the imposition of a Poll Tax of £1 a head, to be levied on all sections of the community, whites, Indians and Africans alike. If the tax had fallen upon the Africans alone the Bill would have had to be reserved for the King's approval, which would have meant delay and possible rejection, but as it affected all races it passed through both Houses without much discussion and became law in *August, 1905.*

There were, however, many people in Natal who believed that the Zulus would deeply resent the new measure:

December 31st: 'This [Bill] has since been made the subject of much opposition, and a scare has been got up that the natives will rise [in protest] and within the last month there has been much vague rumour and uneasiness among the Europeans, but

200

as far as the Government can ascertain the fear of a rising is quite baseless.' [It seems strange that one who had always had such a dread of a Zulu rebellion in the past should brush aside the threat of a rising so lightly now.]

Charles was much more concerned at this time over the fact that the Conservative Government in Great Britain had resigned and been replaced by a Liberal Party government led by Sir Henry Campbell-Bannerman. It was not much comfort to him to find that the new British Secretary of State for the Colonies was no other than his own cousin Lord Elgin, because of course Elgin was a Liberal like the rest. An odd quirk of fate had placed the two men opposite each other, one Colonial Secretary in London – a position of great importance considering the size of the Empire – and the other Colonial Secretary of the British Colony of Natal. Elgin was then fifty-five years old, Charles fifty-two.

Charles wrote to the Earl to renew their acquaintance and remind him of their meetings at Methven Castle long ago, and received a reply dated *January 19th, 1906*, written from his cousin's home, 'Broomhall', in Perthshire:
'Dear Charles,

'Many thanks for your letter of *December 15th* which I had intended to acknowledge before this – but you will understand that I have been a good deal pressed at present.

'I respond most heartily to your two calls: first, to your mention of Methven, (how little we thought then that we should ever correspond in this way!), and secondly to co-operation in strengthening the ties between the Colonies and Mother Country. My task, especially in South Africa, is not an easy one at the moment – but if I am met in the spirit you describe I hope and believe that good work will be done.

'Hoping you will remember I am a cousin, if I can ever be of any use,

'Yours very sincerely,
Elgin.'

Charles was delighted with this friendly letter, and began to look ahead to the New Year more optimistically. The political scene seemed brighter, and his family was flourishing too: David and Mungo had taken the farming work off his hands,

201

Pat was safely recovered from a bad bout of enteric, and Camilla had made him and Margaret grandparents for the first time when she gave birth to a son, Colin Walter Shaw, in *September*. There had, it was true, been an unusually severe snowstorm in *June* which damaged many of his fine pine trees, but the snow brought on the spring grass and his stock had done well.

Charles did not remain cheerful for long. No sooner had officials begun to collect the Poll Tax in *January, 1906*, than the Zulu's pent-up feelings flared into open rebellion; the magistrates of the Umgeni and Greytown districts were defied, two white policemen were stabbed to death, and the white population of Natal was thrown into a state of panic. Some farmers and their families even 'went into *laager*', as the saying was, gathering in some place such as a magistracy or church and preparing to make a stand there if attacked. The Government called out the Volunteers on *February 9th*, and next day proclaimed martial law. A censorship on telegrams was imposed, to prevent alarming reports being spread.

There was no doubt – as an investigating commission found out after the rising – that the Zulus in Natal had had genuine grievances; many of them were very poor as a result of their stock losses in the rinderpest and East Coast fever epidemics, and others were victims of financial extortion at the hands of grasping landlords and usurers. White officials had not had the same contact with the chiefs as in the days of Sir Theophilus Shepstone, and the chiefs found they had no means of making their people's feelings properly understood. There were several other and more subtle causes of unrest in *1906:* for one thing, the new tax had fallen chiefly on the young men, (as kraal heads already liable for hut tax were exempt), some of whom had worked in the gold mines of the Witwatersrand and come under the influence there of the doctrine of 'Ethiopianism' which urged all black men to unite against the whites. Ethiopianism had a strong appeal for Zulus with a smattering of education. At the opposite end of the scale were totally illiterate tribesmen who were deeply suspicious of the Government because a Population Census had been taken in *1904* and they thought some evil motive was behind it.

The Natal Volunteer forces checked the rebellion without

much difficulty in its early stage; assisted by a loyal chief they rounded up a number of Africans concerned in the murder of the two policemen, tried two of them by drumhead court-martial, and shot them without more ado. This over-zealousness on the part of the military put the Natal Government in a serious predicament, as Charles realised only too well when he wrote on *February 14th*:

'I am just afraid that we may get into trouble over it, as though they really deserved it, there may be some legal bother about it, the crime having been committed before martial law was declared.'

The Lieut. Governor, Sir Henry McCallum, had advised Charles to communicate immediately with the officers in the field and forbid any further drum-head trials until the legal position was clear. Charles knew that the British Government was watching the situation in Natal closely:

'There is an urgent cable from Elgin tonight, wanting a full report of the origin and figures of the disturbances for the Imperial Parliament tomorrow, so I shall have to get something ready in the morning.'

Lord Elgin's Parliamentary Under-Secretary for the Colonies at this time was the thirty-one-year-old Winston Churchill, who had crossed the floor of the House to become a Liberal in *1904*. (Churchill said in *August, 1906*, 'All South African business in the House of Commons has been in my hands.') The two held the same political views, broadly speaking, but their partnership was an uneasy one; they regarded each other with what Edward Marsh, Churchill's private secretary, described with amusement as 'qualified esteem', and there is no doubt that the younger man often exasperated the staid ex-Viceroy.

Elgin and Winston were, however, united in their disapproval of the Natal Government's muzzling the press at the start of the Zulu Rebellion, though they misunderstood the reason for it. They insisted that it should cease at once, and in a later letter written on *February 14th* Charles reported:

'We have removed the telegraph censorship today in consequence of Elgin's urgent representations about inter-national complications. One would hardly have thought Natal was so important.'

203

By early *March* twenty-four rebels had been captured, and on the *12th* of that month their trial under martial law began. When the proceedings closed, twelve of the men had been found guilty of murder, public violence and taking up arms against the Government, and had been sentenced to death. The Governor accepted the advice of his Ministers that the sentences should be carried out, and a cable was sent to Lord Elgin to this effect.

Elgin immediately replied that executions under martial law excited strong criticism in Britain. He said that trial of murder cases by civil courts was greatly to be preferred, and ordered that the executions be suspended.

At Charles's prompting, Sir Henry McCallum sent an answer saying that the Prime Minister of Natal regretted he could not authorise the suspension of the executions, which had been confirmed after full and deliberate consideration. (To do so, the Governor would have had to exercise the prerogative of the Crown to cancel death warrants which he had already signed.)

Charles saw that an extremely important constitutional issue had arisen as a result of the Secretary of State's intervention. He decided to make a stand, though it meant risking his position as Premier. He asked the Governor for written instructions, to which he then replied:

'As Your Excellency has thought it necessary to give instructions to suspend the executions which were confirmed by the Executive Council and appointed to be carried out on Friday next, I feel that it is impossible for me to continue in office as Prime Minister, and I beg to tender my resignation. My colleagues are unanimous in supporting me in what, under the present circumstances, appears to be a most important constitutional question.'

The Governor asked Charles to remain in office until he had consulted further with Lord Elgin.

The affair caused a tremendous commotion, not only in Natal but much further afield. Elgin's 'unnecessary interference in the affairs of a self-governing colony', as it was called, was condemned by the Governor-General of Australia, (Sir Henry Stafford Northcote, 1st Baronet), who cabled Elgin saying that a dangerous precedent would be established, affecting all states in the Empire, if he insisted on pursuing this course.

The Secretary of State for the Colonies climbed down. On *March 30th* he sent a cable saying that His Majesty's Government had no intention of interfering with the action of a responsible government in Natal, and that the decision to execute the rebels rested in the hands of the Governor and his Ministers.

The condemned men were shot, in the presence of a large number of other Zulus.

The shooting did not bring the *1906* Rebellion to an end, for a second and far more vigorous phase began, led by a minor chief named Bambata who fled into Zululand and rallied thousands of tribesmen to his side. The rising was crushed only after large-scale operations had been undertaken involving Volunteers from the Transvaal and Cape Colony as well as Natal, but by *mid-September* Bambata was dead and all resistance over. Charles's son Oswald took part in the fighting, as an officer in the Natal Carbineers.

It sounds unlikely, but is a fact, that Gandhi served in the Bambata rebellion (on the Government side), with the rank of Sergeant-Major! He had organised a small Indian ambulance corps which was in the field for a few weeks. A wealthy man now, Gandhi had returned to Natal in *1904*, bought a piece of land at Phoenix, six miles north of Durban, and established a communal farm at which he set up a printing-press to produce the newspaper, 'Indian Opinion'. His motive for serving in the Zulu Rebellion may have been – as in the South African War – to demonstrate that Indians were patriots. Natal Indians naturally sided with the whites against the Zulus, because they knew the latter would make short work of them if they ever got the chance.

When the tragic revolt was at last over, Charles told Lord Elgin:

'There is no doubt a feeling in the Colony that we are rather in the position of a naughty child who is in disgrace, and a feeling of resentment has been created which the Imperial Government could do much to allay if you could send some message from the Government of sympathy with the sacrifices we have made which for a small colony as we are have been very considerable.'

His cousin cabled his congratulations that the emergency had been dealt with successfully.

An interesting sidelight on the Zulu Rebellion is to be found in Randolph Churchill's biography of his father, (Volume Two), in which he mentions a letter which Winston Churchill wrote to Lord Elgin on *September 14th, 1906.* Winston told of a talk he had had with the German Emperor at Breslau military manoeuvres, during which Kaiser Wilhelm II had said, patronisingly, that if a native rising should take place in Cape Colony, the colonists might be glad of the help of German troops from South-West Africa.

Churchill had replied that 'in Natal, on the contrary, our chief difficulty had not been to kill the rebellious natives, but to prevent our colonists, (who so thoroughly understood native warfare), from killing too many of them!'

Charles had ended the letter he wrote to Lord Elgin on *August 4th, 1906,* with the words:

'I must congratulate you on the settlement you have arrived at with regard to the Transvaal constitution. The question was a most difficult one, and your solution of it most fair to all parties.'

He was referring to the fact that the Liberal Government in Britain had decided to grant Responsible Government to the Transvaal as from *December* of that year. It had been largely due to the efforts of Winston Churchill on the British side, and General Smuts on the other, that the former Boer republic was given self-government so soon after the war. The Orange River Colony was granted a constitution similar to the Transvaal's in *November, 1907.*

Charles told Elgin:

'What I hope for within the near future is a union of the Transvaal, Orange River Colony and Natal. The Dutch in the Transvaal would not agree to a union with Natal only, but bringing in the O.R.C. would counterbalance the addition of

206

the British vote in Natal, and I believe they would agree on those terms.'

Charles's desire for union with the former Boer republics may have surprised his cousin, but the reason for it is obvious: Natal's Volunteer forces had put down the recent Zulu rising only with the help of men from other parts of South Africa, and in common with many other white colonists he wanted the assurance that troops from beyond Natal's borders would be available if trouble broke out again.

He felt that the withdrawal of British troops from Natal had left the territory very vulnerable, and in *February*, at the start of the Rebellion, had insisted that soldiers of a Highland regiment stationed in Pretoria should be rushed to Pietermaritzburg; the kilted Highlanders had marched up and down the main streets of the capital with band and pipes, 'to show the natives that the story about the soldiers having gone away for good is untrue'.

But it *was* true; he knew that British regiments were being removed from South Africa one by one. On the other hand, when the Transvaal and Orange River Colony were independent they would revive the old commando system and build up a strong defence force. Charles was well aware that it would be no use Natal looking to Britain for sympathy if another Zulu rebellion occurred, for the events of the previous few months had led to an estrangement between the Liberal Government and the Colony's leaders. An alliance with the Boers seemed the only safe policy.

Charles's views on this and other subjects were not necessarily the views of Natal as a whole. Members of the Legislative Assembly gave him and his Ministers a difficult time during the Parliamentary session of *1906*, and he was seriously harassed by what he called 'Government-baiting' in the House. In *November* he resigned from office as he felt he could not secure a working majority unless he effected a compromise with the Labour party, which was a step he was determined not to take.

Frederick Moor succeeded him as Prime Minister, but as their outlook was much alike Charles seldom clashed with him when he was leader of the Opposition in *1907*; in fact, he supported the Government on most issues.

There was much to interest him at home this year; he had bought another farm adjoining his own lands at Nottingham Road, and David had now gone to live there, naming the place 'Dalcrue'. He subsequently married for a second time, very happily. Oswald had become engaged, and Camilla Shaw had a second son whom she named Victor.

Towards the end of *1907* rumours were rife that the Zulus were plotting further resistance:

'At the beginning of *December* all the active militia and nearly all the first reserves were called out for active service. Martial law was proclaimed in Zululand and the northern districts. Dinizulu [Chief Dinizulu, head of the Zulu royal house] was arrested, and some other chiefs, but there was no sign of resistance on the part of the natives.'

By Christmas time only a small force of police and Volunteers was till active, searching Zululand for stray rebels and arms. Dinizulu was suspended as chief, as the Natal Government believed him to have been the instigator of the *1906* Rebellion and to have stirred up other, more recent, trouble as well. He was imprisoned, pending his trial in a few months' time on twenty-three counts of treason.

CHAPTER FOURTEEN

IN *1908* there was one subject above all others which was discussed and mulled over in the homes of white South Africans from Cape Town to the Limpopo: this was the proposed union or federation of the four semi-independent states in the country – Cape Colony, Natal, the Transvaal and the Orange River Colony – all of which now exercised Responsible Government under the Crown. It was not of course a new concept, for Lord Carnarvon had spent years trying to bring federation about, but it had much stronger appeal now, especially among ex-republicans who saw it as a way of eliminating British influence in South Africa. Many Imperialists were eager for it too, as they thought it would end economic disputes between rival states and result in prosperity and progress. There was a general desire for a uniform policy towards the Africans, to give the whites greater security.

An intercolonial conference in *May, 1908*, recommended that the four states should appoint delegates to a National Convention to prepare a draft constitution for a united South Africa. The number of delegates was to vary according to the size and importance of each colony, and it was finally decided that the Cape should send twelve, the Transvaal eight, and the other two states five each.

Charles Smythe was one of Natal's representatives, the others being Frederick Moor (the Premier), Colonel Edward Greene, William Morcom Q.C., Thomas Watt and Thomas Hyslop, though only five had voting rights. Delegates from the other parts of the country included men with very famous names: from the Transvaal came General Louis Botha, General Jan Smuts, Sir Percy Fitzpatrick, George Farrar and General De la Rey; the Orange Free State sent General J. B. M. Hertzog, General Christiaan De Wet and ex-President Steyn; while among the Cape delegates were Dr. Leander Starr Jameson and John X. Merriman.

The Convention met behind closed doors, first in Durban and later in Cape Town, under the chairmanship of Sir Henry De Villiers, Chief Justice of Cape Colony; their sittings took place between *October, 1908* and *February, 1909*. The conference report was then debated by the colonial Parliaments, and in *May, 1909*, the Convention reassembled in Bloemfontein to consider amendments to the proposed constitution. The amended draft which was produced was quickly approved by the Transvaal, Orange Free State and Cape Colony, but in Natal its publication aroused a storm of protest from voters who declared they had been 'betrayed to the Boers'. The Natal delegates responded by emphasising the economic advantages of union, and were so convincing that when a referendum was held to test public opinion the opposition group was overwhelmingly defeated.

The proceedings of the National Convention were carried on in such secrecy that delegates could not discuss them except amongst themselves, so the letters Charles sent Margaret from Durban and Cape Town mention only the most trivial things. All the same, some of his remarks are diverting:

October 12th, 1908, 8.30 p.m.: 'We had not to wear frock coats today, as it was found out that General De la Rey had not got a top hat. We did not do much this morning beyond settling the rules of procedure, and then adjourned . . . we are to sit from 9.30 to 12.30 and from 3.30 to 5.30, the long interval in the middle of the day being to allow His Honour ex-President Steyn to have a nap as he is not very well. Plowman [Principal Under-Secretary] is very anxious that one of the girls should come to the ball on the *Good Hope* . . . says his wife will chaperone . . . I think it will be an awful crush.'

October 14th, 3.40 p.m.: 'There was a big dinner at the Club last night, 146 people . . . I am writing this at the Convention, Sir L. Mitchell [Sir Lewis Michell, the South African banker, and friend of Rhodes] is speaking and giving a little old South African history. The room is very comfortable, [the Convention sat in Durban's Town Hall, now the main Post Office], all the [Legislative] Assembly tables and chairs, and so far it has been quite cool.'

October 20th: 'The Government has hired a motor car for the

210

use of Natal delegates and . . . I went out after lunch up to Hunt, Leuchars timber yards . . . and then took a drive along the Umbilo Road.' [Motor cars were an innovation in South Africa, and there were very few in Durban.]

October 26th: 'We have been talking all day and done nothing. I see no end to the business.'

November 23rd, from Mount Nelson Hotel, Cape Town: 'We are going to alter the hours of sitting, so as to sit from 9.30 to 1.30 and leave the afternoon free for committees sitting.' [Charles was a member of the franchise, civil service and finance committees.]

December 1st: 'Moor and I are going to lunch with old Jan Hofmeyr tomorrow. He is an historical personage at the Cape. ['Onze Jan' Hofmeyr had been leader of the Afrikaner Bond at the Cape, and wielded great influence.] I had a note from Lady Selborne, last night, asking me to dine with them on Sunday night, which I shall have to accept as they are in the same hotel.' [Lord Selborne was High Commissioner for South Africa after Lord Milner.]

December 16th: 'We went to Simonstown yesterday afternoon, to see the new dock the Imperial Government has built at a cost of two millions . . . it did not look much for the money.' [The Royal Navy's South Atlantic squadron was based at Simonstown.]

There were five main issues to be debated by the delegates to the National Convention. These were, briefly:

(1) Should power be concentrated in the central government, in a Cabinet responsible to Parliament, or divided between the centre and the provinces?

(2) Who should have the right to take part in political elections and hold political offices?

(3) What electoral system should be adopted?

(4) In what way could Afrikaner culture be protected? (The Boers were now known as Afrikaners.)

(5) What should be done about Rhodesia, Basutoland (Lesotho), Bechuanaland (Botswana) and Swaziland?

On the first issue the Natal delegates were unanimous in their desire for a *federation* instead of a close union. Natal was a colony essentially British in tradition, and most of its people

211

were loyal to the Crown – some to the point of jingoism. They had no wish to come under Afrikaner domination and lose their identity, and they believed that in a federation of South African states it would be possible to preserve Natal's unique character. Charles was anxious to see defence, railways and Customs put under central government control, but he wanted other affairs, particularly education, left in the hands of the provincial Parliaments.

He and the other Natal delegates put up a brave fight for federation, but they failed mainly because two powerful champions of their cause were absent from the conference: 'Onze Jan' Hofmeyr had, for some reason of his own, kept out of the fray, and the clever and eloquent William Schreiner, (brother of Olive Schreiner, and a former Premier of Cape Colony), was otherwise committed. Schreiner had given up his legal practice, temporarily, so as to be free to defend Chief Dinizulu at his trial; he believed the chief to be innocent of the treason charges brought against him by the Natal Government. Both he and Hofmeyr were a crippling loss to the pro-federation party.

When the subject of the franchise was raised, the Natal delegates sided with Louis Botha and other members from the Transvaal and Orange Free State who wanted a political colour-bar entrenched in the South African constitution. In no circumstances, they said, would they accept a qualified, non-racial franchise such as Cape Colony (always more liberal in its views than the rest of South Africa), had had. After a long and heated argument the franchise problem was referred to a committee. Eventually, delegates decided not to tamper with the existing voting rights in the four states; the subject was so controversial that they put it aside for the Union Parliament to deal with later.

It was inevitable that while the Convention was debating the franchise issue the question of giving the vote to women should be brought up, for this was a question which, like the coloured vote, aroused strong feelings. The Natal delegates were in favour of granting women voting rights, and Sir Frederick Moor presented a signed petition to that effect. This was followed by three petitions from Cape Colony.

19. The National Convention, Durban, 1908 (*Parliament Library, Cape Town*)

20. South Africa's first Provincial Administrators, 1912. Standing (left to right) J. Rissik (Transvaal), W. Ramsbottom (O.F.S.). Sitting (left to right) C. Smythe (Natal), F. de Waal (Cape)

When the third issue on the agenda came up for discussion, Charles and the other Natal men declared that they wanted an electoral system such as was already in force in their Colony and the Cape, viz a system in which a member of Parliament with an urban constituency represented a much larger number of voters than a member from a rural constituency. (In *1908* the two Natal towns of Pietermaritzburg and Durban contained 38% of Natal's voters but returned only 19% of the members of the Natal Legislative Assembly!) The opposition argued that each M.P. should represent more or less the same number of voters; they won the day, but made important concessions regarding delimitation of constituencies which were later seized upon to give the advantage again to the rural voters.

When the subject of the Afrikaners' heritage was raised the Convention decided that Dutch should be one of South Africa's two official languages, (Afrikaans had not yet been officially recognised), and placed on an equal footing with English.

The final issue on the agenda was more or less shelved, as the British Government would not permit Lesotho, Botswana and Swaziland to be swallowed up in a united South Africa, though the draft Constitution allowed for these territories to become part of the Union at a later date. Rhodesia decided on a policy of 'wait and see'.

Midway through *1909* the governments of the four South African colonies sent delegates to London to confer with Lord Crewe, the Colonial Secretary, (Elgin had been dismissed from office by Herbert Asquith, the new British Prime Minister), and Charles was chosen as one of Natal's representatives. After the conference the British Government was to introduce to Parliament a 'South Africa Bill' advocating the adoption of a constitution for South Africa substantially the same as in the draft drawn up by the National Convenion delegates.

Charles took Effie with him – she was thirty-two now, and they were close companions – and they sailed with other delegates accompanied by wives and/or daughters on the mailship *Kenilworth Castle* in *June*. It was Effie's first trip to

213

England, and she was keenly excited. Charles's diary contains the comment, 'No particularly interesting passengers', but Effie mentioned in a letter that the Indian leader Gandhi was on board, and had a first-class cabin. She felt almost sorry for him, she said, 'shunned by everyone'.

Gandhi was on his way to London with a colleague, Haji Habib, to make a final appeal to the British Government to amend the Transvaal's anti-Asiatic laws. He had begun agitating against this legislation when it was first proposed in *1906*, on his return to Johannesburg after the Zulu Rebellion. (It was at this time that he founded his well-known policy of *Satyagraha* or passive resistance.) In *October, 1906*, he had gone to England to lay the Indians' case before Lord Elgin and had been successful – Elgin refused to assent to the new ordinance. The following year the Transvaal was given self-government and at once passed the law, and Gandhi started organising resistance all over again. He was sent to prison several times in *1908*. (His mission to London in *1909* was to prove fruitless, and he returned to the Transvaal to continue agitating.)

During their stay in London Charles and Effie put up at the Hyde Park Hotel in Knightsbridge:

July 23rd: 'We have been having meetings all this week at the Foreign Office, and have got things pretty well settled with the Imperial Government. Moor, Watt and Plowman and all the Transvaal and Free State delegates arrived last Saturday and are staying here.'

The delegates were made much of in the British capital, and had the honour of being received by Royalty:

July 29th: 'Well, I went to lunch at Buckingham Palace with all the other delegates and their wives, except Mrs. Watt, who is too ill to go. We were shown into a large room and waited there for about half an hour, and all the men stood on one side and the ladies on the other. Then the King and Queen and Prince and Princess of Wales [King Edward VII and Queen Alexandra, and the future King George V and Queen Mary] came in and all shook hands with us. Then the King took the Queen's hand and led her in to the dining-room and we all followed, those who had ladies taking them in. [Daughters were not invited, so Effie could not be there.] We had all had the plans of where we were to sit sent to us the night before.

'There were four round tables, about sixteen people at each. I sat at the Queen's, almost opposite to her, next to Mrs. Botha on one side and Percy Fitzpatrick on the other. We had gold plates and cutlery for everything . . . there was a blaze of gold plate on the sideboards.'

The seating of guests at the Queen's table was as follows: Rt. Hon. H. H. Asquith, Lady Fitzpatrick, Rt. Hon. R. McKenna, Lady Morris, Colonel J. E. B. Seely, Hon. Charles Knollys, General J. B. M. Hertzog, Sir Percy Fitzpatrick, Hon. Charles Smythe, Mrs. Louis Botha, Rt. Hon. J. X. Merriman, Lady Hopwood, Rt. Hon. A. J. Balfour, H.R.H. Princess Victoria (daughter of King Edward VII), and the Marquis of Lansdowne.

Charles's description continues:

'When we were finished we went into the adjoining room. The Queen was wearing the Cullinan diamond as a brooch and pendant, and [Lord] Selborne took me up to her to see it. She held it out for me to look at.' [What Charles saw was, of course, only a small part of the enormous 3,106-carat Cullinan diamond found at Premier Mine near Pretoria in *1905* and presented to King Edward VII by the Transvaal Government. In *1908* it had been sent to Amsterdam for cutting into a number of smaller stones. The largest, a drop-shaped brilliant known as the Star of Africa Number 1, now forms part of the head of the Royal sceptre.]

'Then the men went into an adjoining room, where the King was smoking, and we had cigars. Selborne took me up to the King and told him I had been his Prime Minister in Natal, and he talked to me for a bit. At a quarter past three we shook hands again with them all, and left . . . the Queen is wonderful, does not look more than forty [she was sixty-five], of course they say it is all make-up, but the effect is very good.'

Charles took the opportunity, whilst in London, of visiting relations and friends within easy reach. He and Effie attended At Homes and other official functions, and went to the House of Lords to hear the second reading of the Union of South Africa Bill. Charles took his daughter to dine at the House of Commons several times; on one occasion they were the guests

215

of the Deputy Speaker, Mr. Emmott, and on another of the Birrells. (Augustine Birrell was the Secretary for Ireland.) Commenting on this latter dinner-party in a letter home, Effie wrote:

'Mr. Harcourt and Mr. Haldane dined too. [These were Lewis Harcourt, 1st Viscount, First Commissioner of Works, and Richard Haldane, later Viscount, Secretary of State for War.] Such outsiders ... we were glad to get away, they jarred so much!' [Like Charles, Effie thought Liberals beyond the pale.]

Early in *August* the delegates were invited to go aboard the *S.S. Armadale Castle* at Spithead to watch a Naval review. Effie thoroughly enjoyed this:

'This afternoon the King's yacht came, and he inspected the Fleet, guns boomed and bands played ... then we saw submarines and destroyers and torpedo-boats, all showing off in various ways [At night] all the boats were illuminated, they do look splendid.'

Next day the *Armadale Castle* cruised past the Isle of Wight:

'I discovered this morning that Lieut. Shackleton, the Antarctic man, was on board.' [This was Sir Ernest Shackleton, the British explorer, then at the height of his fame; he had been to the Antarctic with Captain Robert Scott, and had commanded an expedition in *1909* which got to within ninety-seven miles of the South Pole – a record at the time.]

Effie persuaded Sir Ernest to give her his autograph; she had been impressed by the 'awfully nice' speech he made at dinner. She had another thrill a day or two later while watching yacht races at Cowes, for 'the Czar arrived, and there was much flag-wagging and gun-booming'. [The illustrious visitor was the ill-fated Tsar Nicholas II, aboard the Russian Royal yacht with the Tsarina and their children.]

By this time Charles was growing tired of all the public functions he had to attend, and wrote:

'I shall be glad when we get down to Scotland, though I do not think we shall stop there long.'

Now that his parents were dead and Methven let to tenants, he half dreaded going to Perthshire. But before he and Effie set off for the north there was more to be done in London:

August 13th: 'Tomorrow evening we are going to see the fireworks at the Crystal Palace, and on Monday we go to hear the second reading of the Union Bill in the House of Commons.'

Effie described the historic second reading:

'At 4 o'clock we went to the House of Commons to hear our Bill discussed, it was splendid. I stayed till nearly 8 o'clock. We heard Colonel Seely, Mr. Lyttleton, Mr. Keir Hardie, Mr. Balfour, Mr. Asquith. Mr. Balfour was miles the best, such a nice speech and he spoke so well. So glad to have heard him.' [The speakers were: John Seely, (later, 1st Baron Mottistone), Under Secretary for the Colonies; Alfred Lyttleton, a Conservative and former Colonial Secretary; Keir Hardie of the Labour Party; Arthur Balfour, (later, 1st Earl), a former Conservative Prime Minister; and Herbert Asquith, (later, 1st Earl of Oxford and Asquith), Prime Minister *1908–1916*.]

Before leaving for Scotland Charles and Effie visited Westminster Abbey to see the tomb of Dean Stanley and of his wife Augusta, Charles's mother's cousin. Effie noted with pride that they were the only commoners buried in the Royal part of the Abbey, 'by command of Queen Victoria'. The memorial inscription to the Dean's wife read:

> Augusta Elizabeth Frederica,
> 5th daughter of Thomas Bruce
> 7th Earl of Elgin and Kincardine,
> The beloved wife
> Of Arthur Penrhyn Stanley,
> Dean of the Collegiate Church.
> For 30 years a devoted servant
> Of Queen Victoria
> And the Queen's mother and children.
> For 12 years the unwearied friend
> Of the people of Westminister
> And the inseparable partner
> Of her husband's toils and hopes,
> Uniting many hearts from many lands
> And drawing all to things above.
> Born April 3rd, *1822*
> Died March 1st, *1876*.

The visit to Methven was a painful one, though Charles was glad to see his brother David again and meet his wife and little girl. The tenants of Methven were away, and he and David walked in woods 'all looking so pretty', but it was very distressing to hear that the estate must soon be sold. Charles wrote to Margaret:

'Is it not sickening . . . David says there is a dead loss every year, and it is impossible to go on.'

He felt he never wanted to see Methven again; it would have been such joy showing Effie the places he had loved as a boy, 'had it not been for the thought that as far as we are concerned, it is all coming to an end'. But he understood the position, and could not blame David.

This experience made Charles long all the more now to get back to 'Strathearn'. A mental picture rose before his eyes of the house he had built, the trees he had planted and his stock at pasture on green hillsides under a cloudless African sky; he could almost smell the aromatic African grass and the honey-sweetness of wattle bloom. The Natal countryside was where he belonged, and he ached to return to it. Farewell to the Highlands, farewell for ever.

The South Africa Act passed through all its stages in Parliament at Westminster with little difficulty, and as a result the new British Dominion known as the Union of South Africa came into being on *May 31st, 1910.* The South African constitution laid down that a Governor-General should represent the King, and Parliament at Cape Town consist of a Senate and a House of Assembly. The four Provinces were each to have its own Provincial Council under an Administrator. The franchise laws of the two former colonies and two former republics remained untouched.

Looking back, it seems strange that the Liberals did not insist on suitably-qualified non-whites being given the franchise in Natal, the Transvaal and the Orange Free State as they were in the Cape, (no-one in his senses would have asked for one-man-one-vote when many Africans were still utterly ignorant of Western ways), but although the issue was raised it was not taken up seriously. The British Government, very anxious to see South Africa united, realised that the franchise question was a rock on which all their hopes might founder, for no Transvaal or Free State Afrikaner would agree to a black man having the vote, and the whites in Natal were terrified of being swamped by the vast numbers of Zulus and Indians in their province. An insistence on racial equality would have brought about civil war in South Africa, which was the last thing Britain wanted.

Charles Smythe may have thought his political career would come to an end once Natal was absorbed into the Union, for he had refused to stand as a candidate when the election of Senators took place in *February, 1910*. He did not wish to go all the way to Cape Town every year to attend the Parliamentary sessions.

But there was a post awaiting him which was much more to his liking, and the offer of it came in *May*:

'Moor, who was Prime Minister, wired to me on *May 12th* to meet him at Nottingham Road, which I did. He told me he wished to recommend me to Botha as Administrator [of Natal] if I would accept; I said I would. On the *27th* I got a letter from Botha [General Louis Botha had become first Prime Minister of the Union of South Africa] offering me the post which I accepted, and was sworn in on the *31st* . . . I have, therefore, to spend all the week in Pietermaritzburg, only getting home at week-ends. I am appointed for five years, at £2,000 per annum and £20 per month house allowance.'

Charles had no intention of moving into Government House; he would stay at Oswald's home, (Oswald had married in *1909*), from Monday to Friday. He was not going to uproot himself from the country, and knew it would not be right to ask Margaret to do so.

Louis Botha was anxious to put Charles's name forward for the decoration K.C.M.G. (Knight Commander of the Most Distinguished Order of St. Michael and St. George) when he submitted his list for Union honours; this was a decoration conferrable on diplomats and other men who had performed valuable administrative services in countries belonging to the

219

British Empire, and would have brought Charles a knighthood and the right to bear the title 'Sir'. Charles had a great admiration for Botha and did not wish to offend him or appear ungrateful, but so profound was his dislike of the Liberals that he would not accept anything from them. He asked George Plowman, the Provincial Secretary, to send a message for him, declining the offer. The telegram, sent in code to General Botha on his behalf, ran:

'Strictly confidential. In reply to your telegram of 1st September, I have given the matter my most earnest consideration but would prefer that my name should not be put forward for Union honours. I highly appreciate your good feeling towards me and am indeed most grateful for your offer to recommend me for those honours.'

General Botha was probably surprised at this response.

Charles entered upon his new duties with zest, and had important work to do as Chief Executive Officer and Chairman of Natal's Executive Committee. There was a certain amount of entertaining, too, and in *September, 1910*, it fell to him to receive South Africa's first Governor-General when he arrived in Natal on an official visit. The Governor-General was Herbert, Viscount Gladstone, son of the Victorian Prime Minister, W. E. Gladstone. Charles had groomed his eldest daughters to act as hostesses for him at official functions, as Margaret seldom left the farm. In a letter to his sister Bice he described the arrival of the Governor-General's train in Pietermaritzburg station, and how he had introduced himself and Meta, the Mayor and Mayoress of Pietermaritzburg, and about twenty other people to Lord and Lady Gladstone. After the handshaking was over the King's representative inspected the guard-of-honour, and then the official party climbed into their carriages and proceeded to the Town Hall. Gladstone made a speech to the crowd assembled there – 'he spoke very well, but naturally did not commit himself to anything', Charles reported – and the party drove round the town and reached Government House in time for lunch.

Charles now discovered, to his cost, that entertaining the great could be nerve-racking. His letter tells, very amusingly, what happened next:

220

'Plowman had arranged with the military secretary that Meta and I, the Mayor and Mayoress, Sir Duncan and Lady McKenzie, Colonel Warden and Mr. Dove Wilson [the Judge-President of Natal] should also lunch there; well, they told me lunch was ready, so after going over the house we went in. I thought the secretary would have arranged about the seats, but found I had to do it on the spur of the moment. Luckily, Lord and Lady Gladstone took the centre seats opposite each other, and I managed to get the others told off, but it was an awful moment.'

Worse was to come, for the lunch lasted far longer than it was meant to do:

'By a quarter to three we had not got to the dessert, so I told them to cut the rest and bring in the coffee, which they did, but the poor Mayoress was nearly distracted, wanting to get off and change her dress and get down to the Park before 3.30' [where the Governor-General was to attend a garden party in his honour].

Meta also had to change, but was fortunately given a lift in a motor car to Oswald's house, where her garden party clothes were waiting; even so, she and her father only just succeeded in reaching Alexandra Park in time to welcome the Gladstones. It was with relief that Charles saw his distinguished guests off by train later that afternoon. He said afterwards:

'They professed themselves very much pleased, and with the exception of the length of the lunch everything went off all right . . . Thank goodness I shall not be responsible for anything tomorrow beyond the first introductions. [He does not say what function this was.] They are both very friendly, and I could not see any of the "side" people talked about.'

November, 1910, brought more visitors, this time the Duke and Duchess of Connaught and their younger daughter, twenty-four-year-old Princess Patricia. The Duke, Prince Arthur, was the third son of Queen Victoria. This official visit, like the Gladstones', gave Charles plenty to think about; in a note written to Margaret on *November 30th* from his office he said:

'Such a worry I am having. Last night I got a wire from the Duke's secretary, saying that although I was not living at Government House I was still the host, and asking me to send

221

out invitations for a dinner-party tomorrow night, so I had to start this morning and have asked a dinner-party of thirty-eight including the Duke and suite.'

Charles had already arranged a luncheon for the *30th*, and was finding the seating a problem:

'Lady Bale sent this morning to say Sir Henry [who was ill] was so much worse she would not come to the luncheon. This threatened to throw out all our seating, when luckily I thought of Mrs. Fred Moor, [Lady Moor], and wired to her at Estcourt, and got an answer to say she would come. She just fills Lady Bale's place in precedence, so that saved the situation. I have also asked her to the dinner tomorrow.'

The complications were a nightmare:

'Think how awkward it will be: Effie and I will have to go to Government House to receive the guests as hosts, and then wait till they all go away and the Royal party retire, and then get home [to Oswald's house]. I shall have to pack my evening things and get my bag to the station for Plowman to take down [to Durban] by the midnight train, as I cannot take it with me in the Royal train in the morning. I have to go to a dinner on the *Balmoral Castle* on Friday night, and drive all about in the carriage with the Duke and Duchess. *I am sure I shall tread on the Duke's gouty toe*, and shall be as sick of them as they will be of me!'

Reverting to his lunch party plans, Charles ended his note:

'Effie will be between the Duke and Dove Wilson, and I between the Duke and Duchess. There are sixteen at it. Now I must go and dress for this confounded Caledonian dinner!'

The next two years were pleasant ones for Charles, as he enjoyed his work as Administrator and could keep in touch with country affairs at the week-ends. His sons were all grown up now, except Keith, who was still at boarding-school; Mungo was farming 'Howard', while Rowan took his place at 'Strathearn'. Pat intended to be a farmer too, but was at present apprenticed to the local blacksmith as he thought a knowledge of working in iron would be useful to him. Edric had married in *1911*, and was living on a part of 'Howard' named 'Dwaleni', and May, who had married Ken Soutar in *1910*, was at 'Steybraes'. Effie and Meta were still at home, but the youngest daughter, Iris, had been sent to school in Pietermaritzburg.

Tragedy had touched this happy, close-knit family only once recently, when Camilla's third child died as a result of an accident.

Up to this time Charles had always been in excellent health except for bouts of neuralgia caused by tooth decay, but in *1913*, at the age of sixty-one, he fell ill and in *August* he sailed for England – accompanied by Effie – to undergo an operation. He was in a nursing-home for seven weeks, and on his return to Natal he spent a further week in hospital.

In *July, 1914*, he was ill again. He told his sister Bice:

'I have been having a week of bed in Addington Hospital [in Durban] . . . unfortunately, they could not do anything for me. It is a return of the old complaint [prostatitis] and they are unwilling to operate, say I had better leave things alone till some operation is imperative, and meanwhile I am to remain within close touch of medical aid. I do not know what I shall do about going home at the week-ends, as one is so cut off there, but I think I shall risk it and trust to getting somebody to motor me down [to Pietermaritzburg] if I am taken bad there. It is all rather disgusting, after being in England last year and thinking that I was put right at any rate for a few years.' [His stay at Addington Hospital cost him only 14/– per day, 'which covered doctor and everything!']

It will be noticed, from what Charles says in this letter, that he had not yet bought a motor car; but horse-drawn vehicles were beginning to disappear from the South African scene in the country districts as well as in the towns. He had noted in *April, 1914*:

'I hear that the Durban Corporation, who used to be our best customer for horses, are reducing their horse establishment very much, and going in for more motor traction.'

The pace of life was quickening, and the things of the nineteenth-century were soon to be swept into oblivion in South Africa as in the whole of the Western world.

223

CHAPTER FIFTEEN

THE FIRST SEVEN MONTHS of *1914* had been marred for
Charles by poor health, and for South Africa by political
unrest. There had been a Union-wide strike by white railway
employees early in the year, and the Government had declared
martial law, called up 60,000 men of the Defence Force and
commandos and compelled the strike leaders to surrender. At
the same time Gandhi had stirred up the Transvaal Indians'
resistance to discriminatory laws, to the point where it became
an international affair and the Viceroy of India had intervened.

By *August* the threat of further railway strikes had disappeared.
The Indian agitation had subsided too, as General Smuts and
Gandhi – two remarkable men who recognised each other's
genius – had met for discussions which resulted in the amendment of certain Transvaal legislation. The Mahatma had left
South Africa for ever, feeling that he had won a victory over his
wily opponent.

The skies seemed to have cleared in the south, but in the north
they had grown ominously darker week by week and people had
been predicting the outbreak of hostilities in Europe in which
South Africa might become involved. The German Kaiser,
Wilhelm II, had long been building up his fleet and army, and
by *August 3rd* had attacked Russia and ordered his troops into
France and Belgium. Britain sent him an ultimatum demanding
the maintenance of Belgian neutrality, and when it expired at
midnight on *August 4th* all hope of peace had fled: Great Britain
and Germany were at war. The governments of the Dominions
of Canada, Australia and New Zealand at once pledged their
support for the Mother Country, as did the South African
government led by Louis Botha.

Charles and Effie were at an agricultural show at New
Hanover a week after war had been declared, and Charles wrote
to tell his sister how his constituents there had taken the news:

225

'My German friends were rather down on their luck. They say they are quite willing to do what is required by the Union, but they do not want to be called out to fight their own people, which I think is only natural.'

He continued:

'There is to be a great meeting in the Town Hall tonight, to proclaim the patriotism of Pietermaritzburg. I shall go but not speak, as I do not approve of flag-wagging unless there is some object to be gained. Prices of provisions have gone up one third. No sale for our main products – diamonds, feathers, wattle-bark [used in tanning] and wool. Germany was our best customer for the two latter. We are cutting down all expenditure on new works and in every direction. The old Kruger mint in Pretoria is to start again in a fortnight if we are not able to ship the gold output. All our news is most rigidly censored, we are hungering for news of what has happened in the North Sea.'

The few British troops still in South Africa were being recalled to Europe, and it was clear to Charles that his country would in future have to defend herself without outside aid. He wrote:

'I expect Rowan will be called out when the troops leave, [Rowan was a member of the Active Citizen Force] and I shall not be able to avail myself of Pat during his absence, as he is far too busy.'

Fortunately Margaret, who was now sixty years old, was in good health and doing as much as ever to help run the farm. In a letter written about this time her husband said:

'Madge is going to the fat-stock show at Mooi River today, though she is not showing her ox; she wants to see how he compares with the fat-stock shown there.'

The British Government had asked General Botha to equip an expedition to conquer the German colony of South West Africa, and the Premier readily agreed as the German troops stationed there were a serious threat to the Union's security. But Charles's comment was:

August 25th: 'Here we have the Defence Force called out again, in addition to the formation of a Volunteer regiment to be called "Natal Light Horse". Rowan and Keith are both down here [Keith had left school only the year before], encamped in the

226

Park with the Carbineers. They are waiting to be properly equipped, and then, report says, they are to be taken round to Swakopmund and fight their way in from there. I can only hope it is not true, as I consider it utter madness. Much better wait till the Germans attack us; as old Kruger said, "Wait till the tortoise puts out its head..." ' ["and then chop it off"; President Kruger had made this celebrated remark before the Jameson Raid, while waiting for the *Uitlanders*' Reform Committee to make some fatal blunder.]

He was having a wretched time, anxious about Rowan and Keith, and ill again; he had had to go down to Durban for more treatment for his old complaint. His only crumb of comfort was the fact that he had found a suitable man to help Margaret with the farming at 'Strathearn'.

September 8th: 'Both Rowan and Keith have had to go off with the Carbineers. They left suddenly on Saturday night with no information as to where they were bound for, after being camped in Pietermaritzburg for fourteen days. I know their destination, but cannot tell . . . in my opinion it is simply criminal to send raw, untrained boys there, not so much on account of anything they may have to do in the way of fighting, but on account of the climate . . . The natives [in Natal] are a bit scared, naturally, seeing all the Defence Force turned out . . . but there is no fear of scarcity for them, as mealies are plentiful and cheap.'

Botha's decision to take South West Africa had been welcomed by many South Africans, but a certain section among the Afrikaners was bitterly opposed to it. The leader of this dissident group, General Christiaan Beyers, happened to be in a particularly strong position as he was Commandant-General of South Africa's armed forces at this time. He had visited Germany, and as a result of German intrigue had returned home determined to bring about a rebellion in the army; he knew that many Afrikaners were longing to avenge themselves of their defeat by Britain in the Boer War.

Beyers persuaded old General De la Rey to help him raise the revolt, and they met in Pretoria on *September 15th, 1914.* They were on their way to Potchefstroom, where commandos, armed and ready, were awaiting the word to rise, when they encountered a road-block set up by the police to intercept a notorious band of criminals called the 'Foster Gang', which was terrorising the Rand. The car in which the two rebel leaders were travelling did not stop on command, and a shot fired at the tyres ricochetted, struck De la Rey, and killed him instantly. His death was a blow to Beyers, but he went ahead with his plans with the support of another famous guerilla leader, the daring General Christiaan de Wet.

Charles's sister had met Beyers on a voyage some years before, and was of course interested to hear of his activities.

September 22nd: 'You will have seen what a traitorous knave your friend Beyers has turned out. He is now busy stirring up the backveld Boers. Why the bullet which killed the fine old De la Rey should not have taken Beyers, is one of those dispensations of Providence that one cannot understand. Anyway, it [the rebellion] is going to cost South Africa a lot.

'Rowan and Keith are still in Cape Town. At first, for some extraordinary reason, they had 3,000 of them on the *Gascon* without room to turn, but later they camped them out on land. From all I can hear, the organisation, or rather want of it, is shocking, very different from when we had our own Natal organisation.'

October 7th: 'Rowan and Keith sailed for Walfisch Bay on Tuesday, from Cape Town. The more one hears of that country [S.W.A.] the more one regrets that the Imperial Government should ever have asked Botha to conquer it. For sixty miles in from the coast it is a waterless desert, and how our men are ever to get across that, with a well-mounted, well-armed force with superior artillery to anything that we have opposing them, I do not know. But it is no good grumbling . . . .

'I have got to go up to Pretoria tonight, to try and screw some money out of the Treasury to go on with our public works. It is a nuisance having to go, but luckily I am feeling much better and stronger, and I am taking Plowman and a saloon.' [Administrator's private coach on the train.]

The rebellion spread very quickly, and Botha mustered forces to crush it and took the field in person. The loyalists fought fierce battles with the rebels and their German allies, and although they had notable successes in the northern Cape the position in the Transvaal and O.F.S. became very grave, with insurgent bands roving about, commandeering horses, saddles, rifles and provisions.

October 28th: 'We do not know where we stand here; my own opinion is that a very large number of the Dutch are passive rebels, and a few active. The response to Botha's call has been very poor in spite of the newspaper reports.'

'We have heard from Rowan and Keith at Luderitz Bay, where there are 6,000 troops. It is a ghastly hole, no water for sixty miles, and entirely dependent on condensed sea-water, of which there is a very poor supply. The idea is, I believe, to rebuild the railway which the Germans have destroyed as they advance, so as to get water, and make for the junction at Seeheim . . . while Botha advances from Upington [in Cape Province] to which the railway from Prieska is being pushed on. He will have the same difficulty about water . . . as the Germans have destroyed or polluted the few water holes there are. And all the time these forces will be subject to attacks from an enemy well mounted and who know every water hole. Anyway, I hope nothing happens to Botha; were it not for his personal influence we should have had a civil war after De la Rey's funeral.

'You ask if the latter would have been with us; from what I gathered in Pretoria, the old man had gone off his head a bit, he used to sit all day with the Bible in front of him, and though Botha's influence prevented him being openly disloyal he was certainly not on our side.

'I made out my journey to Pretoria all right, and got some money to go on with our [Provincial] works. Botha is looking much thinner, Smuts the same as usual as if he had not a care – wonderful but untrustworthy man, perhaps untrustworthy is not what I mean; *whose word no man relied on* is better.'

October 27th: 'Well, we are going through bad times, what the result is to be no-one can say, and Botha does not know from day to day upon whom he may rely. The line is still open to Pretoria, but we may be cut off at any moment . . . we are still having good rains and everybody would be planting were it not for this unrest . . . Plowman has just been in about the Civil Servants forming a town guard, but as the only weapons we have available are a hundred carbines and we have requests for weapons from all parts I do not think much will come of it. Unfortunately, at the time of the Railway Strike in *January*, 60,000 rifles were issued to the burghers, and the men that have been sent to German S.W.A. have taken a lot. I wish we had them back from Luderitz; much more need of them here now.' [The rebels numbered about 7,000 Free Staters and some 3,000 Transvaalers.]

In *October* loyal troops under General Botha routed Beyers near Rustenburg, and the rebels in the Cape were quelled; two of Beyers's firmest supporters, Generals Kemp and Muller, were heavily defeated in the Transvaal. By *November* only one rebel leader, Christiaan de Wet, remained undefeated, but his influence was immense.

November 9th: 'The steamers' departure from Cape Town is still very erratic, and now we have the additional risk of the trains being stopped by De Wet and his friends. Truly, we are an unfortunate country, between wars and diseases it is marvellous how we progress at all ... There is a muster of all the men in Nottingham Road district today, to see who have rifles and horses ready to turn out. I hope they do not have to go, but there is no saying how far De Wet's rebellion may spread.'

November 17th: 'Things are not at all bright here, I do not like Botha being in the field in person, if anything were to happen to him there is not a man who could fill his place. Even here in Natal the Dutch are not to be trusted, though not actively hostile they will not fight against the rebels. There is talk that the troops are coming back from Luderitz.'

By this time heavy fighting had taken place in Europe. The German armies had marched deeper into France, there had been desperate battles at Mons, Le Cateau and on the Marne, the Russians had been defeated at Tannenberg, and Turkey had allied herself with Germany. Charles commented:

'I see the Staffords, which were the last regiment stationed here, have lost a lot of officers. Their long casualty list makes one wonder what England is going to do for officers even if the men are forthcoming.'

South Africa's own troubles were nearly over. De Wet's 3,500 mounted rebels were decisively beaten at Mushroom

Valley in the Free State at the end of *November*, and he fled with a handful of followers; he was pursued by loyalists in a motorised column, and captured on *December 2nd*. General Beyers was drowned while attempting to escape across the flooded Vaal River.

December 13th: 'We have had some very heavy rains, quite phenomenal ... however, as they had the good result of drowning Beyers one cannot grumble. The only pity is that De Wet was not disposed of in the same way, as it is a difficult question what to do with him.

'I do not know what they intend doing about a session of the Union Parliament: between deaths and rebellion there are about ten seats vacant. There is a good deal of unemployment in Durban, and the Labour men are wanting the Corporation and the Province to start relief works, but as the trade unions will not allow their men to take anything less than the standard wage I am not prepared to do anything beyond the works on the estimates.'

At the end of *December* Charles wrote:

'We had rather a quiet Christmas, only Mungo and Pat here of the boys, but all the girls. I am quite in agreement with the saying, "A son is a son till he gets him a wife, but a daughter's a daughter all the days of her life".' [He was pleased that May and Camilla came to 'Strathearn' as often as they could, with their families; he and Margaret adored their grandchildren.]

The thoughts of all were, of course, with Rowan and Keith in South West Africa:

'They had both been in this last skirmish where, as far as I can make out, had it not been for one of the Germans' guns going off too soon, our men would have ridden right into an ambush. They [the Germans] have an aeroplane dropping bombs among them, but no harm done so far.'

The news that the enemy possessed air power of a sort was disturbing, and Charles was glad to be able to report, early in *1915:*

'I see an Aviation corps has been started, so we will be able to return the German compliments.' [The South African Aviation Corps, renamed in *1920* the South African Air Force, made a very successful debut during the operations in South

231

West Africa; it had only seventeen officers and a hundred and fifty other ranks, flying four Henry Farmons and two other primitive aircraft, but flew 10,000 miles during the campaign.]

On *February 23rd, 1915*, he was writing of the visit to Pietermaritzburg of a party of Belgian delegates who were currently touring South Africa to collect relief funds for a million of their countrymen made homeless by the war. There had been accounts in the newspapers of German atrocities in Belgium:

'The Belgian delegates had a crowded meeting in the Town Hall, but I think the audience came to hear something "bluggy" but were disappointed as the delegates did not expatiate on the horrors as they did at some places . . . we can only hope that Germany may before the finish have a little experience itself of the horrors of war. I wish Italy would make up its mind to join.' [Italy declared war on Austria in *mid-May, 1915.*]

Meanwhile the Union troops based on Luderitz in South West Africa were forcing their way inland:

March 9th: 'They have got to within about twenty miles of the end of the sand desert, but are faced with a very strongly fortified position at Aus, which can only be reached through a pass, and which they cannot get round as they cannot leave the railway for water supply . . . it must be galling to see the Germans pulling up the railway in front of them and dynamiting everything which they have laboriously to repair.'

April 6th: 'I am glad that they have taken Aus without a fight, as that is the beginning of the better country, with trees and grass.'

From this point the mounted men would make for Gibeon, to the north-east; this Southern force was commanded by General Smuts.

Botha, leading the Northern force, had landed at Walvis Bay further up the coast and had advanced on Windhoek in a series of forced marches which were exhausting for his soldiers and their horses and mules but gave the Germans no time to regroup. He was a clever strategist.

Charles studied every move in the campaign with the keenest interest. He had not much Provincial work to do just now:

'We are doing nothing in the way of capital expenditure.

Very little general business, but . . . the usual number of stupid questions to be answered or evaded. The Union Treasurer has announced the increase of the Income Tax to a minimum of 1/– in the £ on incomes over £300, increasing on a sliding scale to 2/– in the £, and the Customs duties are to be put up to 20% ad valorem. I do not intend to introduce any Provincial taxation.'

April 21st, 1915, was Charles's sixty-third birthday:

'As a birthday present I have received a letter from the Government, asking me to continue in the office of Administrator on the understanding that if Parliament should abolish the office at any time I should not make any claim for compensation in respect of any unexpired period. I rather reluctantly am writing to say that I will accept. Though I would rather go home, I feel that with my large family I am not justified in giving up £2,000 per annum when offered to me, and when I cannot stand it any longer I can resign. My health is so much better that I cannot make that an excuse, and after all I suppose I must look on it as a compliment that my administration has been satisfactory.'

South Africa's Southern Force in South West Africa captured Gibeon as planned, but only after stiff fighting:

May 24th: 'We had an anxious time on Monday till the lists appeared of the casualties . . . at Gibeon. We heard from the boys just before they left Garub that they were starting off in heavy marching order, with two days' rations for themselves and their horses. Rowan said the saddles were so heavy they could hardly lift them on to their horses.'

With South African troops pressing them relentlessly from south and west, the Germans retreated northwards. After the fall of Windhoek in *May* they withdrew first to Omaruru, then to Otavi, and finally to Tsumeb.

Charles had had postcards from Rowan and Keith, which told something of the hardships the young men had endured:

'They are still very badly off for any food except mutton, with goat for a change, and Rowan says that even Magindan [an old Zulu living on 'Strathearn'] would look with scorn on their clothes, which are simply rags.'

News from the South West African front was temporarily

overshadowed, later in *May*, by a report from overseas of the torpedoing of the liner *Lusitania* by the Germans; the ship had been sunk off the west coast of Ireland, and two thousand passengers, many of them children, had died. The incident led to violent scenes in Natal, where mobs took revenge on local German residents:

May 18th: 'There have been lively times here. On Thursday . . . a public holiday . . . a mob composed mostly of railway men started destroying the stores of those they thought were Germans . . . Durban was still worse, as they burnt a lot of stores there, among them G – – 's [he mentioned the name of a member of the Provincial Council], but as he was insured against riot with a British company for £80,000 the loss falls on them. Many stores were burnt that did not belong to Germans at all, one very large warehouse belonging to a Dutch company, but the mob does not discriminate. I think it is all over now, but it has shown up the Britisher in a very bad light. We have now had three riots in the last eighteen months – the railway strike riots, the O.F.S. rebellion, and now this. We shall very soon descend to the level of a South American republic . . . May and Ken were down in Durban all through the riots there, and the hotel next to that in which they were staying was destroyed.'

In *June* Charles entertained Viscount Buxton, South Africa's second Governor-General and High Commissioner; he was 'bombarded' with requests for invitations to official dinners and At Homes. 'I think Buxton is an improvement on Gladstone, not quite such a stick, and has rather a humorous vein in his speeches.'

He was far more interested in the return of the troops from South West Africa than in the Buxtons:

June 15th: 'The Natal Light Horse . . . returned here last week . . . and a lot of the Transvaal and Cape men have been sent home, so we are hoping that the Carbineers may soon return . . . It is time that Botha was back to look after his political interests, I am very much afraid that unless by his personal influence he can turn the tide among the Dutch, the next elections which are due to take place at the end of the year will go against him. We British, instead of joining together to support [his South African Party] are running a third party who call themselves Unionists, and who have not a chance of making themselves felt except that they may run three-cornered contests which will result in Labour men getting in.' [The Unionists eventually joined an enlarged South African Party.]

Charles felt it was a pity that the British newspapers eulogised General Botha, 'as it is all cabled out here and furnishes fuel to the fire of the Dutch [i.e. Afrikaner Nationalists] against him.'

July 6th: 'I got a wire from Rowan . . . saying that they had just arrived at Windhoek, both well, and . . . were to be sent home on *Tuesday 10th.* Botha seems to have driven the Germans right up to the end of the railway now, and they will surely have to make a stand soon.' [The general received the Germans' unconditional surrender on *July 9th.*]

'There is a great deal of talk about sending a contingent to Europe, my own opinion is we want all our men here to keep the rebel Boers in order, to say nothing of the natives. It is all very well for Canada and Australia to send men, but we are in a very different position and it would not be much advantage to the Empire if we sent a contingent and lost South Africa. The whole of the Free State, the greater part of the Transvaal, a large part of Cape Colony, and every Dutchman in Natal are rebels at heart and hate us nearly as much as the Germans do.'

The South African contingent for Europe, to which he was referring, was to be raised at the suggestion of Louis Botha, whose offer of help had been gladly received by Britain; the general saw the Great War in its true perspective, and realised that it was entirely in South Africa's interest to support the Allies in every possible way. The contingent was to consist of a brigade of four infantry battalions with heavy artillery, signals and field ambulances, and was to be commanded by Brigadier-General Henry Timson Lukin, Inspector-General of the Union Defence Force. Initially about 15% of the men were Afrikaners, the rest English-speaking, but by the end of the war the proportion of Afrikaner volunteers had risen to about 30%.

The brigade was not due to sail for England until *September* or *October*, as the remainder of the Union troops still in South West Africa would not be back for several weeks. The Natal Carbineers returned before the end of *July*, and their arrival in

Pietermaritzburg was celebrated by 'a thanksgiving service and address by Lord Buxton in Alexandra Park . . . he having motored up from Durban with his wife and daughters'. The Smythes rejoiced to see Rowan and Keith again, and plans were made for the former to resume farming 'Strathearn' and his younger brother to join Mungo at 'Howard'. Neither said anything about wanting to sign on for further service, and it did not occur to their father that they might choose to go overseas.

Charles had not lost sight, all these months, of what was happening on the Western Front in France and in the other theatres of war; in *March* the battle of Neuve Chapelle had been fought, in *April* landings were made at Gallipoli and the Germans used poison-gas for the first time at Ypres.

August 3rd: 'It is too sickening to read the long list of casualties [in France], and we seem to get no further forward. [British losses in 1915 were 73,160 killed, and nearly 240,000 wounded of whom many died later.] There is to be a great meeting here tomorrow, to affirm our loyalty to the Empire and determination to help to carry the war to a successful termination.'

Bice had asked about his German constituents at New Hanover, and he told her:

'The very large majority of them have been naturalised, and unless they have done something wrong are allowed to go about as usual. A few of the unnaturalised ones have been interned in Pietermaritzburg, where we have 4,000 altogether from different parts of South Africa. Others are allowed to go about under bonds for good behaviour. The internment camp has been quite a boon to Pietermaritzburg in these bad times, not only the money spent on and by the prisoners, but there is a regiment called the Veteran Regiment of about 1,200 men to guard them. This is composed of all the old scallywags and stoney brokes in the country, but they are quite good enough for the job.'

In *September*, when the South African military contingent was about to sail for England, Patrick and his brother Rowan announced that they too intended to join up and take part in the fighting in Europe. The news hit Charles very hard, and although he could not have prevented their going he insisted that they serve as officers and not in the ranks. He told his sister:

September 14th: 'Pat and Rowan want to go to serve in Europe, I am not in favour of it, but of course shall put no obstacle in their way, only I object to their going as privates. You may say it is snobbishness on my part, but it is a different thing serving out here as a trooper when all your friends are doing the same, and it is the law, to going to serve as a private in Europe. I am going to send a cable to David, to ask him what chance they would have of getting commissions in either cavalry or Highlanders. A lot of men have gone from here not as well qualified, and have got commissions.'

Charles's letter continued with a complaint that conscientious objectors in Britain were too leniently treated, and he ended with:

'I will not say anything more except this, that with 75% of the Dutch population in passive rebellion, and a native population outnumbering us in Natal by ten to one, who are only watching events, we are allowing our young men to leave the country.'

He signed himself, 'Your rather disgusted brother'.

David Smythe promised his help, (he had retired from the Black Watch with the honorary rank of Colonel), and Charles told Bice:

'Pat and Rowan will probably sail from here [i.e. Durban] on *October 31st.* They want to get commissions in a Highland regiment, the Black Watch for choice. It is a great nuisance their going away, but I cannot stand in their way if they think it is their duty to go. [Pat was twenty-four, Rowan just twenty-three.] I do not know what I shall do about somebody to look after "Strathearn".' [Keith came, though he was very inexperienced.]

It was bad enough having to part with two sons, but to Charles's indignation he now heard that 'Meta had some idea that she ought to go to Europe as a nurse!' He was the typical Victorian father, and his reaction was predictable:

'I promptly suppressed that.'

Poor Meta dared not bring up the subject again.

It was at about this time that Charles read a newspaper

report stating that of fifty-four British officers killed in battle no less than seventeen were only sons, and this roused him to let fly at the British social system of his youth:

'Well, Britain is paying the penalty now for her shortcomings of the past. It was not fashionable to marry early, and it was expensive to have large families. The "classes" [the upper class] did neither. I won't say more, though it is a subject I feel very strongly on when I see our Dutch and German fellow-colonists with their large families, who by force of numbers are bound soon to oust us because the British here suffer from the same complaint as at Home. "A baby fourteen months after another! Oh, shocking!! Think of the poor mother, and how is the father going to pay for the maintenance of such a family!" I know they said it about me, and now they say it about Edric. I say "Carry on!" Now I have rather let my pen run away with me . . . perhaps I am feeling bitter as the time approaches for Pat and Rowan going away.'

Sick at heart, he had one thing at least to console him: ' "Strathearn" is very pretty just now, the orchard a blaze of blossom and the broom hedge to the road a yellow mass!'

The thought of his sons' imminent departure did not lessen his concern over the possible outcome of the South African General Election to be held that year. It was with relief that he was able to report, on *October 26th:*

'I am thankful the elections have gone as well as they have.' [His fears had not been realised, for Botha's South African Party had won 54 seats as against the Nationalists' 27. The Unionists had 40 seats, Labour 3 and Independents 6.]

Charles distinguished between the supporters of the various political parties as follows:

'The South African Party is the moderate man who recognises that this country cannot be governed without the aid of both Dutch and English, needless to say I belong to that section. The Unionists are the blatant Britishers who want everything done in the British way, and the bulk of whom live in the towns, and the Nationalists of course are the extreme Dutch who think the Dutch should be top dog and that the British are intruders.'

He regarded himself as entirely South African now; Britain seemed almost a foreign land, though from force of habit he

238

still referred to it as 'Home'. This explains his telling Bice, just before Pat and Rowan sailed for Europe at the end of *October*:

'I did not mind David going out in the Boer War, or Oswald in the native rebellion, or Rowan and Keith to S.W.A., because I recognised that those were all our own jobs, but I do feel . . . that the rich man ought to use his own flocks and herds before he calls on me to provide my "ewe lambs", however willing they may be to go.'

He was thinking illogically, letting his emotions overcome his common sense for once, for he knew in his heart – as Pat and Rowan did – that Britain was in desperate need of troops, and that if Germany won the war South Africa would fall into her hands and everything he valued would be lost.

So great, in fact, was Britain's need of men at this time, that South Africa was now asked to supply an expeditionary force of mounted men and infantry to help overcome German resistance in Tanganyika, or 'German East Africa' as it was called.

November 23rd: 'There is a great stir on about recruiting for East Africa. I have to speak at a meeting on Thursday night, much against my will as I am no good at flag-wagging.'

He got a rough reception, as he later reported:

'The crowd would not listen to me last week in the Town Hall, there was a strong Labour element with whom I am not a *persona grata*, and as I had a very bad cold and could not make myself heard they made such a row that I retired. This voluntary recruiting is a rotten business. There was no trouble when they turned out the men for South West Africa, under the Defence Act, but now there is any amount of trouble and ill-feeling.'

December 21st: 'I feel too sick this morning at seeing that our troops have been withdrawn from Anzac and Suvla Bay [in Gallipoli], leaving their thousands of dead behind them, as far as I can see, not being a strategist, absolutely wasted.'

Reverting to the subject of the East African campaign, he wrote:

'I believe the East African contingent are to leave Durban on *January 6th*. I should have felt easier about them if they had

239

been under a Colonial rather than Imperial officer, but that, I have no doubt, is prejudice on my part.' [The command was entrusted initially to Britain's General Smith-Dorrien; when he was needed in France General Smuts took command.]

On Christmas Day an overseas cable reached 'Strathearn' from Patrick and Rowan, who were now in Scotland. It told the family that they had been given commissions in the regiment of their choice, The Black Watch.

CHAPTER SIXTEEN

February 16th: 'The last of the East African contingent sailed from Durban yesterday . . . there were 3,000 of them on the one ship, so they would be pretty glad to get to the end of their voyage, which takes about six days . . . everyone here is very pleased that Smuts has been given command in German East. He is a real hustler, and will push things along if it is at all possible. He sailed on Saturday.'

So wrote Charles Smythe early in *1916*. He reported that horses were in great demand in South Africa at that time, as most of the troops going to Tanganyika were mounted men. At a big sale of horses held at Nottingham Road there had been literally hundreds of remounts standing in long lines:

'I believe the military people bought a lot at very good prices for East Africa, where I suppose they will live for [only] a short time.' [As he predicted, horse-sickness took a tragic toll during the campaign, and more than three thousand animals died.]

By a strange coincidence South African troops were fighting in North Africa at the same time as their compatriots were starting their drive against the Germans on the eastern shores of the continent: the South African Infantry Brigade, which had spent two months training in Britain, was now taking part in operations in Egypt.

With so much going on on the various battle fronts Charles found it difficult to concentrate on matters of purely local interest when the Provincial Council session opened that year. It seemed to him almost frivolous to spend hours debating such subjects as, for instance, the future of the big game in Zululand – and yet the large herds of elephants, buffalo, hippo and antelope still found there did much damage to crops and something would have to be done about them. Conservationists wanted to save the animals, but Charles came to the conclusion,

241

regretfully, that farming interests were paramount and that the game would have to go. He did not live to see the creation of the huge Zululand nature reserves of Hluhluwe, Umfolosi, and Mkuzi, where wild life was secure and where the rare white rhino, whose numbers had dwindled almost to the point of extinction, could breed again in safety.

South Africa's Provincial Councils were themselves in danger of extinction in *1916*, as he told his sister:

'They may be abolished by next year, though . . . it is difficult to know what they could be replaced by.

'The Transvaal have made a bad hash of theirs, they got a Labour majority in, who passed free education and free hospitals, with the result of a deficit of £200,000, and this has raised a good deal of opposition to the system.'

He could not keep his thoughts off the greater issues for long, for by the beginning of *May* the reports from East Africa were disheartening:

'The wet weather has set in there, and I am afraid we are having a good deal of malaria among our men. [Casualties due to disease were heavy in this campaign.] When one thinks that the country is bigger than the Union, it means a tough proposition even to get the men over it, without counting German opposition.'

But the East African affair was nothing compared with what was happening further north:

May 23rd: 'There seems to be a frightful slaughter going on on all the European fronts.'

In France a big German offensive had begun on *February 21st*, and the battle of Verdun had claimed thousands of lives; in the east, the Russians were taking tremendous punishment. The South African Brigade, which had left Egypt in *April*, was now in France as part of an otherwise wholly Scottish Ninth Division; it was being initiated into the horrors of trench warfare. Charles was thankful that Pat and Rowan were still in Scotland, but knew they would not be there much longer.

On *July 1st, 1916*, the terrible Battle of the Somme began, in which the South Africans were given the task of capturing Delville Wood, a position which had to be taken at all costs. They succeeded, and held for six days and five nights the most difficult post on the British front, warding off attack after attack by the crack troops of the German army; they only yielded when finally ordered to withdraw. Some idea of the ghastliness of this battle can be gauged by the fact that British losses in a single day's fighting amounted to 57,400! The South African losses had been very great, as Charles learnt to his sorrow:

July 31st: 'The casualty lists have been appalling, I think almost everyone I knew personally in the South African Brigade has been killed or wounded. I think every Government office in this building has had one or two men killed. [502 were dead, 1,735 wounded and 578 missing.] And these are all loyal men, how are we going to combat the Dutch rebels who are all sitting at home?'

The Brigade had suffered so grievously that it had to be reorganised and replacements brought in. It was soon back in the front line on the Somme, in shocking conditions of rain and mud; in ten days during *October*, casualties in the contingent amounted to 1,150.

Charles naturally thought that the Black Watch would be drafted to France, but *September* brought surprising news:

September 27th: 'We heard by the last mail that Pat and Rowan were going to Mesopotamia!'

He was not as relieved at this posting as one might have expected, as the name Mesopotamia was synonymous with lack of organisation, indescribable heat, disease and Turkish brutality. The report of the Commission which had been sent out after the surrender of Kut had been called 'the most distressing document ever submitted to Parliament'. But Charles felt that anything was better than the Western front, and commented:

'I expect they will find the heat pretty bad after Scotland, but I am just as well pleased that they are not going to winter in Flanders.'

The following month his letter to Bice told of the strenuous efforts Natal people were making to collect money for war funds; the Governor-General had set up a charity to help needy dependants of men who had been killed or disabled:

October 23rd: 'Pietermaritzburg is to hold a big War Market

243

on the *23rd* of next month. Durban made £10,000 at theirs, but I do not think Pietermaritzburg will come out as well. Durban is full of money, the port is doing as much trade as all the Cape ports and Delagoa Bay put together, and they had an enormous number of people from up-country during the winter season. We have got old Mrs. F – – [he mentioned a member of a well-known family] at "Strathearn" just now . . . she personifies Durban; well off, hates Botha, thinks Durban the hub of the universe, and utterly ignores the existence of a Dutch population in South Africa larger than the British!'

Turning to another topic he wrote:

'The kaffirs are not coming forward very fast for their contingent of 10,000 which is being got up to do dock work in France. I think the German missionaries are frightening them, as they have some most astounding yarns going about as to what will happen to them.' [Africans recruited in South Africa served as labourers in South West Africa, East Africa and France during the First World War, and 615 of them were drowned when the transport *S.S. Mendi* was sunk.]

The troopship in which Pat and Rowan were making the voyage to the Middle East called at Durban in November, and to the family's great joy the two young men managed to fit in a visit to 'Strathearn'. Oswald drove down to the port in his car to fetch them, and they reached the farm at half-past six one Saturday evening. Camilla and May had of course been told the thrilling news, ('Strathearn' had a telephone now), and they and their husbands and children had arrived, the Karkloof party in their car and the 'Steybraes' family in a 'spider' sent over for them.

'So when Pat and Rowan stepped out of Oswald's motor in their kilts and helmets, looking enormous, there was a crowd to greet them and the elasticity of "Strathearn" was tested as regards accommodation,' Charles wrote delightedly. Besides members of the family already living in the house, there were nineteen extra!

'They had to leave at 5.30 the next morning to motor to Durban by noon, [the main road was not tarred in 1916, and the going was slow] and all got up to see them off, Edric and Kate riding down [from 'Dwaleni'] . . . You may imagine the pleasure it was to us to see them, and the pride their sisters and cousins and nephews and nieces took in their appearance! They say they are frightfully crowded on board, 2,000 men and 170 officers, and the way the men are crowded and fed is disgraceful. I thought after all the Mesopotamia scandals the authorities would have been more careful . . .

'Well, it is a great thing having seen them, just a year since they left, and we can only hope we may see them again when this war is over.'

It had been a bad moment when Oswald's car disappeared from view down the drive, carrying Pat and Rowan away; as Charles took Margaret's arm and they went indoors out of the early morning sunshine they wondered if this had been their last sight of two dearly-loved sons.

It was a relief for them both to turn to farming affairs and the things of the countryside. Charles noted in his diary:

'We are shearing the sheep this week, there have been some record prices for wool, so far 22d per pound, and I remember when we thought 9d was a very good price.'

In *November* there was news that the campaign in East Africa was coming to an end; General Smuts had succeeded in driving the Germans out of their formidable positions, taken possession of Tanganyika's railways and chief towns, and only the remote southern part of the territory remained in enemy hands:

November 23rd: 'A great many men are coming back now, invalided from German East; they expect 8,000 to be back by the middle of next month. Luckily the percentage of deaths is not very high, most of the cases being malaria.'

With final victory in sight, (though the German general, Von Lettow-Vorbeck, carried on guerilla war until after the Armistice), Smuts withdrew most of his white troops and replaced them with men from India and West Africa:

'They are getting in black troops . . . up there now, which is what should have been done at first, instead of sending all these young fellows from here to have their health ruined.'

Pietermaritzburg's big War Market took place in *November*, as planned, and Charles told his sister:

'Botha and Mrs. Botha came down to do the opening . . . He is looking well but getting very stout again. He made his speech

245

in Dutch, which has given great offence to the extremists here who will not believe that he cannot express himself properly in English and that a man in his position cannot run the risk of using a wrong expression when he speaks in public.'

Charles's defence of Botha is not very convincing. One cannot help feeling that it was tactless of the Prime Minister to have spoken only in Dutch in a predominantly English town; he could have read a prepared address, carefully checked beforehand. Possibly he was hoping, by using Dutch and not repeating himself in the other official language, to win over Natal's Afrikaner minority.

Charles had a long talk with him, presumably in English, during his visit to the capital:

'He said that nobody would believe the amount of work and worry he has had to go through in the last three years. I told him I thought of resigning, at which he expressed his great regret.'

A later letter to Bice in *1916* contains Charles's comment on the British political scene, for he had just heard that David Lloyd George had become Prime Minister in succession to Asquith:

'I trust the new English Cabinet will be an improvement, there is no doubt Lloyd George has push, and that is really the great thing wanted now.'

February 14th, 1917: 'Somebody has been stringing mines quite close to the Cape, and three ships, two of them transports, have been struck but no loss of life.'

Beatrice Smythe was still living in the south of France, and Charles wrote:

'I am afraid you must be having a bad time of it; I see everything in France has advanced in price enormously. Were it not for the danger of travelling I should say "Come out here at once", as though prices have gone up there is really nothing to complain of . . . of course if this submarine business continues things may get worse, but things produced in the country are not likely to rise, and if we cannot import we will also be unable to export.'

He had had letters from Pat and Rowan from Mesopotamia,

and knew that so far both were well, although Pat wrote that he had been in the trenches. The young men had reached Mesopotamia just as the vital stage of the campaign on that front began. General Sir Stanley Maude – a tactician of genius – had taken command, transformed the port of Basra (first seized by the British in *November, 1914*, to protect the oil pipeline), and brought about an efficient system of land and river transport. After adequate preparation he had recaptured Kut from the Turks early in *1917*, and was now about to push on to Baghdad.

While his sons in the Black Watch were fighting on the Tigris, Charles was involved in a battle of a very different sort in South Africa:

February 27th, (from Mount Nelson Hotel, Cape Town):

'This unusual address is the outcome of a hurried summons to Cape Town to attend a conference of the four Administrators with the Government in regard to future Provincial financial relations. The Cape, O.F.S. and Natal are quite willing to leave things as they are, rather than risk anything by asking Parliament to make any change, [Parliament had already debated the question of the abolition of the Provincial Councils], but the Transvaal declares that it must have more revenue assigned to it, which means raising the whole question ... we have been arguing all day with no result, and can only hope that tomorrow the Government will take a stand and tell the Transvaal that if it wants more revenue it must tax itself.'

March 15th: 'The result of my visit to Cape Town was that the Provincial Councils are to continue for anyway another three years, and our financial arrangements are to continue, which is quite satisfactory from our point of view.'

By this time Charles had definitely made up his mind to retire from office 'whenever I have got the new Council through its first session, which will probably be in *June*.' At the end of *May* he would have been, as he said, 'seven years at the job'. He would celebrate his sixty-fifth birthday in *April*.

But when his birthday came round neither he nor Margaret was in the mood for celebrations, for they had had bad news:

March 29th: 'We were much concerned at getting a wire from the War Office on the *20th* to say that Rowan had been wounded on the *14th*. No particulars of any kind. We heard

247

nothing more till the *26th*, when we got a wire from Rowan dated *25th* at Basra, the port near the mouth of the Tigris, saying that he was wounded in the groin but was going on well. I sent a wire to him ... and today got a notice ... that the wire cannot be delivered as the addressee has gone to India.' [Rowan had in fact not gone to India; he remained at Basra until discharged from hospital, and then rejoined his regiment.]

Added to Charles's anxiety about his son's condition was the fear that Pat might be killed or wounded, for the British advance in Mesopotamia was in full swing now; Baghdad had fallen, after heavy fighting.

Charles gave thanks daily that none of his other sons was in danger; Mungo, who was to be married shortly, was busy repairing the iron roof of the house at 'Howard', and Keith had just finished reaping millet and teff at 'Strathearn' and had had forty or fifty Zulu women tying the sheaves at 6d per hundred. 'One woman working from sunrise to sunset tied 1,880!' Edric and his family were going up into the Drakensberg in an ox-waggon:

'He and Mungo have hired a farm for winter grazing, and Edric is taking up all the cattle with him. It is about fifty miles by road ... there is no house, but they have a tent and the waggon, and the five children, and the chance of shooting.'

In *April* Charles began to feel more cheerful, despite the fact that the terrible trench-warfare in France was as fierce as ever:

'Surely the war will come to an end soon, now that the United States has joined in and apparently the South American Republics are likely to do the same.'

Then came news which was anything but cheering:

May 1st: 'We got a cable from Simla on Saturday, to say Pat was severely wounded on *21st April*, and in hospital at Baghdad, and then we got one from Pat himself to say that it was a shrapnel wound in the chest but that it was not serious. I hope he told the truth. Anyhow, they are both out of further danger for a bit, for which one is thankful. Our last news of Rowan was "condition improved, would healing".'

Many of Charles's friends and acquaintances in Natal had heard of the death or disablement of their sons, for the South African Brigade in France, which had held trenches at Arras for three months during an appalling winter, had suffered severely in the battle which began on *April 10th*:

'Frightful casualty lists are coming in from the South African Contingent in Flanders. Jim Ross [a farmer in the Nottingham Road district] has lost two out of three sons, killed. Jim Maclean, who lives beyond Soutar, has lost both of his. It is all too sickening.'

May 16th: 'Still we have had no letters from Pat and Rowan ... we got a cable from the War Office on Monday, to say Pat had been moved from Baghdad to Kut-el-Amara ...

'I see they are making a tin god of Smuts in England; what extraordinary people they are!' [Charles never liked General Smuts.]

By the end of *May* his old complaint had begun to trouble him again, and he knew his health was deteriorating:

May 29th: 'I have not been very well lately, and the least bit of a chill seems to upset me. I have now ... settled to retire ... directly the new Provincial Council has finished its session ... Of course in a way one is sorry to sever oneself from the whole business, but I feel that it is not fair on the Province to keep on when I am not able to go about and do things that an Administrator ought to do. The faithful Plowman is much distressed and much against my resigning, but I think I have convinced him that it is my duty ...'

He was grateful for the help Effie gave him:

'This is Effie's birthday (40). To think that I should have a daughter of those mature years! She is a most capable woman, and I do not know how I should get on without her.'

On *June 27th* came a cable to say that Pat was in hospital in Bombay, and that Rowan had been discharged from hospital at Kut. A letter from Pat followed, giving details of his wound: a piece of shrapnel had passed right through his left arm, penetrated his armpit and lodged itself in his chest, where it remained. He was given sick leave until *September 8th*, and to the great delight of everyone at 'Strathearn' was allowed to spend it in South Africa.

After a few weeks at home he went down to Durban to be examined by a medical board on *September 7th*, and was given a further month's leave.

249

'He brought back an X-ray photo showing very clearly the shrapnel bullet lying under his ribs close to his heart. That apparently is why they are afraid to try and take it out.'

Pat was a tall, handsome young man, and looked splendid in officer's uniform. Said his father, proudly:

'How the young ladies of Durban admired him and his kilt, and needless to say Iris was a proud girl when she walked the streets of Maritzburg with her kilted brother.'

Charles was on sick-leave himself while his son was at home. He was to have taken three months off work, but as he was no better this was extended at the Prime Minister's request:

'Botha is very desirous that I should not resign at the end of October, but that I should take another three months' leave in the hope of getting better, but I know it is quite useless; however, he is to write to me and I am not to do anything definite till I hear from him.'

The highlight of Pat's stay at Nottingham Road was Mungo's wedding, at which he acted best man. He looked forward to another fortnight at home, but on the very day after the wedding he had a telephone message from Durban telling him to report there immediately for embarkation on the big transport, *Empress of Britain*. He left in a great hurry, and Charles wrote in his diary, 'So we have seen the last of him for a time.'

Rowan, completely recovered from his wound, was in action again in Mesopotamia:

October 16th: 'Got a letter from Rowan this morning, of *24th August*, he says it is getting a bit cooler, which is a good thing. I am sorry that he did not stick to his billet as Commandant of Samarra [a town on the Tigris, north of Baghdad], as though it may not have been as pleasant as being with the regiment these sort of jobs are the way to get on.'

Pat was now in India, doing light duty at Bangalore.

Charles remained quietly at home for the rest of the year, growing steadily weaker, as all could see; Margaret and his children were desperately worried about his state of health. He was depressed at the thought that his political career was all but over – it was petering out, rather than ending with a flourish – and George Plowman had taken on his work. The newspapers which he still studied carefully gave him no comfort, for in France the battle of Third Ypres, remembered today by the grim name of Passchendaele, had been raging ever since the *31st July* and would last until *mid-November* when British casualties in three and a half months reached the shocking figure of 245,000. The South African Brigade was in the front line in *September* and *October*, and suffered heavily; it was destined to add to the laurels it had won so gloriously at Delville Wood, when in *March* of the following year at the Battle of Marrières Wood it delayed the German advance at its most critical point.

In Natal, Nature took a hand in creating chaos and misery in the spring of *1917*, for the season was the wettest Charles had known during the forty-five years he had been in the country:

'Floods caused great damage, especially on the coast where the Umgeni railway bridge [at Durban] was swept away, along with many others. The pipeline carrying the Durban water supply from the Umlaas was carried away in five different places, and for four days [in October] not a drop could be got in the town except what came off the roofs.'

For weeks afterwards the townspeople had to depend on unfiltered water from the rivers – a hazard to health – until a safe supply could be restored.

Charles's sister Bice received few letters from him in the first two months of *1918*, but on *March 3rd* he wrote:

'This is Sunday afternoon, and I have put off writing to you and must now make the effort. I have just been reminding the family that forty-three years ago today I rode up to "Lynedoch", journeying through the country with no particular object in view, in fact quite at a loose end, and there I remained.'

What images passed before his eyes as he laid down his pen! He remembered so clearly his first sight of Margaret on that day in *1875* – a golden-haired girl coming out to greet him as he rode in at her father's gate – and now she was an elderly woman with eighteen grandchildren. Eighteen, was it, or nineteen? He wasn't sure; the number was increasing so fast.

On *April 12th* he wrote to Bice for the last time:

'The voice is the voice of C.J.S., but the hand is that of Iris ... it's about all I can do now to sign a cheque, much less write

251

a letter. Plowman is making a very good Administrator.'

Incurable illness had laid such a hold on Charles that the family realised the end must come soon. He hobbled about with the aid of two sticks for as long as he could, but he was getting more and more frail and at length took to his bed. Margaret nursed him devotedly, although the strain was very great.

On *May 15th, 1918,* he died.

Six months later Margaret received news of Pat's death from pneumonia in Egypt, just after the Armistice which ended the war.

Meta wrote to her Aunt Bice, on *May 17th, 1918:*

'You will have heard long ere this that Father is no longer with us in the flesh, but we have the consolation of knowing that he is with us still in the spirit. The end was very peaceful, he just slept away, as it were; he became unconscious about three in the afternoon, never regaining consciousness, and died at twenty to eleven that night. The blankness of everything now is more awful than I can express.'

Meta had the greatest admiration for her mother's fortitude and loving care of Charles. She said, simply, 'Only a brave, devoted wife could have held out as she has done.'

The funeral took place privately at 'Strathearn', and Charles was laid to rest in a quiet spot shaded by the pine and oak trees he had planted, and where the silence was broken only by the sounds he had loved to hear: the cries of wild birds, the distant farmyard noises of cattle and sheep and horses, the laughter of children playing in the sunshine. (In time Margaret, who survived him by a few years, was buried there beside him.)

Tributes to Charles's achievements reached his family from many parts of South Africa; his work as Prime Minister and Colonial Secretary of Natal before Union was recalled, and his wise guidance of the Province's affairs as Administrator after *1910.* People remembered him as a kind, charming, unfailingly courteous man, modest and reserved but extremely efficient in all he did. Effie told Aunt Bice that every class of person had sent messages of sympathy, not only the whites but the Indians and Africans too. 'It is nice to know how much our dear Father was appreciated' she said.

But it was the local Zulus, with their deep feeling for family unity, who understood perhaps better than anyone else, just what the loss of a husband and father meant to the Smythes of 'Strathearn'. In a letter to Bice, Meta described how, two days after Charles's passing, a group of his tenants and farm-labourers had come to see her mother and pay their respects. She wrote:

'Today all the native men and women came to offer their sympathy. One man spoke so well, he said, (in his own language), "It is very terrible when the main prop that supports the hut is taken away, but we hope that the lesser posts will stand firm".

'Quite beautifully expressed, I think.'

CHARLES SMYTHE'S DESCENT FROM WILLIAM THE SILENT

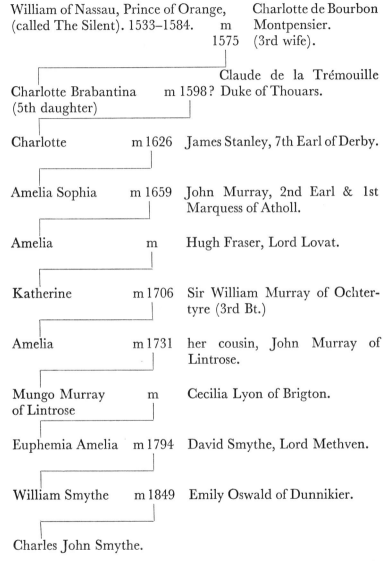

William of Nassau, Prince of Orange, (called The Silent). 1533–1584.   m 1575   Charlotte de Bourbon Montpensier. (3rd wife).

Charlotte Brabantina (5th daughter)   m 1598?   Claude de la Trémouille Duke of Thouars.

Charlotte   m 1626   James Stanley, 7th Earl of Derby.

Amelia Sophia   m 1659   John Murray, 2nd Earl & 1st Marquess of Atholl.

Amelia   m   Hugh Fraser, Lord Lovat.

Katherine   m 1706   Sir William Murray of Ochtertyre (3rd Bt.)

Amelia   m 1731   her cousin, John Murray of Lintrose.

Mungo Murray of Lintrose   m   Cecilia Lyon of Brigton.

Euphemia Amelia   m 1794   David Smythe, Lord Methven.

William Smythe   m 1849   Emily Oswald of Dunnikier.

Charles John Smythe.

Note: Cousin-marriages between the descendants of William's third wife, Charlotte, and fourth wife, Louise, brought forth the *House of Orange* we know today.

The SMYTHE OF METHVEN coat of arms is as follows:

'Az, a burning cup between two chess-rooks in fesse or'.

The crest is 'a dolphin haurient ppr'.

Motto: *Mediis tranquillus in undis*. (Calm amidst the raging waves).

This coat of arms is attributed in Balfour-Paul's Ordinary of Scottish Arms to a family Smith (Smythe) of Braco as granted by George Porteous in 1673.

The motto is the same as the device chosen by William the Silent, Prince of Orange, on the occasion of the birth of his youngest child, Prince Frederick Henry, the son of his fourth wife, Louise de Coligny. This son was destined to become a great ruler 'whose name was to stand for the Golden Age of Dutch history'.

Charles Smythe's ancestor, Patrick Smythe, who bought the lands of Methven in 1664, married as his second wife (in 1682) Janet Haldane, granddaughter of Sir John Haldane, 11th Laird of Gleneagles, a Scottish soldier who had fought in the wars in the Netherlands under Prince Frederick Henry's banner.

Janet would have been delighted to know that her great-great-great-grandson, David Smythe, Lord Methven, would marry Euphemia Murray of Lintrose who could claim direct descent from Prince Frederick Henry's half-sister, Charlotte Brabantina.

APPENDIX II

BISHOP COLENSO

The Colenso controversy of the *1860's* is of great importance because it affected the Anglican fellowship as a whole, not merely the church in South Africa. Up to *1862*, when the dispute began, the British Parliament had been the supreme legislator and court-of-appeal for the State Church, (although many of its members were not Anglicans at all), but when the British colonies received a measure of self-government the relationship between Church and State had to be re-defined; as Bishop B. B. Burnett has said, 'In this the Church of the Province [of South Africa] led the way, and the painful road by which it was arrived at was the Colenso controversy . . .

The solution was eventually found in the Church declaring itself a voluntary association in the colonies, free of government control, but in full communion with the Church of England'.

John William Colenso arrived in Natal as its first Anglican bishop in *1854*. He inclined towards the Evangelicals rather than the 'High Church' group to which most of the clergy in Pietermaritzburg belonged, and was soon involved in disputes over theology and ritual. The real struggle began in *1861*, when he published a book on theology which the bishops in England declared was heretical. It was followed by another in *1862*, which horrified the orthodox. Bishop Robert Gray, the South African Metropolitan (Archbishop) ordered Colenso to stand trial in Cape Town, but he refused to appear and in *December, 1862*, he was deposed from office.

Colenso would not recognise Bishop Gray's authority, and said that the final resort in any ecclesiastical case was the Crown. On appeal the case went to the Privy Council, and they decided that the Letters Patent under which both Gray and Colenso had been appointed ought not to have been issued, as at the time of issue the Cape Colony, (to which Natal was then closely linked), was partly self-ruling under the Responsible Government system. Judgment was given that the Church in a self-governing Colony was no longer 'established' as in England, and was free to order its own affairs. Bishop Gray's deposition of Bishop Colenso was thus upheld.

John William Colenso refused to accept this judgment, and in *1865* he returned to Natal from England as 'Queen's Bishop', drawing authority from the Crown alone. In the meantime many of the clergy and laity in Natal had affirmed their allegiance to Gray and asked for a new bishop. Early in *1869* Bishop Macrorie was consecrated 'Bishop of Pietermaritzburg'. There were now two rival claimants to episcopal authority in Natal, but Colenso won the right to retain control of certain Church property and the income of the endowment of the See. The rival faction built a cathedral in opposition to his church, St. Peter's.

Colenso's supporters gradually dwindled in number, largely because the colonists disliked his championing Chief Langalibalele in *1874*. He died in *1883*, but the breach in the Anglican church in South Africa was destined to remain unhealed for many years longer. Macrorie resigned in *1891*, asking that a new bishop should be appointed who had not been connected with the Natal differences.

His successor, Bishop Baynes, tried to act as peace-maker, but the schism persisted. Bishop Baines, who followed, early in the twentieth century, was more successful, and in time the rift between the two factions practically disappeared. Even in the 1970's, however, there are still South African Anglicans who adhere to the 'Church of England' and remain aloof from the Church of the Province and its Archbishop. This remnant of 'Colenso-ites' is still Evangelical rather than 'High' in its practices.

———

Charles Smythe took an active part in Church affairs, and his diary and letters reveal his views:

July 20th, 1872: 'The Rev. Mr. Shears made rather a donkey of himself at the Macrorie synod the other day, by calling the

Privy Council a despicable tribunal for not turning out Bishop Colenso ... the proposal at the synod not to allow people of Colenso's church to communicate at any of the Macrorie churches seems rather too strong.'

November 10th, 1872: 'I think Colenso as much sinned against as sinning, and that very few know what he really believes or thinks and run away with ideas – certainly he has never forbidden those of the other church to attend his Communion, which is what the Macrorie synod wanted to do, and there seems much more Christian charity in Colenso than in Macrorie. Do not think from this that I am what the people here call a Colenso-ite, as I think both of them are too extreme and unconciliatory in their opinions.'

December 22nd: 'Went to Macrorie's church but did not like the service as it was all so flashy.'

July 12th, 1892: 'There is a chance of there being a settlement of the Church dispute, the Church of England party and the Church of South Africa in Natal having agreed to leave the appointment of a bishop to the Archbishop of Canterbury, and if he will only appoint some moderate man and consecrate him himself, the matter will be settled to the satisfaction of all but a few extremists.'

November 26th, 1893: 'The new bishop [Baynes] arrived and was received by a joint address from the two churches, to which he made a very suitable reply.' [Baynes made such a favourable impression that Charles hoped all would go smoothly from then on.]

April 1st, 1894: 'Baynes is a thoroughly good man, of broad views, but he has unpleasant times before him and ... I doubt if he is quite suited to the difficult task of re-uniting the Church here. [Charles was ready to support him in every way, and had done so at two meetings of the Church Council.]

'The opposition party headed by that Miss Colenso [the late bishop's eldest daughter, Harriette Colenso] are using every means to defeat the object for which the Bishop was sent out, viz the union of the two churches, although he guarantees to protect us against the operation of the Third Proviso which is the only objectionable feature of the South African church.' [This refers to the right of appeal to the Privy Council.]

June 24th, 1894: 'Miss Colenso still keeps up a strenuous opposition [to Bishop Baynes], but she has only a small following, even in her stronghold, Pietermaritzburg.'

In *October, 1894,* Charles had to tell Dr. Thin, who had hitherto officiated at Anglican services at Nottingham Road, that the congregation wished to place themselves in the hands of the Bishop with regard to the choice of clergy and arranging of services. Thin was very angry:

'But we are not going to make ourselves ridiculous by supporting him in opposition. I think there is only one congregation in the Colony now that does not acknowledge the Bishop as head, though many individuals who don't.'

April 28th, 1895: 'We had the Bishop [Baynes] for a couple of days, and he preached at Nottingham Road. It is a pity things will not work smoothly on Church matters, for I think he is a good man and suited to the wants of the people and country, but apt to be led away by injudicious advisers, perhaps a little inclined to think too much of his position in the Church; for instance, I always introduce him as "Bishop Baynes" when introducing him to people who I know are not Church of England. He asked me to introduce him as "the Bishop" – now I say that sort of thing is a mistake in a country where there is no State Church, and where the majority of the people do not belong to the C. of E., and I told him so but he says it is the correct thing ... I consider the great fault of the S. African Church is that they arrogate a position they're not entitled to.'

BIBLIOGRAPHY

BUCHAN, JOHN: History of the South African Forces in France.

BULPIN, T. V.: To the Banks of the Zambesi.

BULPIN, T. V.: To the Shores of Natal.

BURNETT, BISHOP B. B.: Anglicans in Natal.

CHILD, DAPHNE: Saga of the South African Horse.

CHURCHILL, RANDOLPH S.: Winston S. Churchill. Vol. 2.

CHURCHILL, WINSTON S.: Frontiers and Wars.

DU TOIT, ALEX: Geology of South Africa.

FULLER, BASIL: Springbok Round the Corner.

GROSS, FELIX: Rhodes of Africa.

HAGGARD, HENRY RIDER: The Days of My Life.

HAGGARD, LILIAS RIDER: The Cloak That I Left.

HATTERSLEY, PROF. ALAN: The British Settlement of Natal.

HAZLITT, W. CAREW: Faiths and Folklore.

HIERONYMUSSEN, PAUL: Orders, Medals and Decorations of Britain and Europe.

INGRAM, J. FORSYTH: Colony of Natal, Official Handbook, 1895.

LAIDLER AND GELFAND: South Africa: its Medical History.

LEHMANN, JOSEPH: All Sir Garnet.

LLOYD, CHRISTOPHER: The Navy and the Slave Trade.

LOW, CHARLES R.: Memoir of Sir Garnet Wolseley.

MANN, DR. ROBERT: Emigrant's Guide to the Colony of Natal.

MARWICK, ARTHUR: The Deluge.

MICHELL, SIR LEWIS: Life of Rt. Hon. C. J. Rhodes.

MILLAR, RONALD: Kut, the Death of an Army.

MILLIN, SARAH G.: Rhodes.

MURRAY, MARISCHAL: Union Castle Chronicle.

PAYNE, ROBERT: Gandhi.

RADFORD, E. & M.: Encyclopaedia of Superstitions.

ROBINSON, SIR JOHN: Notes on Natal, 1872.

ROSENTHAL, ERIC: Encyclopaedia of Southern Africa.

RUSSELL, ROBERT: Natal, the Land and its Story.

STUART, J.: History of the Zulu Rebellion, 1906.
TYLDEN, G.: The Armed Forces of South Africa.
WALKER, ERIC: Lord de Villiers and His Times.
WALKER, ERIC: A History of Southern Africa.
WALTON, SIR EDGAR: Inner History of the National Convention.
WATSON, R. G. T.: Tongaati.
WEDGWOOD, C. V.: William the Silent.

Who Was Who. 1897–1916.
Encyclopaedia Britannica.
New Cambridge Modern History. Vol. 12.
Oxford History of South Africa. Vol. 2.
Poetical Works of Robert Burns, pub. W. & R. Chambers.
Brewer's Dictionary of Phrase and Fable.
Hoyle's Games.
Burke's Peerage.
Burke's Landed Gentry.

INDEX

Active Citizen Force *see also* Defence Force of South Africa, 212, 225–7, 235

Adamson, Miss, 128, 132

Addington Hospital, 223

Administrators (Provincial), 218–22, 228, 233, 247, 249–50, 252

African Contingent (First World War), 244

African tribes, other than Zulu, 34–5, 40–1, 49, 51–2, 77, 103, 156–7, 165, 173, 186, 191

Afrikaans language, 213

Afrikaners *see also* Boers and Dutch, 206, 209, 211–3, 218–9, 227–30, 234–5, 237–8, 243–4, 246

Afrikaner Bond, 211

Agricultural shows, 64, 69, 134, 167, 225–6

Alexander, Police-Superintendent, 161

Algoa Bay *see* Port Elizabeth

Ammunition, 23, 31, 55, 87, 93, 158

Amos, Maggie, 71

Anglican Church *see also* Church of the Province of South Africa, 23–4, 80, 120, 125, 137, 146 and Appendix II

Annexation
  (a) of Natal, 57
  (b) of Pondoland, 86
  (c) of Transvaal, 74–5, 77
  (d) of Zululand, 131, 167

Antbears, 20, 119

Antelope, *see also* Buck, 241

Anti-Asiatic Laws of Transvaal, 214, 225

Apple trees, 111, 114

Arbuckle, Sir William, 172

Archbishop of Canterbury, see Appendix II

Archer-Houblon, Mrs, 2, 3, 8, 44

Armadale Castle, 216

Armoured Train Disaster, 177

Arnott (farm hand), 88, 98–9, 105, 112

Arras, 248

Artillery, 92, 169, 177, 179–81, 228

Asquith, H. H. (1st Earl of Oxford and Asquith), 213, 215, 217, 246

Athlone, Earl of, *see also* Prince Alexander of Teck, 168

Attorney-General of Natal, 60, 146, 172, 194

Audit Dept of Natal, 172

Aus, 232

Australia, 8, 50, 136, 167, 193, 204, 225, 235

Australian Blue-Gum trees, 32, 122

Aviation Corps, 231–2

Baghdad, 247–9, 250

Baines, Bishop Frederick, see Appendix II

Bale, Sir Henry, 172, 222

Balfour, Arthur (1st Earl), 216–7

Balgowan, 58, 170

Balls, dances, 25–6, 65, 101, 117–8, 134, 138, 140–1, 152, 157, 163–4, 168, 171, 191

Balmoral Castle, 222

Bamangwato, 41

Bambata, Chief, 206

Banks, banking, 17, 85, 97

Bapedi tribe, *see also* Sekukuni, 74, 84

Basra, 247–8

Basuto tribe; Basutoland (Lesotho), 41, 86, 103, 211

Baxter, Mrs, 75–6

Baynes, Bishop Arthur Hamilton, see Appendix II

Bechuanaland (Botswana), 32, 41, 154, 156–7, 211, 213

Belgium, Belgians, 225, 232

Bell, Miss, 118

Bell, Mrs ('Pin'), 6–7

Beyers, Gen. Christiaan, 227–8, 230–1

Biggs, Mrs, 81–2, 94

Binns, Sir Henry, 165–6, 170, 172

Bird, Christopher, 130, 192

Birrell, Augustine, 216

Bishop's Stortford, 2–3, 5, 44

'Black Week', Boer War, 183

Blockhouse system, 195

Bloemfontein, 34, 36–7, 188, 210

Blood River Territory, 79

Boers, *see also* Dutch, Afrikaners, Voortrekkers, 33–4, 36–8, 57, 74–5, 79, 93, 102–4, 123–4, 126, 132–3, 140, 155–6, 163, 169, 173–190, 194, 206–7, 210–1

263

Boer War (South African War), 173–195, 206, 227, 239
Bombay, 155, 249
Botany, 82, 86
Botha, Gen. Louis, 191, 194, 209, 212, 219–20, 225–230, 232, 234–5, 238, 244–6, 250
Botha, Mrs Louis, 215
Botswana, see Bechuanaland
Boyle, Bertie, 135
Boyle, Mimi, 196
Boys, Col E. F., 136
Brand, President Sir Johannes, 129
Branding of Horses, 82
Brickmaking, 67, 104–7, 136
Britain, the British people, see also England, Scotland, 13, 22, 34, 36–7, 50, 54–5, 57, 61, 70, 75, 115, 141, 153, 156, 163, 169, 173–4, 201, 204, 207, 225, 234–5, 237–9
British Govt, also referred to as 'Imperial' or 'Home' Govt, 28, 36, 55, 57, 60–1, 80, 84, 88–9, 100–4, 108, 115, 124, 126, 129–31, 135, 140, 146, 150, 152, 155–6, 158, 163, 169, 173–5, 183, 186, 203, 205–7, 211, 213–4, 219, 225–6, 228, 243, 246
British Army, British troops, 7, 12, 43, 55, 64, 75, 77, 84, 86, 88, 90–5, 103–4, 108, 127, 131, 135–6, 140–1, 147, 152, 156, 158–9, 168–9, 173–7, 181–3, 185–8, 190, 192, 195, 207, 226, 230, 237–8, 242, 244, 246–8, 250
Regiments mentioned by name:
Black Watch, The, 94, 147, 237, 240, 243–8, 250
East Kent Regt (The Buffs), 75, 84
1st Gordon Highlanders (75th Regt), 26
Prince Albert's Somersetshire Light Infantry (13th Regt), 75
Queen's Own Cameron Highlanders (79th Regt), 45–6
1st (Royal) Dragoons, 2, 44
Royal Horse Artillery, 169
Royal Hussars, 140, 168
2nd Royal Irish Rifles (86th Regt), 12
1st Sherwood Foresters (45th Regt), 58, 136
2nd South Staffordshire Regt (80th Regt), 75, 230
York & Lancaster Regt, The, 140–1
British Settlers, Natal, 1849–50, 57–8
British Settlers, Natal, 1872, 16
British South Africa Co., see Chartered Co., 135–6, 141
Bromhead, Lieut, 92

Bruce, Lady Augusta, see also Stanley, 6, 45, 217
Bubonic Plague, 172–3
Buchan, John (Lord Tweedsmuir), 196
Buck (antelope), 24–5, 38, 46, 54, 73, 86, 153
Buckingham Palace, 214–5
Buffalo, 9, 241
Buffalo River, 16, 91
Buller, Gen. Sir Redvers, 90, 182–3, 185, 191–2
Bulwer, Sir Henry, 61, 73
Burgers, President Thomas, 37, 40
Burgess, Rev. Mr, 125, 134
Burns, Robert, 1, 76
Bushman's River, see also Estcourt, 32, 181
Bushmen, 58, 85–6
Butter, 56, 58, 72, 83, 100, 105, 112, 128, 139, 154
Buttermer (friend of Charles Smythe), 15, 18–9, 27, 33–6
Buxton, Viscount, 234, 236

Cable Communication, 92, 141, 203–4, 206, 235, 240, 247–9
Campbell-Bannerman, Sir Henry, 201
Canada, 136, 147, 225, 235
Cancer cure, 132
Cape Carts, see also Post-Carts, 34, 48, 117, 195
Cape Colony, later Cape Province, 12, 32, 39, 44, 57, 69, 77, 79–80, 84, 86–7, 92, 103, 115, 121, 129–30, 133, 139–40, 147, 154–7, 163, 167, 183, 185, 192, 194, 205–6, 209–10, 212, 213, 219, 229–30, 234–5, 244, 247 and Appendix II
Cape of Good Hope, see Cape Town
Cape Town, 1, 9–10, 12–3, 20–1, 39, 47, 54, 125, 161, 182, 196, 210–11, 218–9, 228, 230, 246–7 and Appendix II
Carnarvon, 4th Earl of, 54, 60–1, 69, 75, 104, 209
Carriages, see also 'Spiders', 117, 220, 222
'Castle Line', 2
Casualties in war, 175–8, 180, 182–6, 233, 236, 238–9, 242–5, 247–8, 252
Caterpillar plague, 83
Cats, 82, 133–4
Cattle, 28, 36, 55–6, 58–9, 69, 73, 75, 80–3, 87–8, 99–101, 107–8, 113–4, 121, 129, 133–4, 139, 145, 157–8, 164–5, 176, 180, 183, 199, 202, 218, 248

Cavalry, 90–1, 94, 102, 175, 179, 181, 183, 229, 232, 237
Caversham, 56, 112, 117
Censorship, 202–3, 226
Census, 1904, 202
Cetewayo, Chief (later King), 43, 55, 61, 74, 79–80, 84, 87–90, 93–5, 115, 124
Chadwick, Kathleen, 199
Chamberlain, Joseph, 156, 162–3, 169, 191, 196
Chard, Lieut, 92
Charlestown, 153
Chartered Company (B.S.A. Company), 135–6, 141, 147, 161
Chelmsford, Lord (Lieut Gen. Thesiger), 86, 90–1, 93, 95
Chief Justice of Natal, 60, 194
Chieveley, 177
Christmas, 32, 54, 74, 79, 90, 108, 113, 121, 141, 154, 183–4, 192, 194–5, 208, 231, 240
Chupatties, 118
Church of the Province of South Africa, *see* Anglican Church
Churchill, Winston (later, Sir), 177, 184, 191, 203, 206
Civil Servants' Town Guard, 229–30
Civil Service Committee, 211
Clayton, Walter, 200
Clothes, 26, 52, 56, 59, 70–1, 76, 101, 127, 138, 149, 151, 157, 165–6, 170, 178, 210, 221
Cobalt, 53
Coffee, 18–9, 21–3, 25, 27, 37, 39, 41–2
Colenso (village), 42, 182–3, 193
Colenso, Miss Harriette, see Appendix II
Colenso, Bishop John William, 19, 23–4, 43, 54–5, 80–1, 125 and Appendix II
Colley, Gen. Sir George, 103
Colonial Office Building, Maritzburg 162
Colonial Patriotic Union, 161
Colonial Scouts, 183
Colonial Secretary of Great Britain (Secretary of State for Colonies), 54, 60–1, 69, 124, 152, 156, 162–3, 169, 191, 201, 203–7, 213
Colonial Secretary of Natal, 130, 146, 170–2, 189, 196, 199–207, 252
Commandant of Troops in Natal, 60
Commando (Boer), 178–80, 183, 191, 195, 207, 225, 227
Concentration Camps, 195
Connaught, Duke and Duchess of, 221–2

Conservative Party, 191, 201
Constitution Amendment Bill, 60–1
Cotton, 2–4, 17
Courland, S.S., 161–2
Crewe, Lord, 213
Cricket, 12, 19, 151
Crocodiles, 21, 25
Crown Land, 28, 100, 135
Cullinan Diamond, 215
Curry's Post, 32, 92
Customs Duties, Customs Union, 15, 129–30, 133, 139, 154, 167, 212, 233
Cypress trees, 122

Dagga (hemp), 112
'Dalcrue', 208
Dargle, 67, 87, 116, 152
Dawnay, Hon. Guy, 9–10, 13, 15, 17, 19–21, 26–7, 31–41, 44, 46, 53, 68, 94
Deacon (handyman), 120, 123
De Beers Mining Company, 115
Defence Force of South Africa, *see also* Active Citizen Force, 212, 225–7, 235
Delagoa Bay (Lourenco Marques), 37, 51, 129–30, 140, 163, 173, 244
De La Rey, Gen. Jacobus, 191, 209–10, 227–8, 229
Delville Wood (Somme), 242–3, 251
Dentistry, 124
Deserters, 69, 112, 181
De Villiers, Sir Henry, 210
De Wet, Gen. Christiaan, 191, 209, 228, 230–1
Diamond Fields, *see also* Kimberley, 2, 3, 9, 21, 31, 34–6, 53, 172
Dingaan, King, 43
Dinizulu, Chief, 124, 131, 208, 212
Disenfranchisement Bill, *see also* Gandhi, 150–1, 152, 158
Disraeli, Benjamin, 95
Dogs, 82, 119, 148
Dohl, 101
Donkeys, 164
Doppers, 40
Drakensberg Mountains, 33, 36, 38, 42, 58, 75, 85–6, 99, 248
Drought, 37, 41, 84, 184
Drummond, Frank, 3
Duchess of Edinburgh, 45
Ducks, 82, 113
Duff (farm hand), 99
Duke of York (later, King George V), 193
Duchess of York (later, Queen Mary), 193
Dundee, 173, 175

265

Durban (town), 1, 4, 12–6, 18, 20, 22–
7, 31–2, 42, 44, 46–7, 52, 54–5, 59–60,
67–8, 73, 75, 101, 106, 111, 115, 117,
120, 123, 146, 149–51, 152, 158,
161–3, 172, 177, 182, 192–3, 196, 205,
210–1, 213, 222–3, 227, 231, 234,
236–7, 239, 241, 244, 249–51
Durban's harbour bar, 14, 149
Dutch, *see also* Afrikaners, Boers
Dutch language, 102, 213, 245–6
'Dwaleni', 223, 244

East African Contingent, 239–40, 241–5
East London, 13, 115
'Eberberg', *see also* 'Strathearn', 97–99,
104–9
Edinburgh, 44, 70, 72, 156
Education, *see also* Governess, Tutor,
7–8, 28–9, 34, 58, 100, 118, 123, 128,
137–8, 139, 145, 147, 151, 157–8, 176,
178, 194, 196, 202, 212, 222–3, 242
Egypt, 155, 241–2, 252
Elections, *see also* Franchise, 126, 135,
141–6, 162, 165, 194, 211–2, 234, 238
Electric light, 164
Elephants, 9, 16, 39–40, 46, 53, 241
Elgin, 7th Earl of, 217
Elgin, 8th Earl of, 147
Elgin, 9th Earl of, 147, 152, 201, 203–
7, 213–4
'Elgin Marbles', 6
Ellis, Elizabeth, 57–8, 128, 132, 136,
141, 146, 154, 156, 168
Ellis, Helen, 57, 70
Emmott, Alfred, 215–6
Emperor Frederick, 132
England, *see also* Britain, 21, 44, 74, 191,
214, 223, 249 and Appendices
English language, 116, 144, 213, 245–6
Enteric fever, 154, 169–70, 192, 195,
202
Escombe, Sir Harry, 140, 146, 150,
161–3, 165–6, 184
Eshowe, 93
Estcourt, 32–3, 36–7, 42, 85, 100, 116,
128, 132, 134, 177–8
Ethiopianism, 202
Executive Committee in Natal, 220
Executive Council in Natal, 60, 126,
171, 204

Family Life, 19th century:
(a) in Britain, 6–7, 238
(b) of Natal settlers, 24–5, 63, 72,
119–20
(c) of Zulus, 28–9

Farming, *see also* Sugar, Cattle, Horses,
Hailstorms, etc., 1, 8, 18–23, 27–8,
36–7, 39, 41–2, 55–6, 58–9, 63, 71,
82–3, 87–8, 98, 100, 105, 111–2,
114–6, 119, 121–2, 133, 136–7, 139,
143, 145, 149, 157–8, 167, 172, 175–6,
181–2, 190–1, 195, 222, 226–7, 229,
236, 241–2, 245, 248
Farmers' Association, 121, 152
Farrar, George, 209
Federation of South African states, *see
also* Union, 69–70, 75, 87, 104, 209,
211–2
Fencing (wire), 73–4, 97, 106, 122, 158
Finance Committee, 211
Fireworks display, 64–5, 127, 193, 217
First World War, 225–40, 241–52
Fish, 14, 101, 134–5
Fitzpatrick, Sir Percy, 209, 215
Fitzpatrick, Lady, 215
Fly (farm hand), 106, 111, 114–6, 118,
120, 123, 131
Food, foodstuffs, 24–5, 27, 32, 38, 50,
54, 72–3, 79, 101, 103, 113, 118, 176,
178–80, 184–5, 187–8, 199, 227, 233
Forbes (Perthshireman), 56
'Fordoun', 65, 77, 116
Foreign Office, 214
Fort Nottingham, 56, 58, 67, 112
Foster Gang, 227–8
Fowls, 38, 82
France, 94–5, 197, 225, 230, 236, 242–4,
246, 248, 251
Franchise, *see also* Elections, 60, 150,
152–3, 158, 169, 184, 211–3, 218–9
French, Gen. (later, Field-Marshal) Sir
John, 186
Frere, Sir Bartle, 86–9, 91

Gallipoli, 236, 239
Gambling, 10, 13, 35–6, 50
Game Reserves, 242
Gandhi, Mohandas (Mahatma), 150–2,
158, 161–2, 186, 205, 214, 225
Garub, 233
Gatacre, Gen. Sir William, 183
Germans, Germany, 8, 132, 144–5, 153,
164, 181, 206, 225–9, 230–1, 232–6,
238–9, 242, 244–5, 251
German East Africa, *see* Tanganyika
German language, 8, 144–5
Giant's Castle, 58
Gibeon, 232–3
Giraffe, 9, 46
Gladstone, Herbert, 220–1, 234
Gladstone, William Ewart, 103, 108,
153, 220

Glenalmond (Trinity College), 5, 7, 26, 32, 42, 192
Glencoe, 155, 173, 175
Goats, 28, 36, 82, 99
Gold (builder), 99, 107
Gold Fields of Eastern Transvaal, 26, 32, 34, 44–5, 47–53
Gold, Gold-mines of Witwatersrand, *see also* Johannesburg, 26, 53, 121–2, 125, 129–30, 132–3, 139, 195, 202
Governess, *see also* Adamson, Bell, Wilson, 58, 118, 128, 132, 137–8, 147, 151, 157
Government House, 149, 163–4, 166–8, 171, 191–3, 219–22
Governor-General of South Africa, 168, 218, 220–1, 234
'Gowrie', 58–9, 63, 65, 67–71, 73, 75–6, 78–9, 82, 88, 95, 98–9, 105–6, 108, 112, 114, 132, 169
Grass-fires, 67, 75, 82, 84–5, 123, 190
Gray, Bishop Robert, see Appendix II
Greene, Col Edward, 165, 209–213
Greytown, 194, 202
Grice (friend of Herbert Rhodes), 17–8
Griqualand East, 87
Griqualand West, 36, 87
Griquas, 84
'Groote Schuur', 196
Guerilla warfare, 190, 194–5, 245
Guns (small arms), Gunpowder, 4, 7, 15, 17, 24–5, 31, 35, 38, 47, 55, 79, 87, 90–1, 102, 116, 134, 140, 146, 158, 163, 174–5, 180–1, 186–7, 189, 195, 208, 229–231
'Gun War', 103

Habib, Haji, 214
Haggard, Sir Henry Rider, 29, 32, 83
Hailstorms, 78, 114–5
Haldane, Richard, 216
Half-castes, 32, 41
Hamilton, Susannah, 106–7
Hanover, 8
Harcourt, Lewis, 216
Hardie, Keir, 217
Harrismith, 33, 42, 123, 133
Hartley, Henry, 39–40
Havelock, Sir Arthur, 124, 126
Hay, 100, 114, 149–50, 188
Heidelberg, 37, 39, 41, 53, 153
Helpmekaar, 90
Hely-Hutchinson, Sir Walter, 145, 152, 175
Hertzog, Gen. J. B. M., 209, 215
Highlands, Highlanders, *see also* Perthshire and Scotland, 1, 5, 26, 56, 58, 109, 168, 207, 218, 237

Hime, Col Albert, 170–1, 173, 188–9
Hindus, *see* Indians
Hippopotami ('sea-cows'), 21, 241
Hofmeyr ('Onze Jan'), 211–2
Horses, horse-breeding, 10–11, 18, 20, 23–4, 26, 31, 33–4, 38–9, 41–2, 48, 59, 64–5, 69, 73, 75, 82, 85, 94, 98–9, 101–3, 111, 116–9, 131, 135–9, 144, 153, 164, 169–70, 174–5, 179, 181–3, 187–8, 223, 228, 230, 232–3, 241
Horse-omnibus, 17, 41–2
Horse-racing, 25, 43, 64–5, 167
Horse-sickness, 23, 41, 59, 121, 241
Hospitals and asylums, 107, 172, 178, 188, 195, 242
House-building; Pioneers' houses, 24, 36, 63, 67–70, 72–3, 78, 85, 97, 99, 104–8, 111, 133, 136, 138–9, 168, 178, 181–2, 183
House of Assembly, Cape Town, 218
House of Commons, 203, 215–6, 217
House of Lords, 215
'Howard', 79, 85, 87, 97, 222, 236, 248
Howick, 32, 70, 74, 98, 102, 140, 143, 152, 179
Hunting, 9, 21, 24–5, 38–40, 46, 53, 73, 82, 85–6, 248
Hut Tax, 27, 100, 202
Hutchinson, Miss, 140
Hyaenas, 58
Hyde, Dr, 49
Hyde Park Hotel, 214
Hyslop, Thomas, 200, 209–213

Immigration to Natal (by British, Indians, Voortrekkers), 28, 32, 63, 88, 106, 135–6, 161–2, 172
Imperial Govt, *see* British Govt
'Inchbrakie', *see* 'Vaalkop'
Independence of Transvaal, *see* War of Independence
Independents (election candidates), 238
India, 8, 28, 123, 133, 146, 150, 152, 158, 161, 174, 186, 225, 238, 248, 250
Indians, 27–8, 59, 100–2, 105, 111–2, 114–5, 118–20, 123, 125, 133, 150–3, 155, 157–8, 161–2, 186, 200, 205, 214, 225, 252
Industries, 121, 172
Infantry, 88, 90–1, 179, 181, 183
Ingogo, 103
Inquiry into Jameson Raid, 156, 161
Internment Camp, 236
Iron (galvanised), 36, 67, 78, 104, 107, 114
Ironstone, 75
Isandhlwana, 91–3, 131
Isle of Wight, 216

Italy, 232

Jaffray, Misses, 71
Jameson, Dr Leander Starr, 154—6, 209
Jameson Raid, 154–6, 161, 163, 175, 227
Jingoism, 156, 162–3, 188, 211–2
Johannesburg, see also Witwatersrand, 121, 125, 132–3, 140
John (Zulu groom), 23–6, 31
Joubert, Gen. Petrus (Piet), 103, 181
Justice of the Peace, 130–1

Kaffirs, see also Zulus, Natives, 16, 18, 20, 24–5, 27–9, 31–2, 37, 43, 54–5, 57–8, 63, 67, 69, 72–4, 76–8, 80–1, 83, 87, 89, 92, 98–100, 105, 116, 119, 123, 127, 132–3, 135, 139, 148, 150, 153, 157, 165, 173, 178, 184, 188, 190–1, 200, 202–8, 212, 218–9, 227, 233, 235, 237, 244, 248, 252
Kaffraria, 86
Kaiser Wilhelm II, 132, 206, 225
Karkloof, 140, 196, 199, 244
K.C.M.G., 219–20
Keate, Robert, 16, 21
Kemp, Gen. Christoffel, 230
Kenilworth Castle, 213
Kennedy, Andrew, 18–21, 22–4, 25–6, 31, 42
Kimberley, see also Diamond Fields, 2, 27, 32, 34–6, 44, 115, 140, 185
'Kinfauns Castle', 115
King Edward VII, see also Prince of Wales, 192, 197, 214–6
King George V, see also Duke of York, and Prince of Wales, 193, 214–5
King, Grace, see also Speirs, 57, 64–5, 98, 132, 147
King, James, 57, 59, 64, 67, 69, 73, 79, 91–2, 98, 106, 108, 121, 143, 144–5, 165
King, Janet, 57–8, 66, 70–1, 76, 98, 101, 116, 117, 121, 127–8, 162
King, John, 56–9, 63, 65–6, 75, 97, 101, 114, 117, 121, 132, 162
King, Margaret, see also Smythe, 56–7, 63–6, 70–1
King, Robert, 57, 64–5, 67, 71, 101, 113, 121, 131
Kitchener, Field-Marshal Lord, 183, 185, 195
Klipdrift, 35
Klip River County, 188
Koch, Robert, 164

Kruger, President Paul, 37, 129, 140, 154–5, 163, 169, 174, 227
Kut, 243, 247, 249

Labour, see also Kaffirs, Indians, 20, 27–8, 31, 34–5, 49, 51–2, 58–9, 67–9, 73–4, 84, 87, 99–102, 105–6, 111–4, 123, 132–3, 135–6, 139, 150, 153, 184, 244, 248
Labour Party in Natal, 207, 231, 239
Labour Party, South African, 235, 238
Ladysmith, 27, 33, 37, 90, 130, 133, 169–70, 173, 175–8, 182–4, 185–8, 189, 193
Land Colonisation Company, 79, 97
Land prices, 22, 36–7, 41, 79, 85, 97, 153
Lands and Works, Ministry of, 146
Langalibalele, Chief, 48, 54–5 and Appendix II
Laing's Nek, 103
Lanyon, Sir Owen, 102
Le Cateau, battle of, 230
Legislative Assembly (Lower House under Responsible Govt), 143–6, 149–52, 161–3, 165–8, 196, 200, 207, 210, 213
Legislative Assembly Building, 149, 167, 178
Legislative Council (under Representative Govt), 60, 74, 108, 124, 126, 135
Legislative Council (Upper House under Responsible Govt), 146, 168, 200
Leopards, 58
Leprosy, 172
Lesotho (Basutoland), 86, 103, 211, 213
Liberal Party in Britain, 103–4, 201, 203, 206–7, 216, 218–20
Lieutenant-Governor of Natal, see also Boys, Bulwer, Havelock, Hely-Hutchinson, Keate, MacCallum, Musgrave, Pine, Wolseley, 16, 21, 27, 54, 59, 60–1, 124, 126, 130, 136, 142, 145, 149, 152, 158, 162–4, 166–8, 171, 175, 188–9, 192, 197, 203–5
Lightning, 78, 113
Lions, 38, 58
Lions River (village and electoral division), 85, 108, 141, 143–5, 165, 179, 194
Lloyd-George, David, 246
Lobengula, King, 41, 136, 147
Lobola, see also Kaffirs and Zulus, 80–1
Locusts, 137, 157
London, 1, 3, 5, 45, 125, 161, 213–7
London Convention, 163

Lourenco Marques, *see* Delagoa Bay
Luderitz Bay, 229–30, 232
Lukin, Brigadier-Gen. Henry Timson, 235
Lung-sickness, 129
Lusitania, 234
Lyall, Dr, 21
Lydenburg, 44–5
'Lynedoch', 56–8, 63, 70, 75–6, 88, 98, 108, 112–4, 117, 121, 127–8, 132, 147, 251
Lyttleton, Alfred, 217

MacCallum, Sir Henry, 203–5
MacCallum (friend of Charles Smythe), 47–53
MacCallum (claimant to Breadalbane title), 50–1
McKenna, Reginald, 215
McKenzie, Gen. Sir Duncan, 221
McKenzie, Fanny, 197, 199–200
Maclean, Jim, 249
Macrorie, Bishop William, 23, 125 and Appendix II
Madeira, 10
'*Madumela*' (David Smythe senior), 83
Magersfontein, 183
Magic Lantern, 127
Magistrates, 33, 100, 126, 131, 172, 202
Mail, 14, 21, 39, 68, 92, 179, 185
Mailships, *see also* 'Norseman', 'Union Line', 'Castle Line', etc., 2, 12–3, 44–5, 47, 115, 213–4, 216, 222, 230
Maize (mealies), 25, 27–8, 38, 72–3, 88, 99, 101, 103, 105, 114, 121, 133, 178, 227
Majuba Mountain, 103, 190
Malaria, 51, 242, 245
Malawi, 16, 53
Malloch (farm hand), 106, 108, 111–5, 118, 120, 123, 138, 139
Maritzburg, *see* Pietermaritzburg
Maritzburg College, 157, 178, 196
Marne, battle of, 230
Marriage Custom, 71
Marrières Wood, battle of, 251
Marsh, Edward, 203
Martial Law, 174–5, 202–4, 208, 225
Mashonaland, 135–6, 157
Matabele, 40–1, 147, 156, 161, 196
Matoppo Hills, 161, 196
Mauch, Karl, 40
Maude, Gen. Sir Stanley, 247
Maydon, John, 200
Mealies, *see* Maize
Mechanical Aids (farming), 100, 188
Medical Treatment, *see also* Midwife,

Vaccination, etc., 21, 58, 75–6, 81–3, 98, 101–2, 115–6, 124–5, 127, 128, 131–2, 141, 148–9, 154, 172–3, 178, 188–9, 190, 194–5, 223, 227, 247–50, 252
Merriman, John X., 209, 215
Mesopotamia, 243–4, 246–50
Methuen, Gen. Lord, 183
Methven Castle, 5–6, 23, 44, 57, 72, 85, 92, 94, 108, 120, 133, 168, 201, 216, 218
Meyer, Lukas, 124
Mhlangen (Charles Smythe), 83
Michaelhouse, 190
Michell, Sir Lewis, 210
Middelburg (Nazareth), 53
Midlands of Natal, 56, 58–9, 63, 74, 120
Midwife, 75–6, 81–3, 94, 98, 116, 127–8
Military Cadets, 158
Milk, 38, 73, 81, 100–1, 112, 133, 199
Milner, Lord, 169, 171, 195–6, 211
Minister of Agriculture, 172
Ministry (Cabinet), 146, 151, 158, 162, 165, 170–2, 175, 184, 188–9, 193–4, 196, 199–200, 204–5, 207, 211
Mint, 226
Mitchell, Innes, 26, 42–3, 182
Modder River, 34
Mons, battle of, 230
Mooi River (river and village), 32, 85, 97, 99, 113, 134–5, 178–80, 226
Moor, Sir Frederick, 146, 170–2, 188, 194, 207, 209, 211, 219
Moor, Lady, 222
Morcom, William, 209
Mortgages, 23, 106
Morton (election candidate), 143–5
Mossel Bay, 13
Motor car, 210–1, 221, 223, 244
Mount Nelson Hotel, 211, 247
Mounted Police, 47–8, 84, 135
Mozambique, 173
Mpande, King, 43
Mules, 164, 232
Muller, Gen. Christiaan, 230
Munro (Scottish settler), 56
Murray, Euphemia, 76–7, 109
Murray, Lady Charlotte, 6
Murray, Mungo, 76
Murray, T. K., 146
Murray, Gen. James Wolfe, 192
Musgrave, Anthony, 21, 27, 42, 54
Mushroom Valley, 230–1

Natal, Colony, later Province, of:
(a) Agricultural aspect of, 1–4, 8, 15, 18, 42–3, 58, 137, 164–5, 184

(b) Annexation of Zululand to, 131, 166–7
(c) Boer Colonists of, 102, 186, 189, 230, 235, 237, 246
(d) British Colonists' opinions, 55, 81, 94, 123–4, 135, 202, 205, 207, 211–2, 219, 244
(e) Church affairs of, see Appendix II
(f) Descriptive of, 16, 58, 86, 119
(g) Economic state of, 85, 87, 95, 103, 114–5, 121, 133, 174, 181–2, 183, 190–1, 197, 200, 231
(h) Form of government in, 60–1, 104, 126, 135, 140–2, 146, 162
(i) Indian immigration to, 150
(j) Labour situation in, 27–8, 123, 153
(k) Natalians going to Gold Fields, 122, 125, 132
(l) Rivalry with other South African states, 37, 129, 139–40, 191–2
(m) Transport, Communications, in, 12, 73–4, 77, 108, 121–2, 133
(n) Union with other states, 69–70, 87, 206–7, 209–13
Natal coaster, 12–4, 21
Natal Carbineers, *see also* Volunteers, 158, 163, 170, 174–7, 187, 189–90, 194, 205, 226–7, 234–6
Natal Field Force, 176
Natal Indian Congress, 150–1
Natal Light Horse, 226, 234
Natal men killed in France, 248–9
Natal Mercury, 24, 44, 166
Natal Mounted Police, 47–8, 84, 135
Natal Native Contingent, 88, 90–2
Natal School-cadets, 158
National Convention, 209–13
Nationalists (Afrikaner), 235, 238
Natives, i.e., Africans, *see* Kaffirs, Zulus
Nazareth (Middelburg), 53
Neuve Chapelle, battle of, 236
Newcastle, 37, 48, 77, 103, 141, 175
New Hanover, 144, 153, 225–6, 236
'New Republic', 123–4, 126
New Year celebrations, 75, 113, 121
New Zealand, 225
Newspapers and Periodicals, *see also* *Natal Mercury*, 21, 24, 44, 50, 67, 69, 72, 80, 84, 101–2, 132, 145, 163, 166, 176, 188–9, 197, 203, 205, 229, 235, 237–8
Nicknames (Zulu), 83
Ninth Division (Scottish), 242
Ninth Kaffir War, 77
Nisbett (friend of Charles Smythe), 13–5, 17, 34

Niven, Mary, 114–6, 120, 131
Norseman, 2, 4–5, 9–15
Northcote, Sir Henry Stafford, 204–5
Nottingham Road (village and district), 58, 112, 120–1, 130–1, 134, 137, 139–40, 164, 169–71, 179–81, 191–3, 199–200, 208, 219, 230, 241, 249–50

Oak trees, 6, 111, 122
Oats, 78, 157
Oldham, 191
Omaruru, 233
Operations (surgery), 149, 223
Orange Free State (Orange River Colony), 33, 36–7, 69, 86, 102, 121, 129–30, 133, 163, 167, 175–6, 186, 188, 191, 196, 206–7, 209–10, 212, 214, 218–19, 229–31, 234–5, 247
Orchard, 111, 148, 238
Ostriches, 54, 90
Oswald, Sir John, 6
Otavi, 233
Oxen, 20, 22, 32–3, 36–8, 41, 48, 54, 59, 78, 82, 84, 87–8, 95, 102, 107, 111, 113, 117, 134, 149, 157–8, 164–73, 226
Oxford University, 34, 44, 115
Ox-wagon, 22, 31–3, 40–1, 53–4, 58, 67, 70, 73, 77–8, 84, 88, 91–2, 95, 99, 101–2, 105, 107–8, 113, 117, 120, 157, 164, 187, 199, 248

Paardeberg, 188
Paddock Hill, 'Strathearn', 112, 134, 138
Parliament (Natal), 145–6, 149–50, 151–2, 158, 163, 165–7, 170, 190, 193–4, 196, 199–200, 207
Parliament (South African), 211–2, 218–9, 233, 247
Passchendaele, battle of, 251
Peace of Vereeniging, 195
Peach trees, Peaches, 70, 111, 114
Pearson, Colonel, 90, 93
Peckham (election candidate), 143, 165
Penn-Symons, Gen. Sir William, 173, 175
Perth, Perthshire, 5, 56, 127, 168, 201, 216–8
Petitions, 143, 150, 212
Phillips, Miss, 25–6, 31, 43–4, 56
Phillips, Mrs, 19–20, 24–5, 43–4, 56
Phoenix, 205
Piano, 72, 147
Pietermaritzburg, 16–7, 19, 23, 26, 31–2, 36, 56, 58, 64–5, 67, 73, 75,

77–9, 82, 87–8, 90, 92, 100–1, 104, 107–8, 112, 114, 117, 120–2, 124–5, 127–8, 131, 134, 136, 143, 145–6, 149, 152–3,156,158,162–3,167–8,172,176, 177–9, 184, 190–3, 195, 200, 207, 213, 219–20, 223, 226–7, 232, 234, 235–6, 239, 243–6, 250 and Appendix II
Pigs, 58
Pilgrim's Rest, 48–53
Pine, Sir Benjamin, 54–5
Pine trees, 111, 114, 122, 168, 202
Pioneer Force, 135
Plowman, Sir George, 197, 210, 214, 220–1, 222, 228–9, 249–51
Plum trees, 111
Poll Tax, 200, 202
Polo Club, 146
Polygamy, 80–1
Pondos, Pondoland, 79, 84, 86
Population, 16, 28, 125, 132, 135, 202
Porcupines, 73, 119, 133
Port Elizabeth, 12–3
Port St. John's, 14, 86
Port Shepstone, 193
Portuguese, 40, 173
Post-Carts, *see also* Cape Carts, 36, 41–2, 47–8
Postmaster-General, 60
Posts and Telegraph, Dept of, 172
Potatoes, 100, 119, 133
Potchefstroom, 102, 227
Potgieter's Drift, 185
Presbyterians, 70, 120
Pretoria, 37, 39–41, 44, 53, 75, 85, 93, 103, 140, 182, 184, 190–2, 215, 226–9
Pretoria Convention, 104
Prices (other than of land), 23, 27, 53, 71–3, 75, 84, 87–8, 95, 106, 108, 121–2, 168–9, 173, 223, 226, 245–6
Prieska, 229
Prime Minister of Great Britain, 213, 217, 246
Prime Minister of Natal, 146, 162–3, 165, 170–1, 196, 199–207, 209, 215, 219, 252
Prime Minister of South Africa, 219, 226, 250
Prince Alexander of Teck, *see also* Earl of Athlone, 168
Prince Alfred, 45
Prince Imperial, 94–5
Prince of Wales (later, King Edward VII), 13, 20
Prince of Wales (later, King George V), 214–5
Princess Alice, 168
Princess Patricia, 221–2
Princess Victoria, 215

Princess of Wales (later, Queen Alexandra), 13
Princess of Wales (later, Queen Mary), 214–5
Privy Council, see Appendix II
Protector of Immigrants, 60, 101
Provincial Councils, 211, 218, 232–3, 241, 247, 249

Queen Alexandra, 214–5
Queen Mary, 168, 193, 214–5
Queen Victoria, 6, 13, 45, 69, 94, 127, 146, 163–4, 168, 192–3, 217, 221
Queen Victoria's Birthday (Empire Day), 64–5, 149, 167–8, 170
Queen Victoria's Golden Jubilee, 127
Queen Victoria's Diamond Jubilee, 163–4

Railways, Railway and Harbour Dept, 16, 22, 37, 73–4, 77, 95, 101, 108, 112, 117, 121–2, 127, 129–30, 133, 135, 139–40, 145–6, 149, 151–4, 162, 164, 172, 177–9, 182–3, 190, 193, 195, 212, 222, 225, 228–30, 232, 234–5, 245
Rats, 133
Rebel Boers in Natal (Boer War), 186, 188–9
Rebels (Boer) in 1914, 227–31, 234–5, 237, 243
Redwater, 36, 81
Referendum, 210
Reform Committee, 154–6, 227
Refugees, 175, 182, 195
Relief of Ladysmith, *see also* Ladysmith, 187–9
Religious Services, 10, 19–20, 23, 50, 70, 120, 141, 164 and Appendix II
Representative Government, 28, 60
Responsible Government, 104, 124, 126, 135, 140–4, 146–7, 204–6, 209–14 and Appendix II
Reunion, 19
Rhodes, Cecil John, 2, 32, 34–6, 44, 115, 125, 129, 136, 141, 154–5, 161, 185, 196, 210
Rhodes, Rev. Francis, 2, 3, 44–5
Rhodes, Frank, 2, 4–5, 9, 12–3, 15, 20–1, 26, 32, 34–6, 44, 46, 115, 155–6, 185, 196
Rhodes, Herbert, 2–5, 8–10, 12–3, 15, 17, 19–20, 26, 32, 34, 44–6, 48–51, 53, 141
Rhodesia, 40, 103, 135–6, 141, 147, 156–7, 161, 196, 211, 213

271

Rice, 101, 103, 178
Rifle Associations, 87, 134, 140, 146, 158, 179–82
Rinderpest, 157–8, 164–5, 202
Riots (anti-German), 234
Roads, 31–2, 48, 65, 105, 108, 244
Roberts, Field-Marshal Lord, 183, 188–90, 192
Robinson, Sir John, 16, 146, 162
Rorke's Drift, 92
Ross, George, 180
Ross, Jim, 249
Royal Hotel, Durban, 15, 18–20, 23, 25–6, 31, 47, 117, 193
Royal Navy, 67, 163, 211, 216
Russia, Russians, 45, 225, 230, 242
Rustenburg, 39–41, 230

St. Lucia Estuary, 79
St. Vincent, 92
Samarra, 250
Sand (for building), 105
Satyagraha, 214
Schreiner, Olive, 123, 212
Schreiner, William, 212
Scotland, *see also* Highlands, Perthshire, 3, 5, 8, 21, 27, 44, 51, 57–8, 66, 68, 71, 82, 88, 94, 101, 106, 109, 115, 120–2, 127, 134, 141, 151, 168, 196–7, 216–8, 240, 242–3
Scott (election candidate), 143
Sea Cow Lake, 18–25, 27, 31, 42–3
Seafaring custom, 11
Secretary for Native Affairs, 29, 60, 146, 170, 172, 194
Secretary of State for the Coloniesl *see* Colonial Secretary, Britain
Seeheim, 229
Seely, Colonel J. E. B., 215, 217
Sekukuni, Chief, *see also* Bapedi, 74–5, 84, 86, 90
Selborne, Lord, 211, 215
Selborne, Lady, 211
Senate, South African, 218–9
Shackleton, Lieut (later Sir) Ernest, 216
Shaka Zulu, 16, 28, 43, 89
Shaw, Campbell, 196, 199
Shaw, Colin Walter, 202
Shaw, Victor, 208
Shears, Rev. Mr, 23, 70, 83 and Appendix II
Sheep, 1, 28, 36–8, 59, 67, 69, 78, 82, 87, 98, 108, 112–4, 116, 133–4, 139, 145–6, 176, 179, 184, 202, 218, 245
Shepstone, Sir Theophilus, 29, 43, 55, 75, 79, 81, 202

Shipping, *see also* Mailships, etc., 77, 103, 122, 230, 246
Silver, 53
Simla, 248
Simonstown, 211
Slaves (liberated), 67–8
Sleaford, 3
Sledge, 77, 113
Smallpox, 124–5, 128
Smith-Dorrien, Gen. Sir Horace, 240
Smuts, Gen. (later Field-Marshal) Jan, 169, 191, 194, 206, 209, 225, 229, 232, 240–1, 245, 249
Smythe, Beatrice ('Bice'), 6, 196–7, 220, 223, 228, 236, 246, 251
Smythe, Cecilia Iris, 199, 223, 231, 250–1
Smythe, Charles John (later, the Hon.):
Ancestry, 5–6
Home and boyhood, 5–7
Education 7–8
Choice of career, 7–8
Fails Indian Forestry Service exam., 8
Meets Herbert Rhodes, decides go to Natal, 3–4, 8
Leaves for Natal, 1872, 1–2, 5
Lands at Durban, 14
Goes to stay at Sea Cow Lake, 19
On trek with Guy Dawnay, 31–41
Visits Scotland, 44–6
Returns to South Africa, 1874, 46
At Gold Fields, 48–53
Returns to Natal, 53
Rides to Lynedoch, 1875, meets Kings, 56–7
Accepts partnership at 'Gowrie', 59
Becomes engaged to Margaret King, 65
Builds house on 'Gowrie', 67
Wedding day, 70–1
Becomes father for first time, 75–6
Buys half 'Howard', 79
Buys 'Vaalkop' and other hal 'Howard', 85
Buys 'Eberberg' ('Strathearn'), 97
Begins building house on 'Eberberg', 99
Takes family to live at 'Strathearn', 108
Visits Scotland, 1883, 115–6
Is appointed J.P., 1888, 130–1
Stands as candidate at Natal elections, 1893, 143
Tops poll at election, 145
Is sworn in as M.L.A., 145
Becomes Speaker of Natal Parliament, 1897, 165–6

Is offered post of Colonial Secretary,
and accepts. Becomes Colonial
Secretary, 1899, 170–1
Fears may lose post, as suspected of
being pro-Boer, 188–9
Silver Wedding, 193–4
Mother's death, 196
Ministry defeated: Charles out of
office, Aug., 1903, 196
Given right to retain title 'Honour-
able', 1903, 196–7
Returns to office: becomes P.M. and
Col. Sec., 1905, 199–200
Constitutional crisis during Zulu
Rebellion, 204–5
Resigns as P.M. and Col. Sec., 1906,
207
Is Leader of Opposition, 1907, 207
Is one of Natal's delegates to National
Convention, 1908, 209–13
Is delegate to London Conference,
1909, 213–8
Is appointed first Administrator of
Natal, 1910, 219–20
Becomes ill, undergoes operation,
1913, 223
Second term as Administrator be-
gins, 1915, 233
Plans to resign, 247
Last illness, 249–52
Death, May, 1918, 252
Smythe, David (senior), 6–7, 45–6,
82–3, 85–6, 88–92, 94, 113, 127, 147,
158, 168, 218, 237
Smythe, David William, 94, 98, 113,
118–9, 127, 133–4, 137–9, 147, 151,
157–8, 163–4, 170, 174–7, 182–92,
194–5, 197, 199–201, 208
Smythe, Edric Murray, 127–8, 134,
138, 147, 151, 157, 190, 192, 197, 199,
222, 238, 244, 248
Smythe, Elizabeth Camilla, 116, 124–5,
128–9, 138, 151, 157, 176, 178, 196,
199, 202, 208, 223, 231, 244
Smythe, Emily, 5–8, 45, 48, 59, 63,
66–9, 75–6, 78, 81, 106, 113, 121,
132–3, 134, 138, 141, 196
Smythe, Euphemia Janet, 75–8, 81, 88,
98, 105, 113, 117–8, 119, 121, 127–8,
137–8, 140, 145, 149, 151–2, 154, 157,
163–4, 170, 176, 179–81, 190, 193,
199, 213–8, 220, 222–3, 225, 231, 249,
252
Smythe, Frank, 6, 151, 156, 168, 193–6
Smythe, Graham Haldane, 134
Smythe, John Oswald, 104–5, 116, 137,
139, 148, 151, 157, 173–4, 178–80,
182, 192–3, 196, 199, 205, 208, 219,
221, 239, 244–5
Smythe, Keith fforester, 156, 199, 222,
226–9, 231, 233, 235–6, 237, 239,
248
Smythe, Margaret (Charles's half-
sister), 7, 21
248
Smythe, Margaret (Madge), see also
King, 70–2, 74–7, 81, 83, 89, 94, 98–
101, 104, 106–8, 112–3, 114–120,
124–5 127–8, 131–4, 136, 140–1,
146–8, 154, 156, 168, 176, 178, 178–81,
184, 190, 192–3, 195, 199, 202,
210, 218–21, 226–7, 231, 245, 247ʹ
250–2
Smythe, Margaret Grace (Meta), 98,
113, 116, 128, 134, 151, 154, 157, 168,
170, 176, 192–3, 199, 220–1, 223,
231, 237, 252
Smythe, May Emily, 83, 98, 118–9, 121,
127–8, 137–8, 140, 145, 151, 157, 164,
168, 170, 176, 179, 192–3, 197, 220,
223, 231, 234, 244
Smythe, Mungo Charles, 124–5, 129,
134, 136–7, 138, 147, 151, 157, 176,
190, 193–5, 197, 199, 201, 222, 231,
248, 250
Smythe, Patrick Evelyn, 136–7, 196,
199, 202, 222, 226, 231, 236–40,
242–50, 252
Smythe, Robert, 57
Smythe, Rowan Montrose, 141, 195–6,
199, 222, 226–9, 231, 233, 235–40,
242–50
Smythe, Victor Murray, 112–3, 134
Smythe, Wilfred, 6
Smythe, William, 5, 6, 8, 17, 23, 27,
45, 57, 59, 63, 66–72, 85, 97–8, 105,
121, 141
Snakes, snakebite, 21, 25, 138, 148, 195
Snow, 59, 202
Somaliland, 157
Somme, battle of, 242–3
Soutar, Kenneth, 136–8, 146, 176,
178–81, 184, 199, 223–4, 249
South Africa Bill, 213–8
South African Infantry Brigade, 235–6,
241–3, 248–51
South African League, 156
South African Party, 234–5, 238
South African War, see Boer War
South American Republics, 234, 248
Sout-West Africa, 206, 226–36, 239,
244
Speaker of Natal Parliament, 145, 165–
8, 171–2
Speirs, Bob, 64, 85
Speirs, Charlie, 57, 67, 104, 106, 132

Speirs, Grace, *see also* King, 57, 64–5, 98, 116, 124, 132
Speirs, Jim, 177–8, 189–90
Speirs children (Grace's), 113, 120, 127
'Spider' carriage, 199, 244
Spithead, 216
Stainbank, Henry, 145
Stanley, Lady Augusta, *see also* Bruce, 6, 45, 217
Stanley, Dean, 6, 45, 217
'Steybraes', 146, 223, 244
Steyn, President Marthinus, 209–10
Stone-quarrying, stone-walling, 67, 84 99, 105–6, 112–3
Stormberg, battle of, 183
'Strathearn', *see also* 'Eberberg':
  (a) Is Smythes' family home, 97
  (b) Choice of name, 109
  (c) Water-supply, 111
  (d) Draining of swamp, 112
  (e) Victor buried there, 112
  (f) Storm damage at, 114
  (g) First party at, 117–8
  (h) Family life at, 119–20
  (i) Tree-planting at, 122
  (j) Plague of rats at, 133
  (k) Graham buried at, 134
  (l) Additional wing to house, 136
  (m) House to be left to daughters, 139
  (n) New schoolroom built, 137
  (o) Further alterations to house, 168
  (p) Food hidden at, in Boer War, 178
  (q) Margaret feeds soldiers at, 179–80
  (r) German deserters arrive at, 180–1
  (s) Margaret runs farm in 1914, 227
  (t) Family gathering for Pat and Rowan's visit, 244–5
  (u) Keith runs farm for Rowan, 248
  (v) Pat spends sick-leave there, 249–50
  (w) Charles dies, is buried there, 252
Stretcher-bearers, 186, 205
Strikes, 225, 230, 234
Studdy (friend of Charles Smythe), 9, 11, 13, 32
Sugar, sugar-planters, 1, 4, 15, 18, 19–22, 25, 27, 37, 39–42, 55, 74, 129, 165, 178
Supreme Court of Natal, 142, 151, 196
Sutton, Sir George, 196, 200
Swakopmund, 227
Swaziland, 211, 213

Tamil, Telegu languages, 101, 116, 119

Tanganyika, 239–42, 244–5
Tannenberg, battle of, 230
Tati Gold Fields, 40
Taxation, 74, 139–40, 152, 167, 190, 200, 233, 247
Taxidermy, 23
Tchwala (kaffir beer), 41, 80, 83
Telegraph, 16, 145, 202, 219–20, 235
Telephone, 176, 179, 244, 250
Telescope, 179
Tenants, *see also* Kaffirs, Zulus, 28, 74, 99–100, 139, 168, 202, 216, 252
Theatre, theatricals, 64–5, 101, 127
Thesiger, Lieut Gen. Sir Frederick, *see* Chelmsford
Thin, Dr, see Appendix II
Thorneycroft s Mounted Infantry, 179–80
Ticks, 21, 67, 82
Tigris River, 247–8, 250
Timber (indigenous), *see also* Yellow-wood, 6, 58–9, 67–9, 74, 82, 104–7, 108
Title 'The Honourable', 196–7
Transport, *see* Ox-wagons, Railways, Post-carts, Shipping, etc.
Transvaal Republic, later Province, 33, 37, 40–1, 43, 48, 51, 53, 69–70, 74–5, 77, 79, 84–7, 90, 93, 102–4, 114, 121–4, 129–30, 132–3, 139–40, 153–8, 162, 169, 171, 173–4, 186, 190–1, 195–6, 205–7, 209–10, 212, 214–5, 218–9, 225, 228, 230, 234–5, 242, 247
Traps (vehicles), 25, 114, 199
Treasurer, Treasury of Natal, 60, 146, 172, 200
Tree-planting, 111, 114, 122–3, 218
Trout, 134–5
Tsar Alexander II, 45
Tsar Nicholas II, 216
Tsumeb, 233
Tugela River, 16, 55, 79, 89–93, 182, 185
Turkey, Turks, 230, 243, 247–8
Tutors, *see also* Education, 7–8, 123
Typhoid, 195

Uitlanders, 154–5, 169, 227
Ultimatum, 89, 174, 225
Ulundi, battle of, 94–5
Umgeni Polling Division, 145, 202
Umgeni River, 22, 32, 251
Umgeni Sugar Company, 22
Umhlanga River, 22, 25
Umvoti County, 188
Umzimvubu River, 14
Unionists, 234–5, 238

Union Jack, 75, 164
'Union' Line, 2, 45, 63
Union of South Africa Bill, see South Africa Bill
Union of South African States, see also Federation, 129, 154, 168, 209–19
United States of America, 50, 248
Upington, 229
Utrecht, 90, 93

'Vaalkop' ('Inchbrakie'), 85, 87, 97
Vaal River, 35, 38, 42, 54, 231
Vaccination, 124–5, 128
Van Reenen's Pass, 33, 133, 176
Van Velden, Rev. A., 70–1
Verdun, battle of, 242
Vermin, 23, 47, 82, 102
Verulam, 25
Viceroy of India, 147, 152, 203, 225
Victoria Falls, 9, 27, 39–41
Volunteers, 64, 79, 86, 91–2, 127, 152, 158, 167, 170, 173–6, 178, 183, 185, 187, 189–91, 202–3, 207–8, 226, 235
Von Lettow-Vorbeck, General, 245
Voortrekkers, see also Boers, Dutch, 32, 57
Vultures, 116

Wages, Pay, Fees, Salaries, 20, 23, 27, 47, 49, 51, 69, 74, 76, 82, 87–8, 100, 102, 112, 133, 135–6, 144, 147, 153, 165, 172–3, 183, 190–1, 194, 219, 231, 233, 248
Wakkerstroom, 48
Walfisch Bay (Walvis Bay), 228, 232
Wars:
  Franco-Prussian (1870), 8
  Between Transvaal Boers and Sekukuni (1876), 74–5
  Ninth Kaffir War (1877), 77
  Pondo and Griqua Rising (1878), 84
  2nd Sekukuni War (1878), 84
  Zulu War (1879), 86–95
  Transvaal War of Independence (1880–1881), 102–4
  Matabele Rebellion (1893), 147
  Boer War (1899–1902), 173–95
  Zulu Rebellion (1906), 202–8
War Markets, 243–6

Water, Water-Supply, 22, 37–8, 41, 50, 73, 111, 229, 232, 251
Watt, Thomas, 200, 209
Wattle trees, 122, 218
Weddings, 45, 68, 70–1, 83, 138, 199–200, 250
Weenen County, 188
Westminster Abbey, 217
White, Gen. Sir George, 175–6
White Rhino, 40, 46, 242
Widdringtonia, 86
Wilge River, 33
Willow trees, 122
Wilson, Miss, 58, 147
Wilson, Dove, 222
Winburg, 33
Windhoek, 232–3, 235
Winter, H. D., 165–6, 172, 200
Witchdoctor, see also Zulus, Kaffirs, 78, 83
Witwatersrand, see also Gold and Johannesburg, 26, 121–2, 125, 132, 139, 154–6, 202, 228
Wolseley, Viscount (Sir Garnet), 60–1
Wood, Gen. (later Field-Marshal) Sir Evelyn, 90, 93
Woodhouse (election-agent), 144
Wool, 37, 78, 87–8, 107–8, 114, 133, 176, 245

Yellow-wood trees, see also Timber, 58, 104–7
Yonge, Cecil, 143–5, 152
Ypres, see also Passchendaele, 236, 251

Zambesi River, 9, 53, 157
Zibebu, Chief, 124
Zulus, see also Kaffirs and Natives, 16, 20, 27–9, 31, 54–5, 57–8, 60–1, 73–4, 77–81, 83–4, 86–7, 89–95, 99–100, 116, 119, 123–4, 126–7, 131–3, 135, 139, 148, 150, 153, 165, 173, 184–6, 190, 200, 202–8, 227, 233, 237, 248, 252
Zululand, 16, 26, 38, 43, 55, 61, 74–5, 79–80, 83, 86, 88–95, 115, 124, 126, 131, 167, 186, 190–1, 241–2
Zulu Rebellion (1906), 202–8, 214, 239
Zulu War, 89–95, 102–4, 114, 131